THE
BATUBATSE

Published in 2017 by Footprints Press

website: www.hiltonbarber.co.za

Copyright © Ponele Seshai Shai

Cover design and page layout by Anthony Cuerden
Email: ant@flyingant.co.za

Printed by Pinetown Printers (Pty) Ltd; Pinetown, KwaZulu-Natal

ISBN 978-0-620-70031-3

THE
BATUBATSE

Their Story and Traditions

Our Proud Ancestory

by

ADV. PONELE R. SESHAI (SHAI)

Assisted by Masegare I. Shai

As told to

DAVID HILTON BARBER

ABOUT THE AUTHOR

Ponele R Seshai (Shai), an atheist, culturist and traditionalist is the descendant of the departed chiefs of Batubatse tribes, Masie, Kokontone, Mashishimale, Matome and others of their generation. He is the seventh child in a family of eight, born at Boschplaas near Hammanskraal on 3 March 1948. He grew up in the village of Motsinoni, about six kilometers from Gakgapane in Limpopo and at Gakoranta village in Bolobedu. Life was harsh: he slept on a mat without a pillow, resting his head on his elbow. His late parents, who were illiterate, were among the first generation of Africans to suffer the ravages of the infamous Land Act of 1913 enacted to force the black peasantry into the mainstream economy. Notwithstanding this hindrance his father, Masilo Grant (Korana) Shai Seshai, became a leading businessman in the Bolobedu area. His mother, Makgwedi Mapheya, was the daughter of Chief Maake Maupa ll.

He received his primary education at Krause Bantu School, secondary education at Masalanabo Secondary School and matriculation at Bokgaga High School. His Diploma Iuris and BIuris degree were obtained from the University of Zululand and University of South Africa respectively. He holds LLB and LLM degrees from the University of Limpopo (UL). He trained as a magistrate and was later admitted as an advocate of the High Court of South Africa. With the unbanning of political organizations and the release of Rolihlahla Nelson Mandela from prison he became more active in politics. In the course of his work as a magistrate and during his lifetime, he participated in a number of leadership roles. He spoke up for those who could not speak for themselves. This led to numerous confrontations and disputes with the former Lebowa Government homeland. However, for 39 years he worked with the Department of Justice and retired as a Regional Magistrate on 31 March 2013 but continued to work in a temporary capacity as a relief magistrate to date. He is the author of *My Triumphs, Trials and Tribulations as a Magistrate in the New South Africa* and is presently researching several other historical projects on the history of Batubatse and Baroka tribes.

ACKNOWLEDGEMENT

Naivety is not such a bad thing when beginning a project such as this one. If I had known at the time how much time and energy was required to complete this project, I doubt whether I would have ventured to start it. Throughout the years of the project many people have given me assistance and encouragement when I felt like abandoning the whole thing. Firstly, I acknowledge my debt to Masegare Isaac Shai for convincing me that I had enough time on my hands and the necessary creative energy to complete the task.

Secondly, to David Hilton-Barber I owe much of my anthropological advice, particularly on the editorial side of the project. He always had time for me and was always helpful and consistent with his feedback. I appreciate his "eyes of faith" that enabled him to see the end goal and keep me on track.

Furthermore, I must offer thanks, so often expressed in private, and my indebtedness to the many acquaintances and friends for their support in helping to shape this work during the long road to completion.

With gratitude I recall the many pleasant hours I spent with all Batubatse informants, the initiates, initiators, circumcisers, traditional healers, village headmen and headwomen and senior as well as junior traditional leaders who took the time to tell me about their world. My family members are a lumber spine of my body. They are the last to thank for their support and patience, and their words of encouragement when my confidence in the project or myself wavered.

The opinions expressed in this book are those of the author and should not be attributed to any person who assisted in the work.

PONELE R. SESHAI (SHAI)

FOREWORD

Cultural heritage from a South African point of view encompasses the beliefs and traditions of the many communities in this Rainbow Nation. It plays a significant role in forging a sense of self-identity and belonging especially in this era of globalization. South Africa is a multicultural and multilingual country in which people of many different nations are able to live together. It is through the researching and recording of the past and how it relates to the present that makes our cultural heritage meaningful.

History (Greek historia, meaning "inquiry, knowledge acquired by investigation") is the study of the past, how it relates to humans. Herodotus was the first historian known to collect his materials systematically, test their accuracy, and arrange them in a well-constructed and vivid narrative.

The past does not belongs only to those who lived in it; the past belongs to those who record it and are able to give it meaning for those alive today. It is our duty to revere the memory of our ancestors from the days long gone, not only to hold them in our memory but to place on permanent record the account of their lives and works.

It is through these connections and links between the past and the present that cultural heritage is constructed.

Moral degeneration within the youth of the South African community is a worrying concern. The obsession we see in material consumption, in indulgence in alcohol, drugs and sex, is a cause of concern. It is folly for young people to disregard the lessons from folklore on the pretext that folklore deals with the past.

Cultural heritage represents the wealth of the nation. It is therefore, imperative for us to protect and preserve this for the promotion of self-identity and national pride.

Author Ponele Seshai has given us a splendid insight into the history, culture and identity of the Batubatse people which resonates with the Eskia Mphahlele Centre for African Studies which hosts a qualification in Indigenous Knowledge Systems.

Professor Mokgale Makgopa (DLitt et Phil Unisa)

Dean, School of Human and Social Sciences University of Venda

CONTENTS

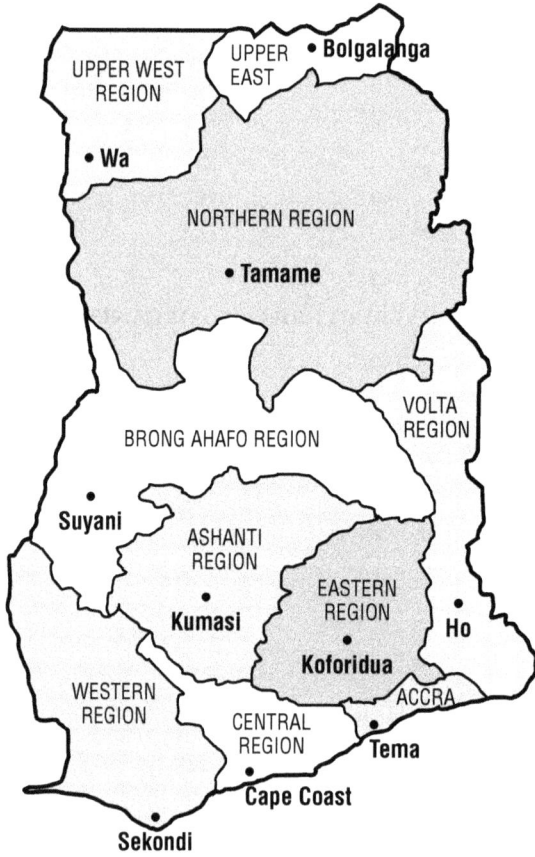

UPPER WEST
REGION

UPPER
EAST

• Bolgalanga

• Wa

NORTHERN REGION

• Tamame

VOLTA
REGION

BRONG AHAFO REGION

•
Suyani

ASHANTI
REGION

•
Kumasi

EASTERN
REGION

•
Koforidua

•
Ho

WESTERN
REGION

CENTRAL
REGION

ACCRA

•
Tema

Cape Coast

•
Sekondi

I
THE PEOPLE AND THEIR JOURNEYS

EARLY ORIGINS

Archaeological and linguistic evidence reveals that the area of present day Ghana (formerly known as the Gold Coast) has been occupied for at least twelve millennia; the first place of human habitation being on the banks of the Oti River (which today forms part of the international border between Ghana and Burkina Faso) in about 10 000 BC, followed by human occupation in the area around Lake Bosumtwi (an ancient meteorite impact crater now considered by Ashanti as a sacred lake) by around 8 000 BC and on the Accra plains in about 4 000 BC. There is also evidence that Neolithic culture with agriculture, domesticated animals, community life, pottery, iron technology and trade existed along the Volta linking the people of the south to the Trans-Sahara trade route to the north by the first century AD. Archaeological research at the ancient site of Shai indicates that the Batubatse of Shai or Shayi people could well be traced back to the Shai Kingdom in ancient Ghana. Their story is a fascinating one of perseverance and resilience.

The Batubatse of Shai and other Batubatse communities were part of a larger group of people known as the Ga-Dangme. Research history has it that the Ga-Dangme migrated from Egypt through Southern Sudan and settled for a period of time at Sameh in Niger and then at Ileife in Nigeria. In the year 1100 AD they migrated again, first to Dahomey and later to Huatsi (Tubatse) in Togo where they stayed for a short season. From Huatsi, they travelled to the eastern banks of the River Volta. They crossed the Volta and established settlements there which endured for over a hundred years. The Ga-Dangme later settled in the Akkra (now Accra) plains, where the capital of the present-day Ghana is situated. The Ga-Dangme still reside in the greater Accra region and their group is made up of the Shai (Se), La, Ningo, Kpong, Osu, Krobo, Gbugbla, Ada and Ga.

The Shai people in Ghana in their secluded highland fortress enjoyed great prosperity and expansion in the 16th and 17th centuries thanks to the coastal trade which they engaged in with the Europeans during the period. Tourists who visited the Shai hills recorded eyewitness accounts on the subject of the government, the culture, architecture and pottery traditions of the locals. One missionary who visited Shai in 1853 recorded in his diary: "The Shai people are well-known potters and as one who knows something of pottery making. I was astonished how they make pots, as beautifully round as if they were turned on a potter's wheel". It is, however, in the area of herbal medicine that the historic Shai have left an important legacy for Ghana and Limpopo. Many of the wild and cultivated medicinal and nutritional plants used by Batubatse people are still known and used by present-day herbalists and nutritionists. There was a darker side to this practice, however, and in 1892 allegations reached the British Administration that the Shai, Krobo and Osudoku people living in the hills of Ghana were offering human sacrifices to their Gods and were sacrificing strangers in particular for annual propitiatory rites and strangers were disappearing without trace. The colonial government of the day sent troops to drive them away from their hills settlements. It was a red letter day for the people who suffered this calamity.

In Egyptian mythology "Shai" meant deification, the transformation of a fictitious person, animal or an object to a God, not a Biblical God. "Shai" in Hebrew means gift or present for a loved one. The tribe, which later became known as Basotswa, Batubatse or Batsubye, adopted this name and years later established themselves in the South African soil as a gift.

Shai settlements in Ghana expanded into large townships by the 1 500s. Due to feuds with neighbouring tribes, members of this tribe moved progressively southwards from Ghana through Nigeria leaving remnants of their people on the way until they settled at Karanga (Bokhalaka/Bokone), the greatest empire in southern Africa, which included the whole of Zimbabwe and parts of Zambia, Mozambique and Botswana. En route to the south and before settling at Karanga they met Tovera who led the ancestors of the Barozwi people from ancient Ethiopia in Sudan to the south. Tovera, the original form of Thobela, was the solar ancestor of Sotho and Ndebele people who include the Basotswa or Batubatse Ba-Shai and other members of the Batubatse of Limpopo. It is for this reason that the Batubatse community is referred to as Matabele from Central Africa or North (Bokone) even today. The name Tovera is etymologically related to Tafari, both names refer to messiah. Tovera himself and his successors were Karangas (Makhalaka/Makgalaka) who left behind a section of Karanga people at Lake Tanganyika on their way southwards. Tovera was succeeded by Changamire Dombo who established the Rozwi (Lozwi) Empire in the 1680s, a domain that endured for over 150 years.

The Rozwi were the first to extract alluvial gold which they traded with merchants on the Indian Ocean. In 1693 Portuguese militia invaded the Rozwi territory in a bid to take control of the gold trade but was repelled. Changamire established his capital at Danamombe, also known as Dhlo-Dhlo (the Ndebele name). From Karanga the Batubatse Ba-Shai people proceeded southwards and settled at the present town of Lobatse (Tubatse) in Botswana before moving northwards. When these Shai people later settle near the present town of Burgersfort, they were considered to be coming from the south and were originally regarded as Transvaal Ndebele from the south.

More than 500 years ago, apart from the Batubatse Ba-Shai and their subjects, there were a number of other tribes sparsely scattered over the whole of the former Northern Transvaal, now Limpopo Province. However, none can trace their ancestry to ancient Ghana. The exact dates of their migrations and their relation to one another are lost in oblivion, but some basic information can be traced from many sources. These other tribes which inhabited the region were the Seoka (Theoka), Ngone (Bakoni/Koni), Ba-Monyela, Ba Shokana and Ba-Sejaphala, people who knew no fire and were living on or eating raw meat, Seja-Phala, mostly offshoots of mixed Sotho and Karanga, and a few so-called Transvaal Ndebele emanating from the far South. Under pressure, the Balobedu royal groups, descendants of Chief Mambo from one of the provinces into which the empire of the Karanga had split up, arrived in the early 1600s or 1700s.

The Laudi, a name which includes the Phalaborwa, Banareng of Mahlo and Letswalo and Bakoni Ba-Matlala, speak of a settlement in the Lowveld of the then Northern Transvaal around 1600 to 1720. The Bakoni left Phalaborwa under the leadership of King Monyewede (meaning the owner of the journey) and eventually gave rise in the area considered to a great chain of tribes such as Bakgaga Ba-Maake (Kingdom), Maupa, Dikgale, Mphahlele, Mashabela, Mametja, Mothapo, Phasha, Molepo, Radingwana, Mashishi, Seopela, Maimela, Poopedi, Matsepe, Marangrang, Rammupudu, Mohlala, Seroka, Kopa, Moloto, to mention but few. All these tribes are grouped under the main tribal name of Baroka. By 1800 other sections of Bakgaga tribe had already occupied a large area around and far beyond Bolebye

Mountain next to JCI (Johannesburg Consolidated Investment) near the present small town of Gravelotte. Between 1800 and 1870 many Sothos scaled the Drakensburg and spread their culture and tradition first among the Balaudi (a praise name of Bakoni Ba-Mametja and Pai) people and through them into Balobedu. The Mafefe tribe, carriers of this culture, ruled several Lowveld tribes for a considerable time.

The Shai people, a senior clan of the Batubatse, were immigrants into the Lowveld from the 1700s. The tribal name of Basotswa, a name only known to a few, was rarely used for security reasons – to disguise their origins from their enemies and those who wanted to overpower them. The Batubatse of Bolebye once used this tribal name after they broke off at Tsubye, but dropped it after they realised there was no danger to them. Besides the Batubatse, led by Shai, these Transvaal Ndebele might be referring to the tribes of Maloma, Maila, Ratau, Masha, Radingwana, Seroka, Morena, Pelane, Maesela, Mathabatha and several others who all have their totem as an elephant and are probably all related to one another. Some of them call themselves Baroka or Bakone since they originate from the North (Bokone).

In other words the Ndebele people in the Transvaal do not form part of the Ndebele of Mzilikazi because those who belong to Mzilikazi arrived later in the Transvaal, and many of them proceeded to Zimbabwe and settled at Matabeleland, with Bulawayo as their capital. Some historians believe that Mzilikazi took this name from Chief Sibindi's tribe, which was known as Ndebele. They say that after Mzilikazi had defeated Chief Sibindi he took all his conquered people and mixed them with his Zulu subjects, whereafter King Shaka expelled him (*motibela*). Mzilikazi also settled with another Ndebele tribe under Chief Manala before proceeding to Zimbabwe. He then started to refer to his Zulu tribe by the name of Ndebele for Shaka to lose any traces of him. Some other tribes, particularly those of Sotho origin, pronounced the name Ndebele as Matabele.

The Shai came as a peaceful group from Central Africa, travelling southwards through the thick lion-infested forests, crossing into the present Matabeleland long before the arrival of Matabele of Mzilikazi. The Batubatse communities are sometimes referred to as Bakone (Nguni/Koni) because originally, like other African tribes, they came down to the south from north (Bokone). Their journey was long and enduring, having taken some centuries. Oral tradition provides that the Shai people settled for a while around the area where Lobatse of the present Botswana is now situated before moving forward into the Transvaal.

Along the way to the Transvaal they successfully overcame several weaker communities that they came across, in order to increase their numbers.

Those subjugated were not permitted to retain their surnames, but were forced to adopt Shai or Shayi surname. That is why, even today, we have many Shai groupings all over South Africa. In generations to come, some of their names, nicknames and behaviours were referred to as their surnames. For some time the tribe settled around the vicinity of Mokopane before it could be known by that name, Tlhogotlou (a hill some 13 or 14 kilometres south of Nebo), the area covering part of the present Loskop, Stoffberg, Mashishing (Lydenburg) and part of Burgersfort. According to one oral tradition and the regimental back-dating system used in many African customs, the information states that these people might be the descendents of the Ndebele-Ndzundza tribe who settled at the present KwaSimkhulu in about 1636.

Another account of history of the Batubatse community and its relation to the land, derived from received oral history, was that the community settled with, or close to, the Ndebele-Ndzundza tribe around 1600 in strongholds on what became known as the Mapoch's Lands, Mabhogo's Lands or Mapochsgronden, not far from Roossenekal. Human habitation of the area could be traced back to the first half of the seventeenth century. The place was named Mapoch's Lands after the Ndebele-Ndzundza tribe was attacked and dispersed by Mzilikazi in 1822 and thereafter by the white settlers. The place is on the edge of the Highveld escarpment in Mpumalanga, northeast of Middelburg and to the east of Groblersdal. Tlhogotlou and Mapoch's Lands appear to have been forming one continuous stretch of land. It is not certain whether Batubatse Ba-Shai, as the senior house, and Ndebele-Ndzudza tribes were one family or not, but both were considered as Ndebele.

Although the origins of South African Ndebele are shrouded in mystery, the history of some Ndebele people can be traced back to Mafana, their first identifiable chief. How his tribe derived the name of Ndebele is not clear. Chief Mafana's successor, Mhlanga, had a son Musi who decide to move away from his Zulu cousin and to settle in the hills of Gauteng near where the capital of Pretoria is situated. After the death of Chief Musi his two sons quarrelled over the chieftainship and the tribe divided into two sections, the Manala and the Ndzundza. The Manala section under Chief Manala remained in the north. In 1820s Mzilikazi overpowered Manala and decided to settle with them. After some time

Mzilikazi, with a clever plan, lured Ndebele (Manala) men away, got the others together and killed them. He then took women and livestock and left the area. The Ndzundza section, also known as the Southern Ndebele, under Chief Ndzundza, travelled to the east and south and became scattered all over Transvaal due to the emergence of the Ndebele of Mzilikazi in 1822. However, some managed to be reunited thereafter and returned to their original place.[7]

In 1883, during the reign of King Mabhogo, war broke out between the Ndzundza tribe and the Boers of the Zuid-Afrikansche Republiek (ZAR). For eight months the Ndebele held out against the onslaught by hiding in their traditional subterranean tunnel in their mountain stronghold at Mapoch's (Mabhogo) Caves. King Mabhogo's brave warriors crept past the enemy line undetected from time to time to fetch water and food nearby. After two of his women were caught as they came to fetch firewood and were tortured, one of them revealed the king's whereabouts. He was attacked and defeated. The tribal land was confiscated, but the Ndebele retained their cultural unit. This happened long after the Batubatse Ba-Shai tribe had moved away near Ndzundza people.

People today commonly referred to as the Ndebele in Zimbabwe are a conglomerate of people of many different origins who migrated from South Africa during the nineteen-century. When the founder of the Ndebele state, Mzilikazi Khumalo, fled from Shaka Zulu in the early 1820s, he was joined by fellow Nguni-speakers and as they moved on, Sotho-speakers, among others, were incorporated into the group. Later, when Mzilikazi settled in today's Matabeleland in 1834, the Shona people were incorporated, mainly by conquest. As a consequence, depending on who their ancestors were at the time of their incorporation into the Ndebele state, an Ndebele today may be of Nguni, Venda, Sotho, Tshwana or Shona origin. In the hierarchical structure of Southern Zimbabwe the Nguni represent a form of aristocracy, termed Zanzi (abeZanzi), while people of Shona origin are categorised according to an older cattle-like division known as Lozwi (abaLozwi) or, pejoratively, Holi (amaHoli).

---

7. The name Mashishing (places of long green grass) is derived from the word leshishi being the place where the Batubatse used to hide themselves in a sort of a fortress which enabled them to attack the enemy with bows and arrows without being seen. Their leader would call out to his people: Re shishimetji, meaning that they must hide in the long green grass. Leshishi could only be found in a deep dense forest on the mountain. In the Lydenburg region, the Batubatse tribe had many such leshishi spots, hence the use of the plural mashshi. Thus, the area was referred to as Mashishing. These fortresses were collectively referred to as Mashishi-a-mogale, meaning the fortresses of a warrior or brave leader. For this reason the chief's tribe or their leader, Masie, who came up with this idea of using long grasses as hiding grounds, was henceforth nicknamed Mashishi-a-mogale. This name was later pronounced Mashishimale, and his great-grandson, Tefo was named after him as Mashishimale Shai I.

SETTLEMENT AT TUBATSE (BURGERSFORT AND STEELPOORT)

Umtubadzi Masie, a warrior and strong leader, led the Batubatse to the present-day Lydenburg or Mashishing after he left Tlhogotlou or Mapoch's Lands. The reason for this community leaving this area is not clear. As we understand it, Umtubadzi's mission to Mashishing was to ensure preservation of the system of his male initiation essential to his tribe and the perpetuation of the tribe as a clear distinctive community away from Ndebele-Ndzudza tribe. It would seem that his tribe also wanted to live under the authority of a King or chief designated by the traditional tribal hierarchy and to occupy an open land, exclusively for them, in accordance with the ancient customs and traditions of the Ndebele people.

Long after the Batubatse had left the area, for reasons that could not be ascertained, and settled along the present Tubatse River, the Boers under the leadership of Andries Potgieter established a settlement, first at Ohrigstad but, following a malaria epidemic in 1850, then at Mashishing. They called the place Lydenburg, a name derived from the Dutch *Lijdenburg* meaning the *Town of Suffering*. The town, now renamed Mashishing, is situated on the Sterkspruit River (later renamed the *Steelpoort* River), a tributary of the Olifants River at the base of the Long Tom Pass.

The Tubatse River flows northeastwards and is a tributary of the Olifants River, joining it at the lower end of its basin. Its source is located at Kwaggaskop, a farm between Dullstroom, Stoffberg and Belfast. The main tributaries of Tubatse River are the Klip, Dwars, Waterval and Spekboom rivers. Together with the Tubatse River these tributaries were the source of sufficient water for the Batubatse people at the time they had settled there.

The newly-built De Hoop Dam on the Tubatse River had been in operation since late 2014. Oral information says that near their said head kraal there was a sacred fountain called Sediba-Sebore in the bush which was regarded as "the place of the Batubatse Gods", the ancestral spirits of the Batubatse. The informant says that the fountain is still there, now fenced off by the present owner. The Batubatse stayed there until, fearful of attack by the strong army of the Sekhukhune's Pedis from Bokgatla, they moved by stages along the banks of the Tubatse River, not occupying any place for long, until they reached the confluence of the Tubatse and Olifants Rivers, where they crossed to Makhutšwi at a place known today as Makalali farm, and proceeded later to Maakene near Mica and settled for a short period at a place known as Matshosing, whereafter they crossed Moholoholo (Drakensberg) Mountains to Makhutšwi at places known today as Enable (Mabye-A-Shosho) and Makalali farms and proceeded later to Mogotle and Maakene or Tsubye near Mica.

It was after this settlement that the tribal name of Batubatse and surname of Šai were adopted. The surname could be spelt Šai, Shayi, Shaai or Shai. This surname, spelt in different ways, is still recognized by all Batubatse or Shai people in its variations for identification purpose. In certain areas of South Africa it is maintained that the name derives from or is associated with the term Šaa, shaya or hlaka meaning to "have nothing, lack something or to suffer". The name also has reference to their misfortunes resulting from a malaria epidemic which nearly exterminated them. The tribe was miserable and devastated because they were unable to protect themselves against malaria. They believed that their hardship was a result of their ancestors deserting them during their travels through parts of the country, or that their suffering was an ancestral gift for greener pasture to come. They equated any natural event, good or bad, to their ancestors.

Due to their wanderings and the fact that they did not have a permanent home, they adopted their ancestral name Shai and identified themselves as Ba-Shai (Ba-Šai) meaning "the have-not people (Bahloki)" and "sufferers or suffering people (Bahlaki)". Notwithstanding the fact that they had no land of their own, they still regarded soil as their livelihood and they survived by ploughing the land, making pots and tending their stock. Besides the protection against enemies they received from their ancestors, they also depended on herbal medicines and witchcraft for security. Many of the Batubatse males were famous traditional healers (witchdoctors) and there were also a few witches among them.

A far cry from the time of settlement by Batubatse of Shai when the area was completely rural, the region is now the centre of an important mining area and the bustling towns of Burgersfort and Steelpoort boast malls and shopping centres, hotels, a casino, a

---

The name of the river Tubatse and the tribe Batubatse is derived from the word Huatsi in Togo, Lobatse in Botswana and Umtubadzi. Ba-Shai settled along the Tubatse River and the area surrounding Maroni Mountains as an independent peaceful people with their own Chief/Kgoshi and Head kraal near the present towns of Burgersfort and Steelpoort. The town of Burgersfort was named in honour of President TF Burgers of the Zuid Afrikaanse Republic. It was also the name of a hexagonal fort built there by the Voortrekkers during the Second War against the Bapedi of Chief Sekhukhune and the remaining section of Batubatse tribe in 1876-1877.

The name Steelpoort is derived from a hunting expedition that took place either in the late 19th or early 20th centuries by a group of Voortrekkers from Natal. A man called Scholtz shot an elephant at dusk and on returning the next morning found the tusks had been removed by a member of Shai clan. The Tubatse River flowing through the poort was then called Steelpoort ('steel' meaning 'steal') River by the Voortrekkers.

convention centre and an entertainment resort.. A man called Scholtz shot an elephant at dusk and on returning the next morning found the tusks had been removed by a member of the Shai clan. The Tubatse River flows northeastwards and is a tributary of the Olifants River, joining it at the lower end of its basin. Its source is located at Kwaggaskop, a farm between Dullstroom, Stoffberg and Belfast. The main tributaries of Tubatse River are the Klip, Dwars, Waterval and Spekboom rivers. Together with the Tubatse River these tributaries were the source of sufficient water for the Batubatse people at the time they had settled there.

A large group of this tribe can still be traced today at Mashishimale (Phalaborwa), Modubeng (Burgersfort), Ga-Mampa, Bokgaga Ga-Maake, Bolobedu, Gauteng, Venda, Sekhukhune, Moletji, Ga-Matlala, Ga-Mogoboya, Ga-Mamabolo, Ga-Sekororo, Ga-Mametja, Matibidi, Mapulaneng, Leboweng, Thabazimbi, Brits, Ga-Selotole Phasha, Mafefe, Rustenburg, Brits, Mashai and Tlhotse areas in Lesotho, Botswana and many other parts of South Africa. At Matatiele there is a place known as Batloung, named after their totem "tlou", inhabited by a number of Batubatse of Shai. This section, as we understand, was part of the Shai group that was left generations ago at Mapulaneng district.

SETTLEMENT AT MAAKENE/TSUBYE (MICA)

Upon arrival at any new place the Batubatse would perform certain rituals to determine whether the area was suitable for them to occupy. They would first choose a spot where these rituals would be performed, after which cattle would be slaughtered by an experienced assegai thrower who would aim the weapon at a relevant part of the body. If the assegai remained in place when the animal fell to its death, this signified that the place was suitable for their settlement. However, if the assegai fell out of the wound when the beast fell to the ground that would mean that the land was not suitable for them to occupy. They would then move off without delay to look for another place for settlement. This is what they did until they reached the Maakene vicinity and the outcome of their ritual practices favoured them to settle there.

The Batubatse Ba-Shai were relative late-comers to the territory which was to become known as Maakene or Tsubye, sometimes spelt as Tshuubye. Their leader then was Chief Tefo Mashishimale Shai I, who was later given the title of Kgoshi Mashishimale Selota I. The only known black inhabitants to have settled at this area were led by one Modiamofe.

Their tribal name has been forgotten. These people appear to have come from the south and they were probably of Sotho origin. Their totem was most likely an elephant since this was the totem of their remnants. Besides Modiamofe and his small group of people who lived there, no information is available of any other community that might have settled at Maakene before the arrival of Batubatse Ba-Shai.

When the Batubatse arrived in the area, there were, therefore, only Modiamofe, whom they acknowledged as the first settler in the area. For a few years they paid tribute of thatching grass and building poles to him in recognition of his position as the first arrival. They even taught him and his people how to make fire to cook their food, instead of eating their meals raw. The area was extensive and well-suited to agriculture, covered with mopane trees (mehlanare) which yielded a fine harvest of mopane worms (mašotše).

After some time, because of his weaknesses and lack of knowledge and skills, Modiamofe and his people were subjugated and ordered to renounce their names in favour of the surname Shai. The Modiamofe community was thus absorbed into Batubatse and never heard of again. However their remnants later became known as the Motodi people and now live in Sekhukhuneland under their senior traditional leader. The Motodi community is now regarded as a tribe with its own traditional authority falling under Greater Tubatse Municipality. Some members of this community consider themselves as Batubatse.

Within the territory lay an important mountain range with some 21 separate hills, each with its own indigenous name: Marakapula, Phetole, Shabeni, Tokela, Kopeni, Kaleke, Lefalafala, Modikwe, Maalwato, Difoinana, Molema, Mafishi, Marapong, Mosekweni, Mogobeng, Leropse, Kgaleke, Moresweni, Kholapedi, Moshabela and Mantsopi. Three of the hills, Marakapula, Phetole and Kgaleke, were identified as Batubatse's ancestral places (Badimong), of which Marakapula was the main one. This was the burial site for members of the Royal Family and the secret place where rainmaking medicines (dipheko) were kept. On top of this hill a special tree known as Semehee, which is still there today, was used for rituals. The present owner, a white farmer, has cordoned it off and it is guarded by security personnel to prevent strangers from going there to pluck its fruits. The so-called Motjatji Flowers also grow widely in the area, the fruits and flowers of which are sold by the farm owner at a good price.

Phetole Hill was where members of the Royal House would exchange their protective medicines used for different purposes. At Kgaleke Hill there was a natural fountain known as Mphoto. It is said that, during those days, the fountain never dried up and had enough water throughout the year, even during droughts.

There was a mine at Tsubye that produced legakabye or legakadima stone used for making indigenous cups and plates. When whites took control of the place it was renamed Gritjie Mine. These hillswere later named Tsubye after one of the hills was set alight to frighten Modiamofe and his people. The Mmolautsi, Sekgoname and Sedibasakwena Rivers provided sufficient water at Tsubye. The head kraal (mošate) of Kgoshi Tefo Mashishimale Shai 1 was erected at this mountain.

Maakene covered a large area between the present towns of Gravelotte and Mica. The eastern boundary was present-day Phalaborwa, today the boundary of Kruger National Park, while towards the west the area stretched up to the present village of The Oaks, which was then the boundary between Maakene and Malepe.

Some distance from Tsubye Mountains, near the present village of The Oaks, was a second mountain range which later became known as Dioke Mountains. This had six hills, two of which had high protruding rocks balanced on top of one another, making it difficult for a person to reach the highest peak. These two hills, naturally, provide an attracting view for people passing by towards Mica and Phalaborwa. The indigenous names of these hills were: Dioke, Diokana, Legapa, Morolwane, Tshwane and Boloka. At Tshwane a large cave (mphoma/lewa/lepatlaka) is said to have hidden black and white soldiers during both World Wars I and II. On Dioke a section of the hill called Lewatla also produced the legakabye or legakadima stone. The Makhutšwe River near Morolwane, which supplied the Dioke area with water, was a tributary of Lepelle (Olifants) River, while Lepeletšane River near Ngwashepankelakahle Hill was a tributary of Makhutšwe River. This was the place where Lethamaga intended to establish his own head kraal before he was brutally killed.

The territory, a large tract of land with rivers, vegetation and mountain ranges, is known collectively as Maakene while the mountains are referred to individually as Tsubye and Dioke. Here are found rock-rabbits (dipela), the typical inhabitants of mountains and hills. They live in burrows in any type of sedimentary rock and soil with suitable cavities. They are found in groups, active during the day, and sometimes during moonlight, where the dominant male keeps a watchful eye for enemies. They feed on a variety of different plants.

Rock-rabbits were hunted since their meat was a source of high quality protein as a side dish for the Batubatse. They were caught in snares (melaba) or killed with a stone or knobkerrie. The meat was prepared in the same way as chicken meat. In China rabbit meat is particularly popular today and some supermarkets sell their frozen meat. Pelts from rock-rabbits were used for clothing and accessories, such as scarves or hats. They were good producers of manure used for fertilizer and their milk was used as a medicine.

Mopane worms, actually caterpillars, were commonly found on mopane trees. Like most caterpillars, their life cycle started when they hatched in summer around November and December, after which they proceeded to eat the foliage in the immediate vicinity. Their diet was not limited to the leaves of mopane trees but included many indigenous trees in the same region, as well as the mango. Thus, the caterpillars could be scattered over a fairly large area. In the bush, they were not considered to belong to the landowner and were collected by anyone in need of them wherever they occurred naturally.

The traditional method of preserving the Mopane worms was to dry them in the sun after which they could be eaten raw as a crisp snack, providing an important source of protein and, together with rock-rabbits represent a healthy primary diet as side dishes for the Batubatse tribes. Other animal species were hunted daily for their meat and their skins were used for various purposes, including rituals.

When they first arrived at Maakene, the Batubatse noticed many reddish ochre (*letsoku*) outcrops protruding from the ground below the Tsubye Hills and caves. These reddish stones were in fact mica, and this gave rise to the whole territory becoming known as Mica. The word was pronounced by the Batubatse in Sotho as *Maakene*. The discovery of mica in the area brought much joy to their lives; this is why the word *Maakene* is widely used in their praise poems. It was not unusual to find a layer of the cave floor impregnated with a wide range of purplish-red pigment to a significant depth, the colour due to the presence of iron oxide.

Within this large tract of land they discovered open pits of clay containing ochre. They would wash the clay to separate out the ochre which was of particular significant for the Batubatse – for painting their bodies, dyeing animal skins, coating weapons and sprinkling the ground of their dwellings. Initiates would be painted with red ochre at the conclusion of circumcisions schools. Women used a mixture of red ochre and animal fats for body decoration to achieve a reddish skin colour. The red ochre mixture was also applied to their hairs for braiding. In fact a paste of ochre was used for decorative purpose in every phase of their life.

The settlement of Batubatse tribe at Maakene was peaceful, the large tract of land providing sufficient water from the Olifants River and its tributaries for grazing for cattle and game alike. The community lived prosperously, growing in number and wealth under their senior traditional leaders. The name Batubatse or Shai (*Šai or Shayi*) had always been their tribal name; however, with the naming of the first mountain ranges, Tsubye, the second tribal name of Batsubye or Tsubye came into being. Maakene became important to this tribe and they considered it as a land given to them by their ancestors. To them the place was a heritage site.

With all this good fortune there was, however, some internal leadership disputes within the Royal House. This led to the departure of several dissatisfied groups or families to other locations while still maintaining Batubatse and Batsubye as their tribal names. Another reason for the exodus was due to the Batsubye policy of rainmaking. This required the sacrifice of a child, usually a boy, from one of the Royal Units in order to make rain medicines from his flesh. When a father became aware that it was his turn to offer a child for rain medicines he would, in most cases, disappear at night with his whole family to avoid the sacrifice of his son. Other families who supported him would join him then or soon thereafter. The next royal unit to offer a son for rain medicines might well do the same. These disappearances were carefully planned to succeed. That is why the Batubatse/Batsubye people are scattered all over South Africa. Interference by the ruling government in the affairs of Batubatse, creating some problems within the tribe, also contributed to the dispersal of the community near and far. Today Maakene is regarded as the centre from which the Batubatse people scattered in numbers in different directions until 1922, when those who remained were forcefully removed to the present reserve at Ga-Mashishimale. Maakene still represents a heritage site for them. When they scatter at Tsubye some sections of the community went to Letlolong and Mphatjong near the present town of Phalaborwa. The Batubatse Ba-Shai enjoyed the long days and nights of Maakene/Tsubye at the time of their settlement there. Now, looking out over vast bushveld plains of the Valley of the Olifants, Mica offers visitors a sense of tranquillity. At the time of settlement by Batubatse of Shai the area was completely rural. There were no towns, shops and mines. Today Namakgale Township and Phalaborwa town, which were part of the territory of Maakene, boast a number of mines, big and small shopping complexes, plazas and malls.

From what has been described above, one can understand that the Batubatse journey was not an easy one. They traversed rough mountains and rivers of present-day Zambia; they went south to the "heel" and "toe" of Karanga or Bokhalaka; they explored the still underdeveloped regions of Zimbabwe and Botswana; they journeyed through bush country infested with poisonous snakes and other dangerous reptiles and animals. The absence of roads and pathways made their journey difficult, sometimes impossible, forcing them to settle at certain territories for ten years or more before moving further. The long journey they travelled, the vastness and harshness of the land to be travelled, the rough and rocky mountainous passes they crossed, the torment of mosquitoes (*zanzare*) bringing serious risk of malaria, and the presence of bad water threatening typhoid fever – all combined to form a seemingly insurmountable barrier to their migration to the south. But they persevered and finally reached their goal.

BATUBATSE WARS

It appears that, by nature, the Batubatse tribe was not a fighting type of people. They did not practice xenophobia – a strong dislike of groups of people from other places – which might have ended in war. Only few wars fought by them could be remembered. But in those days hiding away was an alternative to fighting to protect the family and the entire tribe when the situation was untenable. Caves in the surrounding mountain provided an excellent retreat for the Batubatse. When they were under threat from attacking tribes they would spend the days sleeping in the caves and only awaken at sunset. In the evenings they would look down from the entrance of the caves to locate the fires of their enemies on the plains below. They could also read the stars for guidance against any misfortunes that might visit them.

They could also climb to the summit of the mountains to get a better perspective of the countryside and determine the boundaries of their territory with that of their neighbours, so that they should observe any encroachment and make the necessary preparations. There

---

The area around Maakene (Mica) in Limpopo Province is the only locality where production of muscovite mica of any importance has taken place. This commenced on a commercial scale in 1909, long after the Batubatse had settled in the vicinity. In 1912 the Selati railway line was extended to this mica field, hence the name for the siding (later a station) named Mica. As of now water-ground and dry-ground mica from the area is used for a variety of applications such as filler and brightener for paints, filler in plaster boards, rolled roofing and moulded electrical insulations. In the Mica area, open casting was followed by underground mining.

were occasions when they had to take up arms to resist attacks. They had skirmishes with Chief Sekhukhune on many occasions which led them to venture out from their ancestral place. They also fought a fierce battle with the Pedi of Chief Mafefe near the present Lekgalameetse Nature Reserve, not far from Trichardsdal. All these battles took place in mountainous regions which have provided evidence to later researchers of their military tactics during those warring years.

Maakene, one of the Tsubye hills, had a level summit to which they could retreat on being attacked and roll loose boulders on to their enemies to take them by surprise at the base of the hill. In the early years before the Europeans arrived, tribes constantly fought against each other. Mountainous areas and caves (*mefoma/ mawa/ mapatlaka*) provided protection from the enemy and offered ideal grounds for settlement.

In the early 1800s a courageous Motubatse, Moholoholo Shayi, lived with his family in the verdant rain forest around the present Blyde River Canyon on the slopes of the north-eastern Drakensberg, falling under Mapulaneng. This area provided him with the security of caves and hanging rocks to which he could retreat and roll the rocks against his attackers. During the first Mapulana and Swazi battle, which did not involve the Batubatse, Moholoholo Shai guided the Mapulana people to the places of safety up in the mountains where they could hide themselves and roll rocks against their enemy. In this way the Mapulana were able to crush the Swazis to their first defeat. The same thing happened in the second Mapulana and Swazi battle, and once again the Swazis suffered defeat at the hands of the Mapulana warriors. The final battle of Moholoholo was fought in 1864 at Mariepskop, named after the Mapulana chief, Maripi Mashile, and this resulted in a convincing victory against the Swazis. Moholoholo and his small number of followers played a vital role in all these fierce battles, and to honour him the forest was named Moholoholo. The Batubatse and his descendants revere him to this day for his bravery and courageous conduct during these battles.

* * *

PRESENT SETTLEMENT AND INTERACTION

The black people of South Africa arrived in the country from about AD 300 onwards, during the southern migration. Today they consist of nine separate ethnic groups representing the greater majority of the population of South Africa. The Batubatse are part of the Northern

Sotho tribes who live mainly in the rural areas of what is today Limpopo and Mpumalanga Provinces. For reasons of water availability and land-use patterns, some are living in large settlements and others in more dispersed villages. The arrival of the Voortrekkers and other white settlers during the nineteenth century led to the concentration of population around some of the black chiefdoms, while other tribal capitals were abandoned or destroyed. Many blacks were also attracted to the towns established by European colonisers.

This process led to the establishment of Namakgale Township, near the present town of Phalaborwa, for the Batubatse of Mashishimale and other neighbouring communities of Ga-Makhushane, Ga-Maseke and Ga-Seloane.

With the unification of the Colonies in 1910, and the denial of franchise to blacks, the Governor General, and later the State President, became their overall Paramount Chief. A Department was created and made responsible for the administration of black people in South Africa. Commissioners were appointed as local representatives of the government, and for the administration of its affairs.

The *Bantu Land Act, 1913*, and the *Bantu Land and Trust Act,1936,* provided separate land reserved for blacks, under which Batubatse Ba-Shai and their break-away sections were also confined to reserves. The *Bantu Administration Act* of 1927 provided, among other things, for the recognition or appointment of chiefs and headmen and the granting to them of administrative powers and civil and criminal jurisdiction over their tribes. Later, other acts of parliament created a system of tribal, regional, and territorial authorities with legislative powers as well as civil and criminal jurisdictions in the tribal areas concerned. Various acts also provided for separate schools and universities for the blacks, with control placed in the hands of various communities.

Such was the administrative and legal machinery under which the historical development of the Batubatse continued till 1994 when the new government was democratically elected. By this time the once-united Batubatse tribe had been divided into a number of separate communities and moved to other areas, some without a senior traditional leader. In 1902/03 the Mashishimale section experienced a famine which led to the loss of a large number of their livestock. This resulted in the re-introduction of the hoe for tilling the soil instead of ploughing with cattle. Later donkeys were brought to replace cattle as beasts of burden. The Mashishimale section under Chief Leshwene Shai were removed from their ancestral place at Maakene/Tsubye and the territory around Mohote River to their present reserve at Ga-Mashishimale village near Phalaborwa in 1922. Hence they are sometimes referred to as Baphalaborwa as if this was, or is, their tribal name.

Other sections of this tribe were reluctantly forced to fall under the control of other foreign chiefs who were not part of the Batubatse tribe, and their senior traditional leadership status was not recognised or was unfairly terminated. For instant Ba-Mmanyaba fell under Chief Sekhukhune, Ba-Mohlabe under Chief Sekororo, Ba-Mampa under Chief Mafefe, Ba-Bolebye under King or Paramount Chief Maake, and so on. Only Chief Leshwene Shai of the Batubatse Ba-Shai retained his status as senior traditional leader, which is still recognised even today. The leaders of the above-named Batubatse sections were and are still considered as traditional leaders (headmen) under their respective senior traditional leaders.

Dissatisfaction with the set-up introduced by the government led other Batubatse groups to leave their areas and settle with foreign traditional leaders in other areas. Those who were lucky enough were offered the status of being traditional leaders (headmen). For instant Thatale Shai, Mokhokolo Shai and a few others became traditional leaders under Chief Maupa Maake; Taola Shai and a few others became traditional leaders under Sekororo; Mafedi Maenetja and a few others became traditional leaders under King or Paramount Chief Maake; Kheselo Maenetja and a few others became traditional leaders under Chief Mogoboya; Seanego Maenetja and a few others became traditional leaders under Chieftainess Modjadji; and many more. This is not exhaustive, for the list is endless. Many of these traditional leaders were offered women as their wives by their respective senior traditional leaders.

The efforts of government to introduce more scientifically planned methods of farming, such as the culling of inferior stock and fencing of lands, were resented as changes in the traditional way of life. The so-called agricultural "rangers" who were appointed were despised as government puppets. The mining boom which occurred at some areas, with the opening up of mines in Phalaborwa, Modubeng, Burgersfort, Steelpoort, Gravelotte, Mica and other parts of the country, provided employment for some of them; unfortunately they also caused much of the game to disappear from their areas. Chief Leshwene died on 28 July 1936 after having led his people at Ga-Mashishimale through some relatively peaceful decades. Although there was infighting within the Royal House, the situation was not as serious as in the Royal Houses of other chiefs where members of the inner circle killed one another in order to wrest the throne for themselves.

As of now many of the Batubatse community live in the former Lebowa homeland, many of them in existing residential settlements in homes ranging from traditional dwellings and shacks to brick structures to which households may have formal or informal rights. The settlements with large populations include Ga-Mashishimale, Ga-Mampa, Ga-Mametja, Ga-Sekororo, Ga-Mogoboya, Ga-Mamabolo, Ga-Matlala, Ga-Maake, Motjetene, Modubeng, Shakung, Motloulela, Sekhukhune District, Bolobedu, Leboeng and Matibidi. Others live in more rural areas with minimal access to services and a small or non-existence economic base. Of course these rural Batubatse households have access to a more secure place to live today than they had fifteen years ago. Yet problems facing rural settlement still persist. These include confusion over roles and responsibilities for rural development, a lack of emphasis on provision of land for settlement by the Department of Land Affairs, a lack of capacity to provide housing, a lack of livelihood opportunities to support the occupants of these rural settlements, and so on. These factors impede the development of sustainable rural settlements. The communities stand to be the real losers as a result of the confusion surrounding the provision of settlement services as they have less access to information about the state responsibilities for development support than their urban counterparts do.

Rural communities that do not have the assistance of Non-Government-Organisations (NGOs) may never become aware of the potential support they could access. Those who apply for assistance often become disheartened when, after several years, they have still not received any support. Access to clean water is still a big challenge in most parts of the rural areas. Donkey-carts and wheelbarrows are still being in use to carry water from far from their households. In the olden days they did not experience these challenges since the whole area was theirs; everything belonged to them and was under their control.

"Action does not always lead to happiness, but there is no happiness without action."
– Benjamin Disraeli

Travelling within the Baphalaborwa Municipality towards the Kruger National Park is an African adventure that can be enjoyed at any time. It all depend on what one would like to see, as each season has in tow a range of highlights. Some people enjoy the wet and rainy summer months, where the surroundings are lush and green. Game-viewing is not the ultimate goal as the vegetation is dense at this time. This is the territory where the Batubatse once lived and still live. The avid game-viewing traveller, like a Motubatse man, will obviously want to visit the area in the season in which the wildlife is more prevalent and easy to spot: the dry season within the winter months of May to August. The vegetation is less dense, the plains are open and sparse, and because water is quite scarce a great variety of game is attracted to the watering holes.

2
HABITATION

A habitat is an ecological or environmental area that is inhabited by a particular species of animal, plant, or other type of organism. A place where a living lives is its habitat. It is a place where it can find food, shelter, protection and mates for production. It is the natural environment in which an organism lives or the physical environment that surrounds a species population. A habitat is made up of physical factors such as soil, moisture, range of temperatures, and availability of light as well as food and the presence of predators.

TERRAIN AND FEATURES

This covers the country where the Batubatse previously lived and where they finally settled before they were forcibly removed to their present location, GaMashishimale, not far from Maakene/Tsubye and Bolebye near Mica, Gravelotte and Phalaborwa.

We can picture the areas where the Batubatse once lived:

In summertime, from November to February, the countryside was blessed with high rainfall, with lingering thundershowers interspersed with clear days and occasional soft rain. Heavy rain during this time could lead to rivers bursting their banks. Daytime temperatures were at their most extreme. Vegetation was dense and colourful with many summer flowers in bloom. Food was abundant. Grasses were in seed. Marula fruit attracted animals, birds and insects. Raptors, bee-eaters and other migrants arrived in great numbers. Food was plentiful and summer breeding was at its peak. Birds were most susceptible to snakes at this time of the year as egg-eaters raided their nests. Water birds were abundant along all major rivers. Sunrise would be seen around 05h00 and sunset at around 18h30. December was the height of summer: very hot and humid with occasional regular thundershowers. March and April saw a seasonal shift towards autumn. Daytime temperatures were noticeably lower, and evenings were chilly with occasional sporadic late rains. The insect population declined. Many species fed heavily to improve their condition before winter. In May deciduous trees started dropping their leaves. The fruiting season for most bushveld trees came to an end. In June winter set in; days were mild and evenings cold. The bush dried up significantly and brown replaced green as the predominant colour of the vegetation, except in the mopane-veld where the leaves changed to yellow and orange. In July the winter was at its height. The veld was prone to bush-fires.

The fauna of the area included the "Big Five": elephant, black rhino, leopard, lion and buffalo. Also prevalent were sable antelope, large herds of buffalo, kudu, impala, giraffe and warthog. Zebra were plentiful, especially after the veld was burnt the previous year. Small game such as steenbok and duiker were commonplace and each koppie had its klipspringer and dassie (rock rabbit) population. Several arboreal reptile species were present. Termites (dihlolo) built their anthills (diolo), which offered refuge for numerous frog, lizard and snake species, and when these winged insects came out after rain, large numbers of mammals, birds, reptiles and amphibians fed on them. Termite mounts were either sharply-pointed or rounded, often covered with plants bearing an edible fruit that attract birds.

Today a Motubatse man travelling towards the Kruger National Park would enjoy a fine African adventure, each season having its special attractions. In the wet and rainy summer months the bush is lush and green but game-viewing is restricted. In winter the vegetation is less dense, the plains are open and sparse, allowing for the easy locating and spotting of wildlife, and, with the scarcity of surface water, game is attracted to watering holes, thus further increasing visibility.

The Greater Baphalaborwa Municipality, which includes Ga-Mashishimale, Maakene, Bolebye and Gravelotte, and the Greater Tubatse Municipality comprised Mashishing, Steelpoort, Ohrigstad and Burgersfort, was where the Batubatse people once lived. The area is known as the Middelveld, forming part of the Valley of the Olifants. In certain parts the topography is mountainous, making it unsuitable for habitation. The terrain dictates that most settlement occurred in flat, low-lying areas between the mountain ranges.

At the time of their arrival at Tsubye the early Batubatse people developed a basic knowledge of smelting the iron-bearing ores (legakabye or legakadima) found in the mountainous areas where they lived. They manufactured iron (tshipi) tools, mainly hoes which were often used as marriage goods. The early Batubatse people also cultivated crops, especially in the fertile soils in the lower-lying areas of Burgersfort and Steelpoort, and in the lighter soils of the uplands. On the banks of the main rivers of the area, the Olifants, Steelpoort (Tubatse), Spekboom, Selati and Makhutšwe, the Batubatse grew maize, sorghum, wheat, groundnuts and other crops, and grazed their cattle on the grasslands.

CLIMATE, WIND AND SUNSHINE

Climate encompasses temperature, humidity, atmospheric pressure, wind, rainfall, atmospheric particle count and numerous other meteorological elements in a given region over long period of time.

The area covered by the Greater Baphalaborwa Municipality normally received 360mm of rain per annum. The average daily temperature ranged from 8 - 24⁰C in July and 20 - 30⁰C in January. The highest recorded temperature was 43⁰C in January 2006. The neighbouring Greater Tubatse Municipality recorded about 440mm of rain per year. The weather condition for the Steelpoort, Ohrigstad and Burgersfort region as a whole is sub-tropical and conducive to agricultural production.

GEOLOGY AND SOIL TYPE

Geology is an earth science comprising the study of solid earth, the rocks of which it is composed, and the processes by which they change. It gives insight into the history of the earth by providing the primary evidence for the evolutionary history of life and past climate. It is important for minerals and hydrocarbon exploration and exploitation, understanding of natural hazards, evaluating water resources, the remediation of environmental problem, etc. Rocks provide the primary record of the majority of the geological history of the earth. Different types of rocks may be melted and re-melted. When this is happens, a new rock is formed, from which another rock may once again crystallise.

The ancient Batubatse people had little scientific knowledge of smelting rocks but they did manufacture basic iron (tshipi) by burning a specific rock known as legakabye or legakadima which was plentiful in the Tsubye area, to make hoes. These were widely used as marriage goods.

There were three main types of soil where the Batubate lived: clay, sandy and silt. Clay soil absorbs and holds water, creating a drainage problem which adversely offers healthy root and plant growth. Sandy soil allows water and nutrients to drain away quickly from the root zone. Silt soil holds water but doesn't have good aeration around the root. The Batubatse people were able to convert these three types of soils into loamy and aerated earth which would retain water and nutrients for healthy plant growth. Deep ploughing every few years broke up the hard pan in day soils and improved water drainage.

The soils around Mashishing consist of black and red clay types, of which the black clay usually is to be found in dry areas with inadequate drainage. These soils have a heavy, coarse texture and their ability to retain moisture gives these soils excellent qualities if the rainfall is adequate. The most fertile soils in the region are found in the lower-lying areas of Burgersfort and Steelpoort, which are deep, well drained and suitable for most agricultural purposes provided that they are fertilised adequately.

Several termite mounds occurred within the grassland vegetation around Mashishing. These provided a refuge for frog, lizard and snake species. Large numbers of mammals, birds and reptiles fed on the emerging winged termites. Termite mounds (diolo) were either sharp-pointed or rounded, the former having no vegetation cover and the latter often clad with a plant bearing an edible fruit, apparently transported by birds. Large and small mammal species inhabited the bush and the vegetation unit provided suitable habitat for several arboreal reptile species.

VEGETATION

The vegetation on the uplands of the landscape is dominated by a number of species, depending on the clay content of the soil. Woody species are common in the bottom-lands. Other different species are dominant in the field layer of the landscape on the uplands. The koppies in the landscape give a unique character to the surrounding. The plants occurring on the koppies are usually also unique, and a number of woody species are noted. The riverine vegetation is generally the same all over. January to April is the optimal time for avid bird-watchers. As summer makes its way out, so do the migratory birds their journey, chasing summer. By April the vegetation surrounds begin to reflect the autumn of things. The bush begins to turn from a lush green oasis into a slightly sparser landscape. The temperature begins to cool, and accordingly the sun starts to dwindle too.

During May and June the brown leafless surrounds epitomise the cold of the winter season. The conditions are extremely cold and dry in the months of July and August. At this time the visibility is fantastic and wildlife tends to congregate around the various watering holes. As springs rears its head in September and October, it brings with it the height of the dry season, hot dry winds and colourless sparse vegetation. Rivers and dams are at their lowest at this stage. Game that can be viewed at watering holes is plentiful. As the first rain begin to shower down towards the end of October, the cycle of life and the wild continues regardless, ushering the next generation into play. November and December are usually accompanied by very hot and humid conditions with perpetual rain. It is during this time that many animals give birth to the next generation of wildlife.

Vegetation in the territorial area of Ohrigstad, Tubatse and Lydenburg consists of grassland, but the grasslands have become severely degraded and transformed due to present and historic agricultural practices. Dense patches of the anthropogenic grass occur here and there. The trees-and-shrubs layer increases along the Marabane River. Vegetation and landscape features consist of high-altitude plateaus, undulating plains, mountain peaks and slopes, hills and deep valleys of the Northern Escarpment region. The grassland is very rich in forb species. The vegetation within the mid and lower slopes has now been heavily impacted on by surrounding anthropogenic activities including old land and degraded overgrazed grasslands. The woody vegetation lines are dominated by tall shrub and grass. Dense, sour grassland occurs on slopes of mountains and undulating hills, with scattered clumps of trees and shrubs in sheltered areas. Dense tall grassland can be found on the lower hill slopes, and encroachment by indigenous tree species is common in other places. Today large areas have been deforested to provide for agricultural land, and fairly extensive soil erosion has occurred throughout the country, further spoiling its natural appearance and limiting its economic productivity. The grass covering was once fairly thick, with many plant species. Between the trees and shrubs there was always a good grass coverage which provided excellent grazing. Overstocking, however, has resulted in encroachment by shrubs.

NATURAL RESOURCES

Throughout South Africa, with its poor water supplies, the value of the surface to man, plant and animal was directly related to the amount of available water, whether rain, surface or subterranean water. Farming was and is still an important resource as a wide range of products were cultivated owing to good soil conditions, the sub-tropical climate and reasonable access to water. The main resources that encouraged agricultural production were the Olifants, Steelpoort (Tubatse), Spekboom, Selati, Makhutšwe and other rivers, which provided water to the region. The territory was crisscrossed with a number of lesser tributaries of the main rivers, although very few of these were reasonably consistent, most of them having only sporadic water-supplies in season. As a result there was always enough production of maize, sorghum, wheat, groundnuts and many other products. Potential land for agricultural purpose was found on the river banks. In olden days when people were few and large pieces of land were still available, the Batubatse didn't experience much overgrazing.

Minerals were in abundance in the Bushveld Igneous Complex (mining belt), which has seen the establishment of several mines in the area. Other significant mineral zones which are found in the mining cluster around Phalaborwa region are the Murchison Greenstone Belt from Gravelotte towards Leewkop in the Kruger National Park, the Giyani Greenbelt from Kruger National Park in the south Western direction to the town of Giyani, and the Rooiwater Complex Northern flank of Murchison Greenstone Belt. Potential exists for small-scale mining in the Murchison sequence near Gravelotte and along the East-West ridge of mineralisation south of Phalaborwa and extending to Mica. Within the Tubatse Municipality the eastern limb of the mining belt emerges as an important structuring element. The wilderness area generally comprises bushveld and sparse grassland in limited parts. It was important to preserve the wilderness for posterity and to harvest plant and animal species in a manner that preserve the habitat.

Phalaborwa, originally a mining town and still home to the Batubatse and other tribes, provides the massive open-pit mine, which is Africa's widest man-made hole at almost 2,000 metres wide. The copper mine here is South Africa's deepest and largest open-cast mine, and indeed one of the largest copper mines in the world. The bottom of the open-cast pit is today about 230 metres below sea level. The open-pit mining began in 1964 and ended in 2002 when the pit reached its final economic depth. The operation employed around 1,800 people. The town of Phalaborwa is located near the confluence of the Selati and Olifants rivers, half-way up the eastern border of the Kruger National Park in the lowveld. The rich mineral deposits were already being worked in prehistoric times, as was evidenced by a nearby excavation site in the area.

"Fear is the main source of superstition, and one of the main sources of cruelty.
To conquer fear is the beginning of wisdom."

– Bertrand Russell

3
THE PEOPLE'S WAY OF LIFE

Storytelling (nngane/nkane)

BATUBATSE LANGUAGE

Language learning is unlike other types of learning; we learn it by largely being exposed to it, especially when we are young. Parents are less likely to reinforce their child's correct grammar than they are to attend to the child's meaning. Although the parent is modelling correct grammar, his or her emphasis is in the truth of the statement, not its form. A dialect could be one of two different things. It could be a variety of language that is specific to one group of speakers, because of the area they live in, or because of social class. A dialect could also be a language found within a region or national language, distinguished by vocabulary, grammar and pronunciation. A dialect is always a local or regional variation on a language, usually with a vocabulary and grammatical features that are different from other dialects. A dialect differs from an accent in that the actual words, not just the pronunciation of them, differs from other dialects. Dialects are important because they help to define different regions and identify them.

The San, also known as the Bushmen, populated South Africa long before the arrival of Black-speaking nations, and thousands of years before the arrival of Europeans. It is estimated that there are between 2,000 and 3,000 languages spoken on the African continent, with possibly as many as 8,000 dialects. The language of the San people has only recently been recorded, for they were traditionally illiterate. The same applies to many of the Black nations; it is estimated that there are between 2,000 and 3,000 languages spoken on the African continent, with possibly as many as 8,000 dialects specific to an area or to a social class.

Very little is known about the dialects of the Batubatse Ba-Shai, since most of these ancient languages were never recorded. Today those who live in the south speak Ndebele, which still has a Zulu influence, while the language of the Ndebele of Limpopo is a mixture of Zulu, Sotho and Shangaan. Overall, people with different languages, regions, races, customs and traditions are united by being South African and form part of our country's identity and culture.

People are influenced by the place and the people around them in a country such as South Africa. Many have learned and shared customs, traditions and memories passed on from parents to children. Culture refers to the way of life of a specific group of people. It can be seen in ways of behaving, beliefs, values, customs followed, dress style, personal decorations like make-up and jewellery, relationship with others and special symbols and codes. Culture is passed on from one generation (parents) to the next (children). It is always changing as each generation contributes its experience of the world and discards things that are no longer useful. Furthermore, culture is not something a person was born with, but something learned from the family, tribe/community and religious teachings. A person's identity is made up of his own characters combined with his family and social roots.

Northern Sotho (Sesotho sa Lebowa/Leboa) is referred to as Sepedi in the Constitution. This is, however, inaccurate, as Sepedi is just one of some thirty dialects of the Northern Sotho language, and Northern Sotho itself is one of South Africa's three Sotho languages, each with a different dialect dependent on the area where it is spoken. Historically the missionaries who first developed the orthography of Northern Sotho had contact mainly with the Pedi of the Northern Sotho complex. The standard Northern Sotho was, therefore, incorrectly largely based on Pedi. The name Pedi thus refers specifically to the language of the Pedi people, while Northern Sotho refers to the official language, which is a much broader category than merely Pedi.

The original language of the Batubatse at the time they left Ghana or Central Africa is unknown. It is understood that, at the beginning, the Batubatse lived with the Ndebele

---

The first permanent white settler in the Lowveld was the Rev. Fritz Reuter of the Berlin Missionary Society. He founded the Medingen mission station near Modjadji in October 1881. He was the only white person living in that part of the lowveld. Sometime later Thabeng Mission was established where Pastor Josefa Monare Maenetja was the pioneer minister. He was a member of the Batubatse of Bolebye near the present small town of Gravelotte. He was born in 1881 at Ga-Manamela near Ramokaku in the Tzaneen/Letaba area. It was about the time of the Boer victory over the British at the battle of Majuba Hill in northwest Natal. The family later moved to Moime in the homeland of the Bakgaga Chief, Maake.

people for a long period. Thereafter they lived parallel with the Bakoni, who are sometimes referred to as Baroka, and the Pedis as well. Since they were less in number than the Baroka and Pedi their language was greatly influenced by them. As the time elapsed their language was the local dialect known as "Seroka" among people who were by then living further west. It was a form of Sotho, very localised and shared with other inhabitants of the area where they lived. Although they still use some dialectical terms, at present Northern Sotho is their spoken and written language wherever they are, particularly in the Limpopo Province

WRITING

Writing (mongwalo) is a medium of communication that presents language through the inscription of signs and symbols. In most languages writing was a complement to speech or the spoken language. It is not a language but a form of technology. The result of writing is generally called text, and the recipient of the text is called the reader. Writing has been instrumental in recording history and the dissemination of knowledge, and it has the ability to make a continuous historical consciousness possible. Through writing the command of the narrator, priest or king and his seal could extend far beyond his sight and voice, and survive his death.

From the research conducted there is no evidence that writing ever featured in the history of the Batubatse. Through the recent introduction of European schools and education and contact with colonists or missionary societies in South Africa, a number of Batubatse were exposed to writing and reading. The same had happened to other South African black tribes. Historians draw a sharp distinction between pre-history and history, with history defined by the advent of writing. There are a few Batubatse paintings and informative inscriptions done on clay pots, poles, trees and rocks. These recordings by a prehistoric people could be considered the precursors of writing. Sometimes the shapes, orientation and meaning of certain individual signs can be interpreted – and yet they do not represent writing. Writing (*mongwalo*) is the medium of communication that presents language through the inscription of signs and symbols.

The Batubatse depended on their memory in the administration of their affairs, but with the passage of time the complexity of issues surely outgrew their power of memory. Initially they counted their livestock through memory and by recognition of the animals' distinctive colours. As the number of livestock increased, new means were found; they began to use clay tokens to count their livestock and other items. These tokens would be placed inside a large clay bowl to which only the head of the family had access. He would count his livestock as they entered the cattle-kraal by removing the tokens one by one from the container. If some clay tokens remained after all the livestock had entered the kraal it would mean, of course, that certain cattle were missing.

CONTACT WITH MISSIONARIES

A Motubatse man's original religion was nearer to his beliefs than the imported religions that were taught to him and sometimes even forced upon him. The commonly used method of land-grabbing in Africa by the imperialistic nations of Europe was to send missionaries into the so-called "barbarian" or "heathen" areas under the pretence of saving the souls of the people who lived there by converting them to Christianity. The arrival of the trader became the next step, and hot on their heels came the armed forces to protect the missionary and the trader and to maintain law and order. All that remained was to raise the flag and to proclaim the area as a colony. It was a highly successful method. What followed was not the civilising of the people but the exploiting of the natural resources of the land for the enrichment of the imperialists. The Batubatse people fell into this exploitation trap. Their original beliefs were polluted and sometimes replaced by the Christian missionaries to serve the imperial interests of overseas nations. To a lesser extent Islam also played a role.

The Batubatse understanding of Christianity was not clear. Those who converted to Christianity, by calling on local missionaries and praying with them to solve their problems, only did so after having tried without success all the traditional methods. Because of this, some old rituals have been discarded and forgotten. Although every tribe has a number of converts, these usually live separately in small settlements of their own, leaving the rest of their tribesmen to continue along the lines of the traditional religion. Despite the difficulties it is still possible to build up a picture of the Batubatse religion, which they describe as *borapedi*. In addition to this, the word *tumelo* (faith) is also used for religion.

The words *borapedi* and *tumelo* describe the correct mode of life to be followed, based on a belief in natural forces with the power to ensure a favourable outcome. Little more is known about the creation, except that the unknown creator, be it a God or Nature, provided everything. The Batubatse certainly cannot be said to have a well-conceived creation belief.

Their word for the unknown creator or God was *Modimo*. But they did not pray to a biblical *Modimo*, nor did such a being have any place in their daily life. They had no contact with him, or he with them. However, the arrival of Lutheran, Wesleyan, Anglican, Dutch Reformed, and Roman Catholic missionaries in many parts of the country where the Batubatse lived brought some changes to their way of life and beliefs.

The missionaries opened mission stations throughout South Africa and established schools and hospitals which were central to the education and health of the forefathers of the Batubatse people. These missionaries travelled from one place to another by ox-wagon to bring their services to the populations. Their schools taught blacks to be evangelists, bricklayers, carpenters, plumbers, vegetable growers and crop farmers. Some of the hospitals established by them are still existing and operative today. South Africa owes a great deal to these missionaries, who have played a major role in the well-being of black people in this country. Members of the Batubatse communities, although atheists, culturalists and traditionalists, were exposed to education and health services provided by the missionaries. Some of them became heroes, mavericks, pioneers, ground breakers and legends who have made great strides on the South African stage.

Kudumela (*ditšwa mmeleng*) Shai was a member of Batubatse tribe at Bolebye. Probably he was born there. For reasons unknown he moved to the Mohlaba area (today known as Bridgeway), together with his family and a few others. He died and was buried there. After his death, his son Marabe left the area and settled at Sudane, today known as Shilubane.

Marabe Shai was the first person to settle at Shilubane, about 35 kilometres from Tzaneen. He was later appointed a headman of that area by King or Paramount Chief Maake when the numbers of households increased. When Henri Alexandre Junod established a school for evangelists at Shilubane in 1886, Marabe Shai, as the leading figure in the community, was immediately appointed a Church Steward, among whose duties was to ring the Church gong. He encouraged his fellows to join the Swiss church. Later a hospital was opened at Shilubane to serve people around the area. Marabe died in1939 and was buried near Shilubane Hospital. He had been a member of the Swiss Mission Church for about 54 years. His age was unknown but it was estimated to be over 100.

After Marabe's death his son, Magari, was supposed to succeed him as the headman of the area. However, he declined. He suspected that his father had not died of natural causes but had been killed by jealous people and that if he took over the headmanship he might be killed as well. Magari was the son of Marabe's first wife (he had two wives) Accordingly, Magari, with his younger brother and their mother, left Shilubane for Phepene and thereafter went on to Parare where even today many Batubatse can still be found. Marabe's second wife died and was buried at Sudane/Shilubane.

Swiss missionaries played an important role in explaining Africa to the literate (European) world in the late 19th and early 20th centuries. This book emphasises how these European intellectuals, brought to deep rural areas of south-eastern Africa by their vocation, formulated and ordered knowledge about the continent.

In those days the gospel was unknown in that region and white people had not yet moved in the area. Both his grandfather and father had several wives and were well-known professional rain doctors. People brought gifts and asked them to appeal to the ancestral spirits to send rain. Monare's father was a headman under King or Paramount Chief Maake, and Monare's mother was his first wife. Traditionally Monare was to follow his father as rain doctor. While Monare was a small boy, herding goats, sheep and calves, a terrible drought occurred. The ensuring famine brought great suffering. Children dug edible roots in the bush. There was no food.

People were lying dead alongside the path. Animal skins were eaten and people sent their children to the white farmers on the plateau above the mountains as servants in exchange for maize. Monare became sick with dysentery. One day he tried to run away from a snake and was so weak that he fell unconscious. His father found him. A friend very kindly gave his father a piece of stiff maize porridge. With it they were able to feed the boy and he recovered.

When he was twelve years old Monare went through the tribal initiation rituals just like other boys of his age. There were no schools at all in the area. At the age of fifteen he travelled 320 kilometres to the southwest of Pretoria on foot to earn money for a marriage dowry (*magadi*). There he learned to read and write. He also heard the gospel, became a believer, joined the church and took the name of Josefa. In 1902 he was baptised at the Medingen Lutheran Mission, about fifty kilometres north of his home. He heard about the martyr, Johannes Kgashane Mamatlepa, who had died under the Lobedu Queen, Modjadji, because he tried to witness for Christ and opposed polygamy and ancestral worship.

This martyrdom for the faith must have greatly influenced Josefa Maenetja because, when he returned home and his father died in 1907, he refused to accept the mantle of rain doctor as was required by custom and the family. After marriage he settled down to the normal life of his people involving traditional worship and lost interest in Christianity, but he refrained from marring additional wives. In 1928 his wife became sick and Monare visited a traditional healer to find help for her. While he was there, engaged in writing a letter for the traditional healer, Missionary Abram E Zook from the Thabeng Mission came to visit and asked them to pray. The traditional healer refused but Monare invited the missionary to his homestead and called the family together for prayer. This contact made a great impression upon him. After this contact he began to attend church services at the mission from time to time, and for months he often came to pray at the altar.

In 1931 two missionaries, the Reverends Irvin E Dayhoff and Leon R Sturtevant, visited his home on horseback one Sunday and he invited them to hold a prayer service. He shared his newly found faith with his wife and told her that he felt these missionaries were telling the truth about the way to heaven. They had their first family prayer. Since then they began attending services regularly at Thabeng Mission. Thabeng mission was an eight-kilometre walk across the mountain pass from their home. His first wife, Johanna, died few months later. Monare was a person who was eager to learn, and so he used to follow Brother Sturtevant around everywhere he went. He began going from home to home in the surrounding areas, telling the story of salvation. He entered classes at the mission and became one of the first four converts to be baptised. This was his second baptism, his first being in 1902 at the Medingen Lutheran Mission.

He then became a regular helper in the Lord's work. He married his second wife, Esther. Thereafter he held church services under a tree at his home at Moime and started a small school nearby. This school is today named after him. Due to his influence, King or Paramount Chief Maake became a friend of the mission. The Maenetjas moved from Moime to Thabeng Mission and started another school there. Billy Mohlare took over as teacher at Moime. There was strong opposition from a rival Tsonga school in the valley below Thabeng Mission but one Makasane, a prominent resident whose homestead adjoined the mission, affirmed this to be his school and the Chief's court allowed Monare Maenetja's school to continue.

Esther passed away before her children were grown up and in 1948 Monare married Dorcus, a Christian lady at the mission. Monare Maenetja used to plough a large field with donkeys and would help others with their harvest. It seemed that he believed in sharing and attracted many friends, among both North Sotho and Tsonga tribes in the region. People trusted him and he was known far and wide. He wrote letters and sent money for illiterate people and helping them in every way he could. During the outbreak of the illness of sores (*dikemola*) he helped at the clinic to put on dressings. He established a strong tradition of good fellowship between Bakgaga and Tsonga people in the congregations.

Towards the end of 1941 the missionaries left the Thabeng Mission station. During 1942 and 1943, in the absence of any missionaries at Thabeng Mission, Monare carried the leadership of the work alone. He called people with a cow-horn trumpet. He often walked 20 kilometres for services and he started numerous preaching points. These were consolidated into three permanent congregations: Thabeng Mission, Khopho at Chief Mogoboya's area around the mountain to the west, and Moime, across the mountain in the east. In 1955 Monare Josefa Maenetja was the first Nazarene minister in the Transvaal to retire from the ministry. His work has developed, together with the churches in the Lorraine mission area, into the great North-eastern District. In 1995 this area became a regular district of the Church of the Nazarene. One of his favourite sayings was the ancient N. Sotho proverb: *Go kgona go phala ke go theeletša* literarilly meaning "Ability is better than listening". He died on 12 July 1963.

According to the African Christian Biography, the Rev. Dalton (Wilton) Chenchi Maenetja, the son of Josefa and Johana Maenetja, was born at the homestead of Motjetene (Mapatene) near Sediba sa Tau (the Lion Spring). The totem of their tribe is the elephant, symbolic of the great influence of the Maenetja family in the community. Chenchi grew up *Wilton Chenchi Maenetja* on the Thabeng Mission and broke with a strong tradition of his people by not going through the tribal initiation school as a boy. He attended the Thabeng Mission School and went on to high school around the mountain at the Shilubane Swiss Mission. During the 1940s Chenchi worked as a waiter at a country club in Pretoria. His name was entered wrongly as Wilton instead of Dalton on his official identification document. Therefore he began using Wilton as his official name. In 1944 he testified to being converted. After that he testified publicly that he felt God was calling him to the ministry. He made no firm plans, however, to enrol in Bible College. He decided rather to join the South African Police. When the day came for him to leave for training he went to say farewell to his father. His father reminded him of his testimony about being called to preach the gospel and asked Dalton to join him in praying about it. As a result he abandoned his plan to join the police.

He married Sophie Mankwana Malapane (1930-1996) in 1952. She was born in Sophiatown, Johannesburg, the second daughter of Makhaya John and Mapula Sarah Malapane. She attended school at Thabeng Mission. Maenetja taught at Lorraine, Thabeng and Moime Primary Schools. Mankwana worked on farms in the area. God blessed their home with six sons and two daughters. Pursuing God's call to the ministry, Maenetja worked with missionaries Kenneth and Minnie Singleton at Thabeng preaching at various preaching points including Hobson's Choice, Longridge (Sekhokho), Khopo, Rooi Koppies, Politsi, Rantenburg, Letaba Estates, Mawa, Ramalema and Lenyenye. Sophie supported him faithfully in all of this work.

As the family grew there were too many demands on his time and he was unable to attend a bible college for ministerial training. As the years went by it seemed as if he was missing the basic preparation for his calling. Missionaries and other workers prayed for him.

Shortly before his father died on 12 July 1963, he called his son to his bedside. Josefa Maenetja told Dalton that before he died he had one question that he wished to ask him: "Have my prayers for you, and those of your mother, been in vain?" Dalton Maenetja wept at his father's bedside and promised him that those prayers were not in vain and that he was determined to obey God's call. At the funeral on 15 July Dalton Maenetja went forward to pray at the close of the service by the Rev. Paul S. Dayhoff, although no special invitation had been given. Then he arose and affirmed his decision to follow God's call and enter Bible College the following year.

Matome Mikiel Shai was born in 1884 and grew up in the Mapulaneng (Bushbuckridge) area. He was the son of one of our grandfathers, Mpaseriti Shai, who was part of the section of Ba-Shai clan that settled in Mapulaneng after they separated with the other sector of the tribe, probably at Maakene. His mother was Mokgautjana Sarah from Maake family. Mpaseriti Shai was a traditional healer who apparently died an unnatural death in Mapulaneng after disappearing without trace. The name Mikiele was how the Mapulana people pronounced Michael. When grown up and before his father's disappearance, Mikiele travelled on foot from Mapulaneng to Kimberley to seek employment. While there he came into contact with missionaries who converted him to Christianity. He worked there for few years and returned home with a Bible and started to preach to the people. Later he became a priest of the Zion Christian Church (ZCC).

He had one younger brother and three sisters, Motlatjo, Ngaletjane, and Mapula. After the disappearance of his father he left Mapulaneng together with his mother, young brother and three sisters and settled at a place known as Sepatwene near Sebabane close to Masilo Grant Seshai (Shai) and his father, Thatale. It is not known how Thatale Shai (Seshai) and Mpaseriti Shai were connected to each other except for the surname of Shai. They may have been half-brothers because Thatale's children referred to Matome Mikiele as their half-brother. Matome Mikiele always called Thatale his father and most people around Tzaneen, Duiwelskloof, Mooketsi and surrounding areas considered him to be the biological son of Thatale. Later on he went to Pusela location near Tzaneen where he opened a butchery business of his own in 1950. He was one of the first few blacks to own a bicycle, motor vehicle and a business within the surrounding areas of Tzaneen. He left some of his children at Mashakga. Other children of his went to settle at Moleketla. One of his sons, the late Elia Shai, and his family could still be traced there. From Pusela he went to reside at Lenyenye Township and continued to operate his butchery business there. His mother and brother passed away at Lenyenye and were buried there. He imparted business knowledge and Christianity to some of his children and the community.

Matome Mikiele had four wives. The first was Mamotlatjo, from Machete family, and she gave birth to seven children, Motlatjo Grace, Matoromela Amos, Mapiti Petros, Magdalina, Benjamin, Matome Lazarus and Joseph. The second, Mamodjadji, from the Mogoboya family, gave birth to six children, Modjadji Rebecca, Enoch, Mokopa Elia, David, Johanna and Samuel. The third, Mamohale, from Lebepe kraal gave birth to four children, Matjie, Lesia, Rosina and Mohale Simon. The fourth and last wife, Molatelo Rachael, from Monyela kraal, gave birth to seven children, Maropene Isaac, Makgadi Esther, Ngwako Simion, Moloti Moses, Mapula Anna, Mokone Angelina and Kholofelo Naphtalina.

Matome Mikiele Shai was a powerful force within the community. He was a diligent and independent man, working hard for his family. He appears to have been a person devoted to his work, faith and business commitments, toiling the earth with virtually no time even to read and build his consciousness. He earned what he had, not through corrupt deals or misusing public funds, but through his natural skills and the acquired knowledge he got from his employers. He left the earth aged 99 years in August 1983 at Lenyenye and was buried there. He belongs to Matome House of Batubatse Ba-Shai Royal blood.

We know why families were created with all their imperfections. They humanise you.

They are made to make you forget yourself occasionally, so that the beautiful balance of life is not destroyed. Heads of such families sometimes dedicates much of their time and energy to make people to understand the other side of our life. Amongst those heads of families was the most caring, inclusive and generous Matome Shai-Ragoboya. His passing away might have not had the attention it deserves, but there is no question that history will regard him as one of the leading figures of our time, especially amongst the category of writers and spiritual healers.

Matome Uriah Ragoboya Shai, also known a Nelson, was born to the late Pheagane Segwate Isaac Shai and Mmapeu Rebecca (nee Morerwa) on 15 March 1909 at Nareng village near Tzaneen, Limpopo Province. He was the first child in a family of six siblings. He started his schooling at Madibeng village in Botlokwa near Soekmekaar. He went on to do his Standard Six at Kgokong Higher Primary School, Ga-Mamabolo, near the present University of Limpopo. This was after his parental family had moved from Madibeng village to Kgwareng village, Ga-Mamabolo. Later he went to Lemana Teacher's Training College, not far from Elim Hospital, where he completed his teacher's training. Lemana was located in the district of Watervaal, Venda, on the outskirts of the present town of Louis Trichardt (Makhado).

He started his teaching career in 1935 and taught at Malesa, Makgodu, Segopye and Megoring Primary schools, where he was a principal of the schools until 1968. During his tenure as a teacher he was called to the priesthood and joined the Malesa Lutheran Church in 1964 at Vierfontein near Turfloop. Being a teacher and priest at the same time did not bother him. He was later sent to lead the churches under Carlsruhe Parish near Styloop from 1967 till 1980. In September 1968 he left teaching altogether and became a full-time priest to lead the parish. He retired from active service at the end of 1980, but occasionally became a self-supporting pastor to assist the church. Beyond his educational and religious duties, Matome Ragoboya Shai was highly esteemed in every community he moved into. He would give voice to people who would otherwise not be heard. As I understand it, he was not out to appease or to please anybody, unlike his predecessors. He knew the education and religious terrain like the back of his hand.

He was married to Mantsha Matilda (nee Modiba) and they were blessed with eight children, to wit Makoma Rebecca, Pheagane Isaac, Nakampe Jacob, Madintši Hilda, Mapeu Martina, Maatle Lucas, Mankete Naomi and Mokanthyana Moses. His wife Mantsha passed away in 1968. He then married Dikgomo Josephine (nee Matlhare), who left the earth in 1988. I am told that Matome Ragoboya was suave, polite, charismatic, comfortable in his own skin, a natty dresser, erudite and articulate, with a voice that commanded authority. His interest was in writing and he was an accomplished author; some of his books were translated into German and could be found in German libraries. When ultimately their families move away from Segopye, Ga-Mamabolo, he was the first person among the Batubatse to purchase a plot at Harriswich (Garawešo) in the present Blouberg Municipality in Limpopo Province. Ragoboya, as he was commonly known, has run his race. He left a fine legacy when he left this world on 29 September 1997 aged 89.

CONTACT AND RELATIONSHIP WITH OTHER TRIBES

A tribe is viewed historically as a social group existing before the development of, or outside of, the state. Many people used the term "tribal society", especially with reference to familial groups. A customary tribe in these terms is an extended family bound by kinship and strong ties to a particular location. Much of tribal history deals with inter-tribal warfare, although in those times it is likely that these intertribal encounters were less serious affairs. While it would be impossible to give a comprehensive account of the complex pattern of inter-tribal relations in early historical times, a summary of such relations may throw some light on the conditions prevailing at the time.

The Batubatse tribe did not consist of an amalgamation of different people. Their sphere of influence comprised tribes living mostly in close proximity to them. This led to a large degree of cultural assimilation among these tribes, but there were still cultural differences between them. They could not be described as a nation but rather an inter-connected group built by marriage with neighbouring tribes. There was no inter-tribal fighting between Batubatse and their neighbours. The few minor conflicts that arose were amicably resolved without any bloodshed. They lived in peace with their fellow citizens and they offered help where it was needed. For instance, when the two Pedi brothers, Mafefe and Ntwampe, were engaged in aleadership squabble, Kgoshi Mmanyaba Shai came to the rescue of Ntwampe and arranged for him to find refuge near Seokodibeng together with a section of the Batubatse of Mampa.

The royal households exchanged daughters with each other to become tribal wives. It was customary, as with the Pedis, to extinguish all fires in their village on the arrival of a tribal wife. All fires would then be re-lighted from the fire started in her homestead. In this manner the whole tribe becomes related to her and the two tribes involved. For instance a daughter from Batubatse Ba-Shai was offered to Kgoshi Malatji as a tribal wife. The same was done with Kgoshi Maake. Batubatse Ba-Mohlabe also offered a daughter to Kgoshi Mametja as a tribal wife. At Modubeng the tribal wife for Kgoshi Mmanyaba came from one of the chiefs falling under Paramount Chief Sekhukhune. Masetla Makutuma of Batubatse married his second wife from Kgoshi Malatji Makhushane.

Each of these very marriages posed challenges and required determination and tolerance on both sides. No two marriages were alike, not even those of twins married to another set of twins. Just as there were bad inter-tribal marriages, there were equally perfect examples of what an ideal marriage should be. A woman who married outside her tribe had to be understanding and sensitive to the ways of her new family.

Around Phalaborwa the neighbouring chiefs to Kgoshi Mashishimale Shai included Kgoshi Makhushane Malatji, Kgoshi Maseke Malatji and Kgoshi Seloane. Although these neighbouring chiefs were independent, they regularly brought a greeting tribute (*madume*) to Kgoshi Shai at Maakene and later at Ga-Mshishimale. Some of these neighbouring chiefs would wait for Kgoshi Shai to open a circumcision school before they could do the same. The tribes generally maintained a friendly relationship with each other. The boundaries between them were roughly defined by natural features such as rivers or mountain ranges.

Visiting between these tribes occurred frequently. Most of these tribes had a fair knowledge of the affairs of another. Although it is generally preferred that people marry within their tribe, inter-tribal marriages did occurs quite often. There was also a measure of inter-tribal trade in the sale of pottery or the products of other craft. Traditional healers with a wide reputation also attempted to extend their practice beyond tribal boundaries. Neighbouring chiefs visited Batubatse chiefs. They also informed one another of important events in their tribes, such as initiation or the death of predecessors. Visiting chiefs were well entertained. If a visiting chief stayed overnight it was customary to give him the choice of the young woman to spend the night with him.

All formal and diplomatic relation between the tribes was maintained by an extensive system of appointed intermediaries (*batseta*). Any person who wished to approach the chief of another tribe had to call on the intercession of this official intermediary in the tribe of that chief. The position of all intermediaries was mostly hereditary and was held by the unit *koru* for many generations. These intermediaries were fully conversant with the affairs of those tribes whom they represent.

BATUBATSE HOMESTEAD AND FAMILY

Batubatse customary law permits polygamy, which allows men to marry as many wives as they wish and can afford. With each new marriage the wife and her children establish a separate house (*lapa*). The houses are not of equal status, but are ranked according to the status of the wife, and this denotes their location. Wives must accord one another the respect due to their rank in the household, and the husband must treat all wives equally. As far as property is concerned, a principle of separate estates must be strictly observed. If a wife consents to a transfer of property from one house to another, an inter-house debt is created, and it must eventually be repaid. The homestead is laid out in accordance with the right-hand/left-hand opposition, but the order of succession is determined by the rank of the houses, which in turn is determined by the date of marriage.

A homestead consists of one or more huts standing in a courtyard enclosed by a wall. In the centre or side of the unit a fire-hut (*setlhaka*) is built for cooking on rainy days. The erection of this fire-hut was begun by placing a number of poles upright in a circle. These poles are then enclosed within a mud-wall (*leboto*) from which only the forked tops of the poles protrude. Then a row of other poles, concentric to the first, is placed outside the first row. A conical thatched roof is then built resting on the poles protruding from the mud-wall, and on the outer ring of the poles. Separate or behind this fire-hut there are one or more main huts. The whole unit is enclosed by an angular wall of about eight metres high, which encloses the area so that homesteads which are built adjoining one another fall into a circular formation.

Enough space is left around the huts for a fairly large courtyard where guests are entertained. There are two entrances of the courtyard; the one in front (*sefero*) is used by both the family and visitors, and the one in the back (*seferwana*) is a private entrance used only by the family. The courtyard in front is called the *lapa* and is a public place for guests. This lapa contains the main fire-place (*sebesho*) for cooking. The back courtyard (*mafuri*) is a private place for family members. Visitors enter this place on invitation and in the company of a family member only. All entrances of the huts face the *lapa*. All floors and mud-walls are smeared by hand with a protective layer of cattle-dung. The whole unit or homestead is called by the same name as the public courtyard – *lapa* – and if these are many they are called *malapa*.

To enable all people to have reasonable access to their land, Batubtse villages were usually built in a fairly extensive, sprawling manner and homesteads might even be separated from one another by one or more hills or valleys. A man who wished to build a new lapa had to consult his relatives. As soon as the site of a new homestead had been identified, the man would employ the services of a traditional healer to arrange for the protection of the new lapa against witchcraft. The man and the traditional healer would meet at night on the site and would undress completely to avoid harmful influences which might attach to their clothes. The traditional healer would mix some protective medicine which would prevent any witches from entering the homestead. All persons who lived in the new lapa would have the protective medicine rubbed into small incisions on their joints to protect them from witches. Once all this had been completed the building of the lapa would begin.

The main decision regarding the siting of the lapa concerned the position of the front entrance, because entrances of homesteads were placed in a specific order according to rank. The living arrangements within a lapa depended on various circumstances. For instance if the homestead was inherited and the husband's mother was still alive, the mother would continue living in the main hut, and the young couple would use one of the huts at the back. If a man had more than one wife the man had to build the homestead of his wives in a special order, according to their rank, in the form of semi-circle with the senior hut or homestead in the middle. In many homesteads there were always separate huts for boys and girls. From an age of about seven or eight years boys and girls were separated, with younger children of both sexes sleeping with the girls. Another hut was used for storing clothes, utensils and food. Usually homesteads of Batubatse were built within a patrilineal group, which consisted of a complex of homestead situated at the foot of a mountain, on rocky and broken terrain.

All the daughters-in-law of a woman started their family life in their homesteads with their husbands. However, the youngest son in any homestead remained in the lapa permanently. Sometimes the wives of a polygamist did not get on well together, so they built their homesteads some distance away from each other. Each wife had to have her own homestead, and the husband was equally at home in all of them. All Batubatse homesteads were built on the same basic pattern and only differed in the number of smaller huts within the units. A normal homestead was always occupied by a wife and from four to five children. An unmarried mother would either have the child secretly killed or it would be married with her, and belong to the man who married her. If a divorced woman remained unmarried her children would finally be incorporated into the group of their mother. Her sons, on their marriage, would build their own homesteads for their wives.

A married couple with a new-born child was entitled to a homestead of their own which was built among those of the relatives of the husband, or they occupied an existing homestead inherited from the husband's relatives. It was only at this stage that the marriage produced a family and the husband and wife fully acquired the status of adulthood with all social, political and jural implications involved. Like the Baroka, Pedi and other black tribes, the Batubatse had no specific word for a family. But the word could mean those of your house (*ba ntlo ya gago*) or a compound with more than one homestead, those of your village (*ba motse wa gago*). A family was a basic and fundamental social unit. It was a cohesive, corporate group, practising its own subsistence economy and performing internal cultural and jural functions. A family was considered an addition to the existing kin group. The whole tribe acted as a single unit, with the individual families operating not for their own benefit but also for the benefit of the whole community. The chief, as head of the tribe and symbol of its unity, played a leading role. The family lived in a dwelling unit called a *kgoro*. This was the most important corporate unit within the tribal community and the whole tribal life hinged on it.

No family could on its own approach the ancestors for rain, or in connection with an epidemic. A family approached its own ancestors concerning its own personal desires, which affected it alone. To a large extent the affairs within a *kgoro* were also concluded on the level of extended families. In every compound family the rule of *patria potestas* obtained, and the father was responsible for the orderly conduct of the family affairs. He also represented the family in all the outward dealings. The senior male member of an extended family, as its genealogical head, had considerable influence and power to deal with any matter amongst the constituent related families of the group. All official matters were always dealt with first within the extended family before the head of the *kgoro* could be approached.

The principal vehicle for settling disputes outside the official courts was the mediation within or between family groups. Disputes within an extended families or family group would always be discussed with the relatives concerned. Only trifling disputes were tried at the family level, and only appeared before the official courts after they had become too involved for the family groups to settle. Traditional family structures were profoundly affected by colonisation and various forces associated with it such as missionaries, urbanisation, wage labour, policies of segregation and apartheid. Of these forces, Christianity was the first. Missionaries demanded that converts complied with the Christian vision of marriage which was deemed monogamous union.

Polygamy was denounced together with levirate and sororate unions, and some churches went as far as branding the preferred forms of cousin-marriage as incestuous. Family composition, structure and relationship were also profoundly affected by the process of urbanisation. While *lobola* was still paid, the spouses' families no longer played an active role in the formation of the unions. Men nevertheless claimed their traditional patriarchal privileges. A force less conspicuous than urbanisation, but more profound in its effect on family life, was the migrant labour system. Employers discouraged male labourers from bringing their wives and children to the mines. The forces indicated above had so destabilised the extended family that the structure now survives as a traditional ideal, not a reality within the Batubatse communities. Nevertheless, tradition may well persist alongside the new forms of family structures.

MAIN HUT, OTHER HUTS AND SHELTERS FOR RITUALS

Long ago people sought safety in a walled village. Settlements were surrounded by a strong mud or stone wall (*morako,* plural *merako)* with a ditch outside it. Outside the wall was a thick barrier formed by a circle of trees tall enough to hide the homestead. Later people resorted to live in compounds, also surrounded by a hedge to keep cattle out of the gardens. The Batubatse had the same word for a house and a hut although the structures were quite different; a hut was a primitive dwelling, the first building to be built after the temporary or seasonal structure of a shelter used when moving between seasonal grazing areas such as mountainous and lowland pastures. A house, of course was durable, a well-built dwelling. In general most Batubatse houses were built of readily-available material such as wood, stones, branches, hides and mud, roofed by grass, using techniques passed down through the generations. Some were built with large stones, particularly on rocky mountains, and also roofed by rocks. Usually they would be constructed with poles with the spaces between filled with stones and mud.

Traditionally, Batubatse villages grew up around the homestead of the most senior person in the community. His house and the houses of his various wives would be formed in a semi-circle, with the cattle kraal in front. If he was a chief, a gathering place for men would be set out adjacent to the homestead. Other dependents and strangers would settle in increasing distance from this original core. The whole area would be surrounded by agricultural fields and grazing pastures.

The traditional dwelling can be described as a cone-on-cylinder type of structure. Essentially it consists of a circular wall of poles or stones, plastered or not plastered with clay or mud, topped with a conical roof of thatched poles. The floor was beaten earth smeared over with cow dung. The outside wall would be decorated, usually with geometrical patterns applied in different earth colours in ochre or cow dung. A number of such dwellings belonging to an extended family would be linked to one another but separated by walling, also decorated with coloured patterns. A special hut for a retreat for the family head was sometimes built.

The homesteads traditionally ranged in sizes from two to ten buildings for a small family and to twenty buildings for a larger one, arranged according to a well-established pattern. When setting up a new home or family homestead a man first decided on the position of the fence and the gate. He would then build a house for his first wife opposite the gate, close to the fence and another one, the main house, for himself in the middle of the compound.

When he took a second wife, her house would be built on the right of the first wife's house as viewed by a person entering the gate, and then a third wife's house would be built on the left, and so on. Each wife would also have at least one granary beside her house. Young unmarried men traditionally slept in a hut close to the gate-way, and unmarried girls stayed with old women in a nearby village or with their grandmother if she lived inside their father's compound. When the boys grew up and found wives of their own, they would build their houses outside the fence. The first son would build on the right as you leave the gate and the second son on the left. The same pattern, as illustrated above, would be followed when they took more than one wife. The number of houses depended on the size of the family when it grew up. The basic social group was the extended family consisting of a husband, his wives and their unmarried children. Although the chief should also have the same households, his should be surrounded by other households and there should be a cattle kraal and a gathering place for tribal court.

The houses were round in shape, with sloping cone-shaped roof of thatch with overhanging eaves. The roof was frame in lighter material. The wall would be plastered, inside and outside, with a mixture of clay and cow dung, the straw in the dung binding the mixture together. The roof was thatched with grass or reeds, depending on what was available. Decorative patterns would be applied to the outside the house. The walls were smeared with cow dung to cut down on dust and resultant infections from the insects that hide there. The walls of the house would be resurfaced every year and the thatch, too, would have to be replaced periodically every four or five years. Unlike today, grass used for thatching was freely available on the land lying fallow (*magola*), and sometimes poor-quality grass could be found on virgin arable land (*hwiting*).

Back to the subject of a shelter used as a temporary structure: these shelters were a top priority in most survival emergencies. Severe weather conditions could kill within a few hours if one did not have some type of shelter to defend one from the elements, particularly for hunters and gatherers. The Batubatse people used to live near rivers and chose natural rock shelters on low mountains and caves which they also used for rituals. Most Batubatse traditional healers kept their medicines inside a shelter and would sometimes communicate with their ancestors' spirits there. Besides the traditional healer himself, only a few people had access to such shelters. When the traditional healer died that rock or cave shelter became sacred.

Large shelters were difficult to heat and took more materials, but were more comfortable and could disperse smoke better than a small shelter. The poorer the quality of thatch, the steeper the pitch of the roof had to be in order to deflect heavy rain. A high roof of the shelter handled smoke much better whereas a low roof was easier to heat. According to local conditions, some shelters were made underground, while others were constructed on a temporary or permanent basis.

STORYTELLING, RIDDLES, IDIOMS AND GAMES

Storytelling *(polelo ya dinnkane/ dinonnwane),* the conveying of events in words, has been shared in every culture as a means of entertainment, cultural preservation and the instilling of moral values. Storytelling pre-dates writing, with the earliest form of storytelling combining gesture and expressions for emphasis. It has been a tradition which varies all over the world, yet has many things in common. Many people today, like the author, are rediscovering the pleasure of telling stories, especially if it has been largely lost in their traditional culture. It must be remembered that in many old traditions storytelling was synonymous with song, chant, music or epic poetry.

Traditionally Africans have revered good stories, and storytelling was rooted in oral culture and traditions. Oral African storytelling was essentially a communal experience. Everyone participated in formal and informal storytelling as an interactive oral performance. Such participation was an essential part of traditional African communal life, and basic training in a particular culture's oral arts and skills. It was an essential part of children's traditional indigenous education on their way to initiation into full human-ness. Some short stories, referred to as fairy tales, were clearly not intended to be understood as true. They were full of clearly defined incidents with little or no connection to reality. There were also stories that were supposed to have actually happened at a particular time and place. These are referred to as legends. Ghost and lover's leap stories belong to this category.

In indigenous culture of Batubatse storytelling was typically passed on by oral means in a quiet and relaxing environment, which usually coincides with family or tribal community gathering and official events such as family occasions, rituals, or ceremonial practices. The most accomplished storytellers were initiates, who had mastered many complex verbal, musical and memory skills after years of specialised training. This training often included a strong spiritual and ethical dimension, required to control the special energy believed to be released by spoken or sung words in oral performances. Elders, parents and grandparents were typically involved, among the Batubatse, in teaching the children the cultural beliefs, along with history, community values and teaching of land. The emphases on attentiveness to surrounding events and important of oral tradition teaches children the skill of keen attention. In oral traditions, stories were kept alive by being told again and again.

In order to ensure that each member or child had equal access to the elders and the storyteller during storytelling, listeners seated themselves in a circle, which promoted a feeling of unity because no person was at the head. During the telling of the story, children might act as participants by asking questions, acting out the story, or telling minor parts of the story. Furthermore, stories were not often told in the same manner twice, resulting in many variations of a single myth. This is because narrators might choose to insert new elements into old stories, depending upon the relationship between the storyteller and the audience, making the story correspond to each unique situation. During the evening children would persuade an old woman to tell them stories (*dinngane*). She would start by saying *nnkane-nnkane* (story-story) and they would reply by saying *nnkane* (story). Then she would go on to tell them the story. Today storytelling has almost died out, which is a pity as it was an important part of our cultural training.

There are various stories which were used to instruct children about cultural values and lessons. For example the Batubatse would use the tale of an owl snatching away misbehaving children as a means to correct inappropriate behaviour and promote cooperation. Young boys were often told the story of a young man who never took care of his body, and as a result his feet failed to run when he tried to escape from predators. Children would be taught not to be forgetful. They would be told that there was a man who had six donkeys which he loved. These donkeys used to return home on their own, all of them together. But on a certain day only one returned. The boy was distressed and mounted that donkey to look in the bush for the remaining five donkeys that did not return home. To his joy he found them, but was surprised to see only five donkeys instead of six. He looked for the sixth donkey but did not find it. Sadly he drove the five donkeys home and kraaled them. Unaware that he had climbed off the other donkey, he counted them before he could close the kraal. To his surprise he saw all six of his donkeys and did not know where the sixth donkey came from. Annoyed with himself and tired, he went to sleep.

Legends talked about cultural heroes and important ancestors who were intelligent, courageous and generous. Young people learned about these illustrious ancestors through storytelling. Within the Batubatse people the young groom would research his family history that had been passed down through legends and chose an important ancestor to emulate as his role model. In a real sense these ancestors participated in and influenced the lives of people today.

Storytelling would also be derived from a poem (*sereto*, plural *direto*). Praise poems were and are still being composed by praise poets whenever an appropriate occasion arose. A poet could compose a praise poem about virtually anything. There are praise poems about people, animals, natural phenomena, good or bad important events, life and death. Poems were composed on the spur of the moment. An African praise poet might be a special poet for a chief or king. The only qualification that one needs was expertise in praise singing.

The Batubatse were also involved in a game of riddles (*dithai*) mainly for entertainment and stimulation. Riddles are not just a form of entertainment; they play an important role in the social and cultural education of children. They are useful tools in the children's cognitive development. They teach rules of behaviour, explain and interpret natural phenomena and are an acceptable medium for questioning social taboos and restricted subjects. Riddles provide a safe avenue for transmitting restricted information as well as intimate and vital knowledge. Riddles, unlike storytelling, were brief and based on observations of nature. The listener was expected to guess the answer to a question or the meaning of a statement. For instance, during the evening while seated with others around the fire, a child would say "witches are dancing on the thorns", which was a riddle meaning "hail-stones bounce as they fall on the grass". Today riddles, like storytelling, have almost died out, which is a pity as they were an important part of our cultural training.

Proverbs (*diema*) and idioms (*dika*) were found in almost every African culture, Batubatse being no exception. There was a world of wisdom contained in these sayings and, and apart from being a source of entertainment, they were learning tools by which of Africa's history has been passed on through the generation.

Indigenous games were played, their objective being to train the young minds, eyes, hands and feet as well as general motor co-ordination. They were divided according to gender. For instance boys played *moruba* – a game played by two contenders moving pips or stones along lines of holes ranging from ten to twenty in length and four in breadth, or *morabaraba* where the objects were shifted along lines drawn on the ground. Another game was *moswe* played by hopping while sitting on your heels in a frog-like position. For girls there was *kgati* in which two girls swing a rope and one or more skip over it in the middle; *diketo* or *dinketo* played by girls seated around a number of small stones on the ground, one player throwing a stone in the air and, before catching it again, rearranging the other stones on the ground, thus improving eye-hand co-ordination; *tseretsere* where players push a flat stone with their toes across rectangular lines drawn on the ground; *banana* in which stones were used to portray family members in this world of make-believe; and many other games.

ARTS AND CRAFTS

Traditional art played an important role in the lives of the Batubatse people as it did with the 3,000 ethnic groups of indigenous people from tribal societies all over Africa. Art embraced various creative activities – imaginative designs, sounds and ideas – considered by the community to have artistic merit. Art served not only to beautify the human environment. The beauty of Batubatse art was simply an element of its function, for these objects would not be effective if they were not aesthetically pleasing. Its beauty and its content thus combine to make art the vehicle that ensures the survival of tradition. The Batubatse were noted for their traditional arts and crafts and for their expertise in the exploitation of a range of resources to produce items needed for everyday household use and survival activities.

Household utensils included different sizes of clay pots (*dipitša tša letsopa/botsopa*), heated and hardened for longevity, used for cooking, brewing beer and storing milk, water and other liquids, clay being resistant to contamination and able to withstand heat. *Pit ša* was a wide- mouthed clay pot for cooking family meals; *moeta* and *motjega* were clay pots used to contain drinks and keep them cool. From grass and reeds they were able to produce *legogo or legogwa* or *pate,* a woven mat used for sitting or sleeping; *moseamo*, a rolled mat to rest one's head when resting; *seroto*, a grass-woven deep grain basket; *serotwana*, a smaller version of *seroto* used as a kitchen utensil; *seshego*, a large basket for the long-term storage of grains; *lehlotlo*, a traditional strainer in the brewing of home-made beer; and *lefielo or leswielo*, a short broom made from a bunch of grass to sweep the yard.

Wood provided implements such as spoons (*mago*, single *lego*), shorter and broader, which helped in the preparation of porridge and samp and for dishing out food; porridge-stirrers (*mafehlo*, single *lefehlo*), long sticks with thin bark strips attached to them for stirring soft porridge; *lehuduo*, a long wooden spoon for stirring cooked food; *leselo*, a large shallow woven tray used for winnowing grain (*go fefera*); *tsaana or tselwana*, a small shallow woven tray used to hold seed or cover food; *kgamelo*, a deep wooden milking-pail also used as a household container; *mogopo*, a wooden bowl used to keep food fresh and warm for the head of the family; *telo*, a wooden bowl like a plate used to serve food for other members of the family; and *mese* and *mahudu*, pestle and mortar used to grind grains into meal. *Mokgopu*, made out of a gourd, was a scoop to pour liquids into a container, especially home-brewed beer. *Kgapa* was a large calabash with a narrow mouth for the storing of milk; *sego* was a gourd or a wide-mouthed calabash used as a cup to hold water, milk or traditional beer; *sefago* was a large round *kgapa* cut in half; and *sefagwana* was a small calabash used to shovel meal out of a bigger container. *Leselo* and *tsaana* were made from a hard-wood tree known as *mogaletlwa,* found mainly on river banks. In addition to the above, wood was used to make pillows (*meseamo*), knobkerries (*dithoka*), chairs (*didulo*), and the handles (*mekgoko*) of many tools including assegais (*marumo*). They were also adept at carving animals and other objects from clay or wood. They worked metal into weapons such as spears and knives as well as implements such as axes (*dilepe*) and hoes (*matjepe*). As regards clothing, the early Batubatse didn't wear much due to the heat but for special ceremonies and meetings they wore loin-cloths and feather headdresses, made typically from animal skins and birds. Later traditional clothing was made from the skins of wild and domestic animals. Hides were used for making ropes, sandals, belts and footwear. For instance *letheba* was a traditional blanket made of animal hide while *kotse* was a traditional shield made of cowhide used by warriors to protect themselves from the spears of the enemy.

The oldest cultural artifacts of the Batubatse were stone tools -- hand axes, cleavers and choppers – and other tools of bone, wood and shell as well as beads, jewellery, grinding stones, clothing and fishing materials. Certain items were used to sanctify burials and are linked to their cosmology and religious beliefs, and they were decorated with variety of beads and other ornaments.

A particular white stone (*legakadima or legakabye*) was trimmed in order to make spears and knives used for carving wood and cutting in general. Sculptures were historically carved in wood and other natural materials that have only survived from a few centuries ago. Traditional music and dancing was largely a communal affair – singing, chanting, and hand-clapping as an accompaniment of dance during various rituals. Musical instruments included drums, rattles, whistles, and stringed instruments.

The emergence of pottery in culture has often been linked with important changes in life-style and this was the case with the Batubatse, representing a highly significant cultural development in their history. Clay pots and figurines served ritual and medical purposes. For the Batubatse pottery was symbolic in the transformation from wet to dry, soft to hard, raw to cooked, natural to cultural and impure to pure through operation of heat. Throughout the ages fine powders of mica have been used for various purposes, including decorations. In art they used ochre of various colours for decoration. Powdered mica was used to decorate water clay pots.

Pottery was primarily a female activity and women were also engaged in beadwork, the weaving of sleeping mats, the finishing and decorating of floors and walls of huts and courtyards. All other crafts were practised by men: woodwork, basket-making, hides and leatherwork, metallurgy, carpentry, ceramic-work and thatching. Specialist iron-smiths used a particular wood commonly found at Maakene/Tsubye for produce a high degree of heat to transform certain minerals into iron for assegais, hoes and other metal tools. Although both "art" and "craft" are creative skills – the former representing a higher degree of intellectual involvement and the latter a more repetitive or purely functional action – the Batubatse did not distinguish between the two. The idea that artists are somehow superior because they create things of beauty, while craftsmen perform a lesser skill in "hands-on" craftsmanship in branches of the decorative arts, was not an issue. Perhaps the only distinction was that a Motubatse craftsman could predict what he was going to create, whereas another Motubatse artist could not predict what he was going to create until he had created it.

Sadly some of the crafts created by Batubatse people have perished or have been bartered away by European exploiters. These crafts included crocheting, knitting, lace-making, weaving, woodcarving, wood-turning, pottery, stoneware, engraving, etc. Weaving, in particular, was a traditional Batubatse craft form – the working with dried grass to create necklaces, bracelets and mats. On the other hand the artworks they created which are still remembered were the drawings and paintings in oil and water-colours, sculpture in metal, stone and wood, and their talents in music and dance.

TRADITIONAL WEAPONS

Long before drive-by shootings and police stabbings, our forefathers used some "badass" traditional weapons, having ceremonial tribal significance, against one another. They seemed to have a knack for finding the most gruesome and painful ways to attack each other; one could even argue that no modern weapons were able to inflict the same level of suffering as these ancient ones. The most commonly weapons used by the Batubatse were assegais/spears (*marumo*, single *lerumo*) and knobkerries. Knives, the rolling of large stones and rocks, bows and arrows, axes, poisons and medicine (*muti*) were included in their arsenal. Knives, axes, serrated blades and spears made of forged iron attest to the skill of the Batubatse blacksmiths. Many exhibited inventive workmanship beyond what was functionally necessary not only as weapons but also for ceremonial or ritual use, or displayed for prestige or status.

By definition, a shield's main purpose was for defence in combat – a warrior would shield himself while at the same time attacking the enemy with his assegai. Yet it was also an object of ostentatious display. A shield could be brandished on a feast day, in a ritual dance or a parade, as its presence in the tournaments of the medieval period makes abundantly clear. According to Batubatse tradition, shields were used not only as defensive weapons, but also as decorative or ritual objects with symbolic meaning. These shields could be carved from wood, or woven, or made from a variety of hides and even metals.

African tribes were renowned for the use of shields and assegais, the latter usually comprising a shaft tipped with a blade for throwing and stabbing. Axes were used as a weapon but also for chopping. Early axes were made of wood and stone (*petwane*). The manufacture of stone blades led to stone spears, points, barbs, and shaped stone knives and scrapers. Stones were used to erect walls (*merako*) forming a strong defence around a fort, and they were also used in the building of kraals. Knives made from a white stone (*legakadima*) were also used in stabbing at a close range.

CATTLES, DONKEY, SHEEP AND GOAT ENCLOSURES

There is archaeological evidence of the presence of domestic cattle in East Africa from an early date. Many breeds of cattle found today originate from the introduction of un-humped cattle from Eurasia and humped cattle from Asia. Whether cattle domestication occurred independently on the African continent is a controversial question. One theory is that Africa's earliest cattle were introduced from south-west Asia through the Nile Valley or via the Horn of Africa. In most of Africa, including the Batubatse tribes, cattle carry a proportionate high value and are linked to prestige and political power. In certain areas cattle ownership was restricted to members of the royal families. Of all livestock, cattle needed special care and enclosure.

Among the Batubatse communities, domesticated animals were raised in an agricultural setting to produce food and hides, and as a source of labour and profit. This had been practised since the transition to farming from their hunter-gather lifestyle. Manure collected from livestock enclosures was used for plastering walls and floors, and as fuel for fire. The kraal (*mašaka*) , an Afrikaans word for an enclosure for cattle or other livestock, was made of poles, stones and thorn-bushes. The term is also used for a settlement and a typical Motubatse kraal consisted of a number of round huts grouped in a circle or crescent, with the cattle-kraal placed in the centre for defensive purpose and to prevent stock theft.

This would also protect the animals from attack by lions. Enclosures were inexpensive to build and maintain and were only occupied by livestock at night. Donkeys needed additional shelter from the elements as well as protection from predators. This was provided by a barn enclosure near the cattle-kraal contiguous to an open pasture. Among the Batubatse sheep and goats were also kept as pets as were easy to handle and responded well to human attention. However, they were more vulnerable to attacks by predators such as dogs and jackals. Their shelter, therefore, was placed within the cattle-kraal and was kept dry to prevent hoof or other disease problems.

TRANSPORT

The primary means of transport in for the early Batubatse was walking or riding on a beast of burden. The condition of paths and tracks was generally very poor and changing weather was always a challenge. Batubatse men were generally depicted carrying loads on yokes, on their backs or on their shoulders. Their women appear to have balanced loads on their heads or supported them with their hips. A day's march was between 20 and 40 kilometres. Elderly people mostly used walking-sticks at times, as did travellers. The walking stick served both as a weapon against robbers and as a walking aid. With the passing of time the use of sleds, sledges or sleighs as their mode of transport were introduced. Wooden sledges date back to 7,000 BC and communities living by hunting and fishing probably used dogs to pull them. Later more sophisticated sleighs were developed with a smooth underside providing low-friction travel for passengers and goods across the ground, on mud, grass or even smooth stones.

For the Batubatse there was only one vehicle, the sleigh (*selei*) being their general term for any design. Sleighs were typically drawn by two or four, sometimes even six, beasts of burden. They were made of wooden poles and were used to convey a variety of materials, even heavy blocks of stone. The history of transport was largely one of technological innovation. Advances in technology have allowed people to travel further, explore more territory, and expand their influence over larger and larger areas. As new inventions and discoveries were applied to transport problems, travel time decreased while the ability to move more and larger loads increased.

Various beasts of burden have been used for ploughing and transporting goods dating back to ancient times. Donkey domestication happened first in northern Africa about a thousand years ago, but this mode of transport used to carry loads, to pull carts and to do heavy work came late for most South African tribes, between the end of the nineteenth and the beginning of the twentieth century, Batubatse included. Today donkeys are often conceived of as animals of the poor, and little is known about their breeding. The Batubatse used oxen, usually in pairs, for transporting heavy materials. A yoke was put on the animal's neck, so that the weight of the load being pulled or transported was distributed equally across the shoulders.

Cattle used for transport were referred to as *makaba*. The nose of a *lekaba* (single pack ox) was pierced through for a rope to be inserted for control and to direct them to the desired direction. Young riders would climb *makaba* and use the ropes on their noses to guide them in the direction they wished to go. *Makaba* were mostly used to drive other cattle home and to carry light goods. Today, of course, the Batubatse use modern means of transport for this purpose.

"Freedom is a package deal – with it comes responsibilities and consequences."
- Unknown

4
CULTURAL PRACTICES AND BELIEFS

Bone reading as practiced by a traditional African diviner

Statues of Batubatse Gods

ANCESTORS WORSHIP

Ancestor worship is the most universal cultural religion of Africa. Though Islam has conquered much of North Africa and Christianity, as the world sees it, has conquered the rest, the surviving belief over all is the power of ancestor worship. It is common knowledge that the African preachers of the leading denominations consult witchdoctors, now referred as traditional healers. The most popular denominations openly combine Christianity with ancestor worship, much as Roman Catholicism combined idolatry and Christianity in centuries past. It makes no difference whether a person is educated or not. It has happened in the past that when someone had stolen something, the victim of theft would seriously consider calling a witchdoctor to determine who did it. That threat worked, for the stolen item would be returned within a short space of time.

The practice of ancestor's worship by the Batubatse people is closely associated with that of the neighbouring Bapedi of Sekhukhune, Baroka and other African tribes, with important similarities in their religious values such as the belief in life after death. Ancestor reverence is a continental-wide cultural practice, and the idea of a Biblical God, who sends misfortune on people for unknown reasons and causes dreadful sufferings to mankind, is uncommon. Since living people were unable to communicate with him, they could not truly believe in his existence.

Unlike most other religions, traditional Batubatse ancestor worship was practised every day, not just on Sundays. Whenever a major step was taken, the Gods were informed. The spirit of the dead are said to live on as long as there is someone to remember them. As a consequence the kings, chiefs and heroes, who were celebrated by oral tradition, live on for centuries, while the spirits of common people may vanish in the turn of a few generations.

Libation was part of ancient Egyptian culture to honour the various divinities, sacred ancestors and important people. It spread out to other regions in Africa and elsewhere – it was practiced in Rome, in China and other countries. Africans – those at home and in the Diaspora – pour libations to their ancestors. This pouring of a drink offering to the Gods is done in the belief that people do not "pass away" but "pass on"; it is to ensure that the bond between the departed, the living and those yet to be born is not broken and is an offering to Gods or spirits in memory of those who have died. Various substances are used for libation, usually water and oil. The strengthening and protection of a person's spirit (*seriti*) was essential during his or her life to protect it from any harm which may cause death to the body.

The Batubatse ritual pouring of a libation was also an essential ceremonial giving homage to the ancestors, and inviting their participation in public functions. The ritual was generally performed by an elder of the tribe or household. Libation was poured during traditional marriage ceremonies and at the installation of kings and chiefs. It is believed that the *seriti* in conjunction with the breathing of air (*moya*) attains such supernatural powers that it is worshiped by living Batubatse people as a whole.

Ancestor worship, sometimes called "animism", is often perceived as a religion of fear. The believers were in fear of angering the ancestors. When things go wrong the witchdoctor was consulted. Invariably the diagnosis was that the worshipper had angered the ancestors and that a feast must be held to put matters right. A feast was expensive because the whole community was allowed to come and eat. A cow or a goat would be killed by the witchdoctor in a traditional way, much beer brewed and great pots of stiff corn meal porridge prepared. Relatives, friends and neighbours would attend, many getting drunk in the process. Of course the witchdoctor received a large fee for his services, plus the best piece of meat. Older people were especially honoured because they would soon become ancestors. It would be to one's advantage if the old person liked you. Then he or she would be willing to help you from the spirit world.

Children were taught that ancestors' spirits have to be respected, honoured and obeyed, this being manifested in sacrifices. Ancestors have power over the living, a belief also held by the Israelis and other tribes, who worshipped their own ancestors. When a group of people abandoned this traditional ancestor worship after the birth of Jesus Christ and turned instead to worship only one God, called Jehovah, this proved problematical.

When the missionaries introduced Christianity in Africa, people were enjoined to believe that the ancestral spirit to whom the Christians pray was the only real God. Most people resisted since their own ancestral spirit was their real God – one who had power over their life and death, their sickness and health, and their poverty and prosperity. The teaching of the wisdom of the ancestors was essential for their prosperity. That knowledge must be understood and the same rituals performed lest their logic be lost. They believed that colonialism replaced African traditional beliefs with Eurocentric mis-education and that colonialists distorted, disfigured and destroyed the past of the oppressed people. Colonialists regarded those who prayed to their Ancestors, rather than to the Biblical God, as sinful. As a consequence Africans suffered cultural amnesia.

The Batubatse believed that their ancestors were vested with mystical powers and authority, and that they retained a functional role in the world of the living, specifically in the lives of their living kinsmen. Indeed an African kinship-group is often described as a community of both the living and the dead. This relationship can be described as ambivalent, punitive and benevolent, sometime even capricious. In general ancestral benevolence was assured through propitiation and sacrifice; neglect was believed to bring about punishment. Ancestors were intimately involved with the welfare of their kinship-group through the authority of the elders, the elders thus being the true representatives of the ancestors and the mediators between them and the kinship-group. The Batubatse's emphasis was clearly not on life after death but rather on the manner in which the dead affect the living.

The ancestral spirit, to the Batubatse, was the real God and, no matter how educated one may be, one should never believe in someone else's God or promote that God to the exclusion of this ancestral spirit. It is their firm belief that one's ancestors have power over life and death, over sickness and health, and over poverty and prosperity. The wisdom of the ancestors was a reality that had to be accepted and understood; that there was logic in the performing of certain rituals to tap into that wisdom. Without proper mental training this logic would be lost to their descendants. In this context colonialism replaced the African traditional belief system with Eurocentric malediction, and colonialists by perverted logic distorted, disfigured and destroyed the past of the oppressed people. The author cites the following event: on 7 May 2008 he was involved in a motor vehicle accident in which both his legs were broken and he had to undergo several operations in hospital. The first thing that came to his mind, he says, was to pray to his ancestor for survival. He implored his sisters, brothers, cousins and other relatives to do likewise to their respective ancestral spirits. The result was a speedy and complete recovery, which astounded the medical staff. Today he can walk, run, jump and *toyi-toyi* as well as if not better than before the accident. What is more, on the day he was informed by the doctor that he would be discharged from hospital, he was given a Mercedes Benz C220 diesel car by his nephew, Mabu Johannes Mmola, a vehicle that he had been longing to own for some time. This was the outcome of praying to his ancestors. His good fortune continued and in the same year on 21 August and 22 October 2008 he bought a new 4×4 Dodge Nitro and Gonow 2.2i X-space vehicles respectively. Not someone's God, but his ancestor, gave him these vehicles.

Despite what members of other religious cults or faiths say about their ancestors, he is steadfast in his conviction that what the ancestor spirits desire is to be remembered by their descendants as he did himself. Living persons must associate themselves with their ancestors' spirit just as a group of people in Israel associated themselves with the spirit of Jesus through prayers. The author's belief is that if this had been done faithfully, the reward to the living would be good health for themselves and their live-stock, plentiful rains and good harvests. In the present day this is no longer happening because people have distanced themselves from their God or ancestral spirits.

Not every ancestor qualifies to be worshipped as a *Modimo* (God), but only those who occupied an exalted position in their lifetime. For instance, the spirits of young people, especially children, go to their forefathers – they do not become Gods. The understanding is that only a man or woman who has become sterile through old age can become an ancestor spirit. Such persons would normally have children and grandchildren who could honour them as a *Modimo* (God). The spirits of young parents who die after already having children would be worshipped by those children, but it would be even better to worship the ancestors of those people. According to Batubatse belief, if one should dream of a dead person, even of a child, it would be proper to make a small sacrifice to such a spirits.

We have been taught that all the dead live in the world of the ancestors (*Badimong*), whether they become Gods or not. But those who died prematurely and were not buried properly with all the necessary rites cannot reside in that world. Such people's spirits become ghosts (*sepoko*/*setšhoša*) which haunt their graves in the form of a bright light, and also haunt the homes of their descendants, making life unpleasant for them. This happening could be prevented by the offspring carrying out the proper rites – slaughtering an animal (goat, sheep or beast) and offering beer. When appeased in this way the spirit will depart to the ancestral world and become a normal ancestor spirit. The author proudly states, without mincing words, that to this day all the deceased members of the Batubatse community have been buried in accordance with the necessary burial rites. The place of abode of the *Badimo* is without doubt a land of plenty, where the grass is always green, the cattle plentiful and fat, and everybody happy; otherwise these spirits would return to where we live and cause suffering and hardship.

Although the Chief is the most important living man, *Badimo* stands above him. It follows naturally that the spirits of departed chiefs are the supreme ancestor spirits of the whole tribe. Thus the spirits of the departed Chiefs of Batubatse Ba-Shai are similarly regarded. Our worship of *Badimo* follows throughout the structural order. Households worship the ancestors of the head of the household; the members of a family offer thanksgiving to, or beg forgiveness from, their own forefathers. The Batubatse people do not worship their ancestors for more than two or three generation back. In the normal course of events the most recently deceased relative is the most influential ancestor spirit. In my case my late father, Masilo Koranta Seshai, and his three deceased wives are the most influential ancestor spirits in my life and any occurrence which affected me is considered to have been brought about by them. In our prayers we refer to our ancestors of more than two or three generations through our recent ancestral spirits. There is definitely no relationship with the Jewish God.

The main method of communication between the ancestor spirits and the living descendants are dreams (*ditoro*). While one can talk with *Modimo* directly, the ancestor cannot speak directly to one as a living person, but can express his desires by visiting the person in dreams. While in hospital after the motor vehicle accident as mentioned above, the author's ancestral spirit communicated twice with him. This happened after he spoke to his late father and mother and asked them if he could join them in their after-life. He saw his lovely parents, Masilo Koranta and Makgwedi Mapheya, sitting together looking at him in pain. His father told him that they were with him and that his broken legs would become functional again. His mother was nodding her head as a sign of agreement. Behind them were seated two unknown old men. In his dream he stood up and walked directly to them but as he approached they waved their right hands to indicate that he should not come nearer. When he continued to walk slowly towards them it suddenly became dark and he could not see them. Behind him the way was clear so he turned back to where he was.

The second vision revealed his father with his three wives and his father told him that it was still early for him to join them. He was ordered to go back to the Batubatse people to carry out the duties that were still required of him. He woke up to realise that the time was not ripe for him to die.

All dreams are not necessarily important, but those that one remembers are assumed to be a sign from ancestors, especially if one is troubled by a dream, or if it coincides with some distressing event; then one would know that this was a sign from *Badimo*. This is precisely what happened to the author before he was involved in the accident. That is why he gave instructions while still at the private hospital in Pretoria to the effect that prayer *(go rapela)* or sacrifice *(go phasa)* should be done to appease his ancestors.

Ancestor spirits are sometimes seen or heard during the night. There was a saying that some hundred years ago one could see the great Shai ancestral spirits just before sunrise every morning near the mountains of Tsubye, Rita and other locations, driving their livestock and carrying their possessions across a path. These names are commemorated in Batubatse praise poems *(direto)* as well as in the names of the Sediba-Sebore fountain, Tubatse, Bolebye and certain animals. The ancestors could also be heard playing their drums *(meropa)* near the same mountains. There is a Rita Mountain near the present township of Lenyenye, but the one referred to in poems is in Bokhalaka from where most of the black tribes emanated or passed en route to the south.

Worship of the ancestors involved a complex series of prayers, the sacrifice of a holy cow, drinking of traditional beer with much dancing, singing and drumming, all of which followed strict rites to appease the ancestors. The ritual, similar to a church gathering, was known as *go phasa Badimo*, and was attended by relatives, young and old, well-wishers and other members of the community. A libation of sorghum beer would be poured by an appropriate elder at the *Lekatlelo*, a special place in the corner of a household earmarked for this purpose. During this process the elder would recount to the immediate ancestor the fortunes and misfortunes being experiencing by the family and would recite a praise poem *(sereto)*. When this had been done, the guests would return to the feast, eating the rest of the meat and drinking the remaining beer. The same process was followed during traditional rain ceremonies. To complete the ritual all the bones would be collected and burned or placed on the grave of one of the ancestors.

Sacrifice to the ancestors of the family unit (*kgoro*) was done by all members, with each household contributing its share. Before the meat of the slaughtered animal could be prepared for consumption, a portion of heart, nose, tongue or ear would be placed on the special place for sacrifice. The ancestors would then be requested to ensure that the livestock of that particular animal would flourish. Traditionally no salt would be added to the meat cooked for the event and all the meat had to be consumed, with no portion being taken from the household where the sacrifice was taking place. The skin of the slaughtered beast was cut into small bracelets for each member of the family to wear on the left arm, and this would be witnessed by the ancestor.

At the beginning of the year, before they could eat any new fruits and vegetables, they would gather at a specific place to perform certain rituals and drink soft beer mixed with medicine. If any member of the unit was not present they would pour the soft beer into a calabash representing the absent person. They would also cook a vegetable known as *mogopu* and consume it without adding any salt. Thereafter another ritual would be performed at the entrance of the kraal, which had to be trampled on by the cattle, donkeys, sheep and goats when they left the enclosure. Having performed all of these rites, the family could now eat the fruits and vegetables harvested in the new season.

There is also oral evidence of human sacrifices when captured enemies were thrown off mountains as a victory thanksgiving sacrifice to the ancestors.

In the event of the death of someone far from home, usually a hunter, soldier or a women gathering firewood, the body would be carried back home. During the journey, if the carriers stopped to rest and laid the corpse on the side of the path, this resting place was treated with great respect. Once the corpse of the dead person had been taken home for burial, a large stone was placed where the corpse had been laid. This would be the start of a mound (*seotlo*). Any persons passing this site would place a stone or a twig on the mound without looking at it. Everyone, whether related to the dead person or not was expected to follow this practice. Sometime a person spat saliva on the mound. This was the origin of the large heaps of stones found at various places. There were also other holy places for the Batubatse associated with their ancestors where sacrifices were occasionally made at the direction of the diviner.

Ancestor worship is a component of faith, almost as old as religion itself and is embraced in various forms by societies throughout the world. Like other aspects of faith, it has no tangible form and is predicated on an abiding and firm acceptance of its existence, rooted deeply both in history and culture. Regrettably it can be preyed upon by persons using elaborate fraudulent schemes to exploit such beliefs to their own profit, at the same time causing harm, injury and grief to the victims. These callous deceivers obtain money from unsuspecting victims with promises to cure their ailments, solve their personal problems and secure their health and wealth through the medium of their ancestors. Those seduced by these offers would, unsuspectingly, either make their way or be led to the so-called traditional healers, the end-result being the loss of their hard-earned money to the fraudsters who might be arrested but more likely would disappear without a trace.

SACRED PLACES OF BATUBATSE AND PRACTICES

The Batubatse held their ancestors in sacred esteem but also revered certain symbols and places as sacred. Objects used for spiritual purposes such as the worship of ancestors are considered holy or sacred and play a part in every religion. Sacred objects include land, water, people, plants and animals that have been recognised as having a "sacred quality" and "value" to humanity and that enhance all life on our Mother Earth, and that deserve to be specially honoured, acknowledged, protected and shared.

Sacred land includes sacred caves and shelters of the ancients that have been recognised as having spiritual significance or symbolism. Sacred water consists of springs, water-holes and water sources, rivers, waterfalls, lakes and estuaries deemed to have spiritual and sacred healing properties. All burial sites and graves are considered sacred ground. Sacred plants include indigenous seeds that have spiritual significance or healing properties. Sacred animals are those that have been recognised as having spiritual significance.

Since ancient time sacred sites have had a mysterious allure for the Batubatse tribes in common with many people in South Africa. The country has thousands of places regarded as sacred, for there are as many sacred sites as there are beliefs and cultures. Sacred communion with the spirit world would take place at certain mountain ranges, fountains and caves, sacred sites only known to the few. Some are still carefully guarded by indigenous people and are sites of secret ceremonies and prayers. Legends and contemporary reports tell us of the extraordinary experiences people have had while visiting these places. Different sacred sites had the power to heal the body, enlighten the mind and inspire the heart. Tsubye was truly the "Land of Legends" since there were so many beliefs and stories about the supernatural that could only be experienced during an extend visit. In Limpopo there are a number of sites sacred to the people living in the province, which are considered to be "the place of unity and strength" or what many spiritualists believe are "energy centres" and which outsiders are seldom allowed to visit. These sacred sites are reputed to be the places of sacrifice for the tribe or people who once lived there or nearby.

One concept vital to Batubatse traditional religion was that life itself was held to be sacred. The birth of a child was the most significant event of humanity. Life must be given, must be lived, must be enjoyed, must be made honourable. Therefore, in the true setting of the Batubatse, abortion or even contraception was a rarity, if not an impossibility. Sacredness of life is interlinked to immortality. The person is body and soul at the same time. Death was not considered to be the end of man but a change of state. Death was regarded as a journey into a better world where a person lives for ever. In that world of the dead, the person was not just indifferent to what happens among the living. He was so alive that he was interested, and actually takes part, in the affair of the living.

Before moving to Maakene, the Batubatse settled in the vicinity of Stoffberg in the Greater Tubatse Municipality. It is said that the sacred fountain in the bush near their Head kraal, called "Sediba-Sebore", was regarded as "The place of the Batubatse Gods" and "The Mother of the Batubatse tribes". Apparently the fountain never dried up. At night the sound of drumming and singing could be heard, seemingly emanating from the pool of water. It is understood that one of the earlier leaders of the Batubatse was buried or disappeared near that fountain. The place was reputedly haunted by ghosts, so few people dared to approach it. It is here that the ancestral spirits of the Batubatse could be located. It is said that the fountain is still there and had been cordoned with a fence by the present owner. The Batubatse lived there until the threat of being attacked by a strong army of the Pedi of Sekhukhune from Bokgatla persuaded them to leave. Permission to visit the fountain is rarely granted, but once a year some of the Batubatse members, with the agreement of the owner, visit the fountain to offer sacrifices. The spirits of the Batubatse are associated with mountains, rivers and symbols, and were treated with awe and fear. They firmly believe their Great Ancestor guided them from the mountains at Mashishing to where they settled at Tsubye Mountain.

One of the peaks of Tsubye Mountain was sacred since some ancestors were buried there. If anyone climbed it he would never return or would go mad. They say the river rising at the peak never stopped flowing during the dry season or at the time of drought. One of the legends surrounding the sacred cave in the Tsubye Mountain, Maakene, is that a senior traditional healer who entered the cave to collect ochre for rain-making medicine never returned but could be seen, at a distance, walking nearby.

Another legend was that the cave was the home of a python. At the start of spring a person from the Royal House would leave a calabash of millet beer at the entrance of the cave. If on his return he found the calabash empty, it would mean that the coming season would be fruitful. If not, then an appeal would be made to the ancestral spirits to bless the season. Before anyone approached the cave certain rituals were performed to ensure his safe passage.

Close by the cave is the Tsubye forest where a sacred white lion is alleged to protect the graves of the royal family members buried there. The forest was also the habitat of the sacred python which, so they say, required human wives to visit it at night. Then there were the sacred baboons living on the nearby Tsubye Hills which warned the Batubatse people of approaching enemies. Beer, snuff and grain were placed on a sacred stone at the foot of the hill to appease the ancestral spirits.

Even to this day the sound of drums can be heard on the Tsubye Mountain, played by the ancestors who come alive at night. The sound of wailing is interpreted as the weeping of the Batubatse ancestors for the land from which they have come. Some say two elephants can be seen dancing to the drum-beat. Tsubye Mountain has thus a special meaning in the life of Batubatse people.

In the foothills of the mountain the bellowing of cattle could be heard. It was here that the Batubatse Ba-Shai circumcision ceremony usually took place. One could not climb the mountain without being circumcised, and even if one was, there were certain rituals that had to be performed, otherwise one would never return. Bolebye Mountain (Kasteelkop) near Gravelotte was also considered sacred. This was where an offshoot of the Batubatse, led by Masetla Makutuma Maenetja Shai, settled after they broke away from the main tribe. This was also a burial place for their ancestors, and the same strange and mysterious things as at Tsubye are said to have taken place here. The circumcision ceremonies were also performed here.

Kgoshi Mafedi of the Balebye tribe, like his father Masetla, was a herbalist who regularly visited Kasteelkop, where he kept his medicines. One day he didn't come back and was later found dead in the cave. The royal family closed the mouth of the cave with stones while his body was inside. Since then the cave has become a sacred place which is regularly visited by the Batubatse to perform certain rituals and sacrifices to their ancestors.

Among the Batubatse, even beads may be sacred. They treasured glass beads, which were undoubtedly of ancient origin. All the beads were cut from the same glass tube after it had cooled down, and were strung in the same order that they were cut. The beads were said to contain the spirit of an ancestor which could be seen as a cloud inside the glass.

With the support of the government, the Batubatse tribes can now qualify for the formal registration of their sacred sites with the South Africa Heritage Resource Agency. All the concerned groups should be engaged in negotiations, dialogue and discussions to ensure that they fully understand and approve the full contents of the documentation. We are hopeful for a successful outcome that will set a precedent for registering all sacred sites within the network. The community should be encouraged to approach "The Mupo Foundation" to initiate a process for their natural sacred sites.

IMPURITY AND TABOOS

A lack of respect towards one's superiors in Batubatse culture implies a lack of respect to the ancestors. Children were taught to respect seniors during their lifetime and after their death. Among the Batubatse when a respectable elderly person breaks wind (*a pshinya/sula*) in the presence of his children and grandchildren, the disgusting noise and the foul smell are blamed on the nearest baby or toddler. If there was no baby or toddler nearby those present would suffer the smell in silence and collectively pretend that nothing had happened. That was good old Batubatse politeness. We knowingly blame the innocent or endure smelly realities peacefully rather than name or shame the gods. Some truths are not told, no matter how obvious and well understood they may be. It is not easy in South Africa and in Africa at large to publicly criticise Rolihlahla Nelson Mandela and still keep your good name among families and friends.

---

*The taboos within the Batubatse communities include the following: * Women were not to sit with men. * A daughter-in-law was not supposed to enter the sleeping place of her father-in-law * Men or women in a condition of impurity should not enter the hut/house where birth has taken place. *A man should not have sexual intercourse with menstruating woman, a woman who has had abortion or miscarriage, a pregnant prostitute or a widow before she has been cured or washed. * No one in a condition of impurity should enter the cattle-kraal, work on the land, or attend any religious function * Youngsters were not supposed to drink alcohol. * Adult children were not allowed to have sexual intercourse before the funeral of their recently deceased parents. * Couples should not marry before the ceremony of "second" birth. * Incest, cheating others and stealing constituted taboo. * It was taboo to sit on a cooking stone. * Sisters and brothers should not look on one another while bathing. * Referring to genitals directly in conversation was taboo. * The young or junior wife was not permitted to plant or harvest before the first or senior wife.*

For us, it was rare for a villager to admonish an elder for unhygienic behaviour, or to identify exactly where the disturbing noise and foul smell emanated. Such candour would attract needless attention to oneself for raising issues that all of us know but are either too polite or too cowardly to mention out loud. This kind of disrespect is frowned upon by our ancestors. One cannot shun the unwritten rules of African decorum to expose issues many dare not talk about. Of all the forms of respect expected of a person, the one due to the ancestors is the most important of all.

To despise or anger the ancestors (*go nyatša Badimo*) is regarded as the worst of form. A person was expected to respect certain taboos. Rituals must be observed at all times. Ritual purification was and is still a feature of many religions. The aim of these rituals is to remove specifically defined uncleanliness prior to a particular type of activity, and especially prior to the worship of a deity. The ritual uncleanliness is not identical with ordinary physical impurity, such as dirt stains. Deities are frequently expressed as having human form. In religious belief a deity is a supernatural being, who may be thought holy, godly, or sacred. Some define a deity as "a being" with powers greater than those of ordinary human beings, but who interact with humans, positively or negatively, in ways that carry us to new levels of consciousness beyond the grounded preoccupations of ordinary life.

They are often thought to be immortal, and are assumed to have personality and to possess consciousness, intellect, desires, and emotions comparable (but usually superior) to human beings. Immortality is eternal life: the ability to live for ever.

Natural phenomena whose causes were not well understood, such as lightning and catastrophes such as earthquakes and floods, were attributed to deities.

The concept of impurity (*ditshila*) refers particularly to ritual. A woman giving birth, the foetus of an unborn child, the placenta and the hut where the birth has taken place, are impurities. The same applies to a woman who has a miscarriage, children who are born malformed, children who are born with teeth, children who are born feet first, a pregnant woman as a result of prostitution, and a woman who had abortion.

There is also the concept of shadow (*moriti*), which is conceived of as an evil power, which may infect both people and objects. A person may transmit a shadow to persons and things. Sickness and death are impure as well. A person who attended a funeral or who has lost a close relative is believed to have been infected by the death. A woman who gave birth to a child or has had a miscarriage was believed to have *moriti*. Certain tribes believe that twins have such a strong shadow that if they come near a sick person he will die: hence twins must be killed. A person whose upper teeth appear before the lower or whose molars appear first was full of *moriti* and should be killed. However, such beliefs had no substance within the Batubatse. To them, having twins was a blessing from our ancestors. Among the Batubatse a number of twins had been born, and while some died, others remained alive. Ramoshaba Seshai Shai had two sets of twins. The first set both died immediately, while of the second set only one died. The one who survived was Rakau Jonathan Seshai. Mamakobe Asariel Seshai had twins. Motlatjo Seshai, married to Ramasobane, had twins called Matlala and Mokgadi. The author, Ponele Seshai Shai, also had twins by his third wife, called Ntima and Ntimana. His eldest son from his first marriage was Phaile, whose upper teeth appeared before the lower ones. Nothing was said and nothing has happened to this very day. All these parents were delighted with their children and family members.

In the past albinism (*bohwetlhe*), a deficiency of melanin pigmentation in the skin, hair and eyes which provides protection from the sun's ultraviolet rays, was considered an impure condition. Albinos (*mahwetlhe*, singular *lehwetlhe*) were shunned as they were believed **to** bring misfortune at home and within the community. An albino is believed to be deficient in organic substance and therefore unable to think. People suffering from this condition were discriminated against and persecuted, driven from the community or even killed in many African countries. In Tanzania they are killed and dismembered due to a widespread belief that charms made from their body-parts bring fortune and prosperity. Such ritual killings have occurred in neighbouring Burundi and other areas. Today albino body-parts can fetch thousands of dollars in Tanzania, particularly around the country's Mwanza region where many of the murders have occurred. Among the Batubatse discrimination and ritual killing of the albinos was never practised. Of course albinos are entitled to live like any other human beings. Whyever not?

The condition of impurity is related to the contact disease, *Makhuma* (derived from the verb *go khuma* – to touch). *Makhuma* (to mix together) is a condition similar to *moriti*, but the sickness infects the immediate host, who cannot transmit it to others. If a man has sexual intercourse with a widow, a menstruating woman, a woman who has had miscarriage or an abortion, or a pregnant prostitute, he will contact *makhuma*.

If a man or an impure woman enters the hut where a birth has taken place, the newborn child will get *makhuma*. One may *khuma* if, after an absence from home during which a death occurred, one eats food without taking precautionary measures. A woman who has lost a child will cause her next child to *khuma* if she allows it to suck her breasts before being doctored. Cattle may *khuma* after a death in the village or if a woman enters the kraal. The symptoms of *makhuma* were usually associated with the stomach, but some tribes extend the condition into other parts of the body.

Impurity is not a sanction connected to ancestor spirits. It is an evil which is feared and should be avoided. All conditions of impurity are contaminated with heat, and the ritual cleansing consists largely of applying measures of coolness. Therefore malformed children are put to death and buried in cool, wet soil, to cleanse and protect the mother from producing such children again. The same remedy is applied to after-births and to the foetuses of aborted women. Beer is regarded as cool. Also the green, partly digested food (*moswane*) in the stomach of the sacrificial animal, placed on the grave, is cool.

There is also the concept of taboo (*diila or dikidišwa*) which in some instances overlaps with impurity, but is distinct from it. It is derived from the word to avoid (*go ila*). Taboos may be sometimes ambiguous. However, they should be seen as a social and religious custom placing prohibition or restriction on a particular thing or person: those acts, behaviours or tendencies that are prohibited or restricted by social custom. A taboo can also be seen as something that was designated as sacred and prohibited. Taboos have been formulated a long time ago by the forefathers. Most have their roots in the history or the myths of a community and initiation into a deity service. They can be changed or wiped away, or have others devised and added to the list, depending on the prevailing circumstances and challenges, geographical location, culture and people's perception towards their resources and heritage.

Taboo is a prohibition against certain actions in social life in order to keep peace and harmony and to avoid sickness or famine considered to be a curse from ancestors or spirits. A taboo is "something that you should not do in front of people or something that is strictly prohibited in a given community". Taboos may not always be directly spelled out. Even though all taboos were not supposed to be broken, some were so important as to be punishable by death.

Batubatse children learned about taboos from their parents and grandparents during day-to-day activities, communal ceremonies, initiation and when arranging for bride wealth. Eating certain food and raising cows of a certain color was sometimes regarded as taboo, as was the killing or eating of the totem animals, which in the case of the Batubatse were the elephant and lion.

Other taboo actions were the cutting of certain grasses or reeds from the time of sowing until the crop has been harvested. It was also taboo to kill or disturb certain animals, birds – such as the hammerhead (*Mašianoke*) – and large spiders (*sehuku*).

Other prohibitions, also described as taboo (*diila/dikidišwa*), are sanctioned by the tribal courts. The Batubatse people, like other members of the Bakgaga/Baroka tribes, were against the killing of big birds such as the secretary bird (*hlame*), legendary bird (*mogolodi*), stork (*leakabosana*) and other birds which could not be identified (*mogwale* and *legama*). These birds are protected because they kill snakes, locusts and rodents and are considered valuable.

Sanctions may be either magical, brought about by the ancestral spirits, legal (*melao*) or a combination of both. Transgression invoked immediate sanctions from the ancestral spirits and was held in contempt not only by the Batubatse Ba-Shai people but by the Bapedi, Bakgaga/Baroka and other African communities.

When a taboo had been broken, the perpetrator or his relatives was punished by death, expulsion from the community, being made insane, fined a goat or sheep, sickness, dissolution of marriage, corporal punishment, curse, a warning, and many other sanctions. Sometimes the whole community would be directly punished through famine because of the breaking of taboos by individuals, and children born of incest would die.

In general, the breaking of any taboo had a negative impact on the family and the community. Damage caused by a person due to a breaking of a taboo would not be final until the ancestors, who seem to be most involved in taboos, were appeased. The rituals in such a process, often involved the slaughtering of a goat or cow. Libations should be made to venerate ancestors.

Taboos served as a moral guidance bringing peace and security in the community, helping in the upbringing of children and providing rules for marriage. In ancient times taboos were a means of control, and without them there would have been much chaos. Taboos were significant in a number of ways:

- They were a means of preserving the life and well-being of people.
- They helped people to realise that an improper behaviour would have disastrous consequences.

- They were an expression of a general set of rules commonly understood by all human beings.
- They were used to convey moral values, especially to children, and could be described as "teaching aids".

In the eyes of the Batubatse, disrespecting elders, committing adultery, incest, stealing and being quarrelsome were considered the most important taboos.

WITCHCRAFT AND SORCERY

Witchcraft and sorcery are general terms for magical practices. On one hand witchcraft (*boloi*) broadly means the practice of, and belief in, magical skills exercised by persons with esoteric secret knowledge. On the other hand sorcery means the use of magical powers of evil spirits especially for necromancy (talking to the spirits of dead people) for evil purpose. Sorcery commonly involves working through an intermediary who could take the form of God, spirits, an angel or the workers. Sorcery's intent is always evil and can be distinguished from witchcraft, which can be either good or bad. Both represent all that is evil and destructive in African culture and are generally loathed and feared. Today in South Africa it is illegal to accuse someone of witchcraft or to call someone a witch, but it will be difficult to enforce this law as certain people believe they can identify witches. Ill-educated people are still convinced that evil witches exist and react violently in what they consider to be self-defence. Witchcraft practiced by night without the use of spells or medicine is known as *boloi bja bošigo* and by day, when such items are used, as *boloi bja mosegare*.

The belief of witchcraft and sorcery has existed in the culture and life of ancient African communities, Batubatse included, as it has among primitive and highly advanced cultures and religions worldwide since the dawn of history. Witches could be either male or female. However, in Ghana women are more often accused of witchcraft and attacked by neighbours. "Witch Camps", dating back over a hundred years and housing thousands of women, have been set up in the country where women suspected of being witches can seek

The report by the South Africa Commission of Inquiry into Witchcraft, Violence and Ritual Killings in May 1996 revealed that thousands of people accused of witchcraft had been expelled from their communities and lost their property. More than 300 had been killed by vigilante mobs over the previous ten years. The victims were accused of "shape-shifting" themselves from human form into bats and birds, of converting people into zombies, and of causing death by calling down lightning or through the use of toxic medicines. Victims accused of witchcraft were typically women between 55 and 72 years of age. These beliefs are similar to those which circulated during the witch-burning craze of the Middle Ages and the Renaissance in Europe circa 1450 to 1792 CE.

refuge. Now the Ghanaian government has announced the closure of these camps and seeks instead to convince the population that witches do not exist. It is doubtful, however, if this will remove the belief of the existence of witchcraft among the majority of African cultures.

In Kuwait, Saudi Arabia and many other countries the death penalty is applicable for practicing sorcery. A Saudi man was beheaded on charges of sorcery and witchcraft in June 2012. Ethiopians have been deported for practicing sorcery. In Malawi it is common practice to accuse children of witchcraft and many children have been abandoned, abused and even killed as a result. In Nigeria churches are numerous and competition for congregation is strong. Pastors here benefit from the lucrative witch-finding and exorcism business which in the past was the exclusive domain of the witchdoctors or traditional healers. Because of this, over the past decade around one thousand children were murdered. In the Indian provinces of Assam and West Bengal some 750 people were killed as witches between 2003 and 2008. Even in America this belief prevailed and between 1645 and 1663, about 80 people in Massachusetts Bay Colony were accused of practicing witchcraft. Thirteen women and two men were executed in a witch-hunt that lasted throughout the period. Witchcraft and sorcery trials occurred frequently in seventh-century Russia. Sources of ecclesiastical witchcraft jurisdiction in Russia date back as early as the second half of the eleventh century, one being Vladimir the Great's first edition of his Statute or Ustav. The sentence

---

According to reports Thatale Shai Seshai, a traditional healer, once taunted a day-witch to approach him, saying he was strong enough to resist. He went to his home in order to prepare a medicine to repel witches. Whilst the concoction was still boiling inside the calabash, a bolt of lightning reportedly struck him unconscious, as well as his wife Maafbyana, his daughter Mankhiti and one of his sons, Ponele. When they revived, the calabash was found some distance away but still bubbling. The following day Thatale left his home early in the morning without talking to anybody, apparently going to apologise to that witch or to inform him that he failed to carry the bubbling calabash away with him.   Notwithstanding this setback, Thatale possessed skills of great magic which he applied to the advantage of those who employed his services. Another story told by oral sources states that one morning the community found one of Chief Maupa's sons, Tjako Maake, mounted at the top of a tall tree, supposedly by a witch. Thatale was summoned and, after applying his medicines around the tree, convinced the victim to jump into his arms, which he did. The witch who was responsible for this deed became ill and subsequently died. Thatale was said to be able to predict rain or drought, the coming of war, the outcome of a journey, where one could find a lost or stolen object or strayed cattle and also whether these could be ascribed to any supernatural cause. It is believed that he could make zombies, conjured by night-witches, visible to the community and for the person responsible to be mocked in public. He was the dispensers of leech craft. Thatale had a hypnotic influence over stock. For instance, once when the blood of an antelope (pudibudu) was required for medication to cure a sick person, he went into the kraal, spoke to the animal in a loud voice and it emerged and followed him. He made it lie down and threw a cord over its body. It lay there, completely pacified, while the blood was taken, until he removed the thong. He had the ability to predict, in time of tribal war, which group was going to win. He was the most popular and trusted traditional healer at Chief Maupa's court as he could tell if a witnesses was lying. Amongst the Batubatse people there were many diviners. Apart from Thatale there were Matome Mokhokolo, Mpaseriti and many others, all having learned this skill from their forebears and grandfathers.

for witchcraft or sorcery during that time, and in previous centuries, included burning at the stake or being tested with the "ordeal of cold water" in terms of which accused persons who sank down when immersed were considered innocent, and ecclesiastical authorities would proclaim them "brought back", but those who floated were considered guilty. Tsar Ivan the Terrible, an avid believer in witchcraft, was convinced that sorcery accounted for the death of his wife, Anastasia, in 1560.

Among the Batubatse, when a child was born with the innate ability of witchcraft, he or she was identified by another witch and taught how to make use of this ability. Witches are said to pray to their own ancestors and sacrifice humans to them. The night-witches resurrect dead persons (*dithuri*) from their graves and give life in a manner known only by the witches. These zombies have no will of their own, but act at the will of the witches. They are sent at night to steal things that the *baloi* requires, or are made to plough lands, thresh the corn and bring it home, or fetch firewood and water. Those who are dumb are known as *tholwane* while those who can talk are *setseetse* and mislead you during the night into thinking that they are relatives or friends.

It is a common belief that all witches are well off and have plenty of food provided by their *dithuri*, but are seldom seen working. It is not known whether their souls have gone to the ancestor, and the *baloi* use only the flesh. Witches also teach certain animals to carry out their wishes. Day-witchcraft, practised by men and women, works solely to the detriment of others while night-witchcraft uses the same magical medicines and is practised by women. The former bewitch a person by speaking the victim's name over the medicines and stating what the desired results should be. This impels the victim to eat or to drink (*go ješa or go leša*) something into which they have put their medicines. This results in the disease known as *sej ešo or sele šo* .

A witch has the power to send a swarm of bees to attack a victim or cause hail to damage his crops. A witch can also cause lightning to strike a person (*go itia/ betha tladi*), a common means of harming one's enemies. "Natural" lightning is accompanied by rain and is believed to strike only trees or rocks far from villages. It is caused by the lightning bird, which has blue feathers and resembles a goose with large feet. This bird feeds on the blue-headed tree lizard. "Sent" lightning, on the other hand, strikes near the village, killing people or animals. It is more terrifying than that of the lightning bird. If lightning causes no harm it is natural; if it strikes any one or destroys anything in the village it is "sent" by witches (*tladimothwana*). One who controlled lightning was able to prevent it from striking him by piercing his flash with a medicated axe or spear, telling it to go elsewhere. Traditional healers frequently measure one another up by sending lightning.

Other forms of magic not classified as witchcraft include the use of medicines to discourage theft, "*setopa*". Applying these medicines where the object was stolen would cause festering wounds on the hands of the thief, only to be healed after the thief had admitted his guilt or returned the stolen items. Similarly it was not magic to create a mock snake (*noga*) to protect the house from thieves.

The eldest male child in the witch's family would be taught by his father the witchcraft secrets and rain-making medicines. The eldest female child was responsible for the safe-keeping of medicines for sacrifices. She performed rituals and spoke to the ancestors.

DIVINATION, MAGIC AND MEDICINE

In South African tradition the three classifications of people with special powers are the witch, *moloi*, a spiteful person who operates in secret to harm others; the diviner, *mokome*, similar to a fortune-teller, who detects illness, predicts futures, advises on which path to take or identifies the guilty party in a crime; and the traditional healer, *ngaka,* who cures illness and injury and provides customers with magical medicines for everyday use.

Moloi was motivated either by malice or for the pleasure derived from doing evil, but the victim of such action could not, in court, claim that he was bewitched and that the witch was guilty. For any misfortune the *ngaka* was there to establish the source and also prescribe the remedy or preventative measure which should be administered. Amongst the Batubatse communities were many such diviners – Thatale, Mokhokolo, Mpaseriti and others who were taught by their fathers, grandfathers or ancestors.

The technique of divination by casting may involve small objects, such as bones, nuts, cowry shells, stones, strips of leather, or flat pieces of wood, or the use of sacred wooden plates (*ditelo*). Divination was often performed within a circle on the ground, the results being interpreted in different ways:

a) how the small objects fall according to their markings or whether they touch one another after casting in terms of predetermined criteria or

b) how symbolic articles indicate specific conditions – certain bones might indicate travel, a round stone pregnancy and a bird's foot emotion. A hyena bone signified a thief and would provide information about what had been stolen. Each object had a special significance to human life.

The casting and reading of bones was performed by gifted psychics who provided answers to the questions posed by their clients. In the traditions of some culture, the bones, shells, and nuts would be left in their natural state; in others, such as the Batubatse, they would be shaped and marked, much like a dice, dominoes, or cut cowries shells. The Batubatse *ngaka* diviners used a large set of bones and other natural curios, such as the 18 items shown in the wooden bowl below.

Well-trained witchdoctors used divination bones (*ditaola*, derived from the verb to control *golaola*) to deduce whether a mishap should be ascribed to witchcraft or to the dissatisfaction of an ancestral spirit. By this method they could identify the witch or the unsatisfied ancestor, what magic should be applied against the witch or what sacrifice should be made to the ancestor.

Diviners were in demand for their wisdom as counsellors and for their knowledge of herbal medicine. This applied also in ancient Greece where oracles were considered the mouthpiece of the deities and were highly valued by the Greeks.

The witchdoctor could neutralise the evil spell of a witch, using the same methods that the witch used. Thus the witchdoctor was socially respected and his work viewed with appreciation, whereas witches were loathed and feared. Most traditional healers could predict rain or drought, the cause of war, the results of a journey or any other future event about which one wishes to know, as well as the precautionary measures which should be taken to ensure the desired results. They could show where lost or stolen objects or strayed cattle could be found and whether these could be ascribed to any supernatural cause. They prevented night-witches from stealing by making them visible to the community and be mocked in public through the use of *dithuri and dirongwa*.

When a person consults a diviner he describes the problem that he wants resolved. The diviner gets him to blow air into a bag made from the skin of a velvet monkey/rabbit (*mankobo*) or squirrel (*sesete*) containing the divination set, and he then throws all the pieces of bone on the floor. This throwing of the set (*go phekola*) is derived from the name of protective medicine (*pheko*). The diviner recites the praise-poem of the particular combination into which the pieces have fallen. Then the interpretation will follow and the session will proceed with information given in turn by the diviner and the patient.

The throwing of bones may be repeated before the diviner gives his final response. This is usually of such a general nature that the patient can easily apply it to his own circumstances and is satisfied with the result. The diviner would invariably know the history of his community, the prevailing disputes and feuds, who was sorrowful and who joyful, and would thus be aware of the social affiliation and family background of each patient.

In contrast to the diviners, prophets (*didupe*) made direct spiritual contact with the ancestor spirits (*malopo*). The cult of the *malopo* was widely believed within the Batubatse Ba-Shai, Bakgaga Ba-Maupa and other tribes. These prophets were mainly women whose chief task was to exorcise spirits sent by ancestors or witches to take possession of people. They would do this by singing and dancing to the accompaniment of a drum (*moropa*). When the patient began chanting in the same note she was believed to be in communication with the spirit. Different medicines were used for the spirits sent by ancestors and those sent by witches.

Disease was also believed to be caused by supernatural forces, the remedy for which would be natural medicines (*dihlare*) administered internally or externally or placed at strategic points for protection. Another medicine, *pheko*, would bring relief. Most Batubatse medicines were derived from vegetable matter, although some were made of animal and soil substances. Apart from healing disease, these medicines were used to strengthen or protect the dignity (*seriti*) of a man, and also to heal any disease that has weakened his dignity. Sometimes human flesh was used in the traditional rain-medicine. "Serpent men" in the Batubatse community believed themselves immune from snake venom and possessed the power to cure those who had been poisoned.

Although *pheko* cannot provide protection against the wrath of ancestral spirits, it can protect a person from witchcraft or magical forces. The medicine most frequently used is a black powder, *tshidi*, made from the roots of the *mohlakola* tree. The roots are dried, burnt to charcoal in a pot and mixed with the seeds of the *sebejane* and the fat of a goat. The potion was placed at the entrance to the hut of a sick person. *Tshidi* mixed with fat and red ochre (*letsoku*) is considered to be the most powerful *pheko* against witchcraft and ensures safe travelling, good fortune in a wide range of endeavours, as well as preventing quarrels, and it can even be used as a love potion.

Medicines could be administered orally, applied to the eyes or ears, rubbed into incisions or on afflicted parts of the body, inserted anally, inhaled as a vapour and even smoked in a pipe. Medicines are also used for the treatment of livestock. Traditional healers have accumulated knowledge of various plants over the years by trial and error and can tell which are poisonous, or which have no effect on any disease at all.

Despite the existence of European hospitals and clinics, *ngaka* still retain a psychological hold over the majority of the community, who turn to them for the treatment of practically all diseases and for the preparation of all protective medicines. Most Batubatse people have an unshaken faith in their ability to divine and to cure despite the measures taken against the practice of witchcraft.

The *ngaka* is generally a man who has inherited the profession, but anyone can receive training from a qualified traditional healer provided he can afford it. The training takes over a year and covers divination, the use and application of medicines and much more. Not all the sons of a traditional healer will automatically follow in the footsteps of their father – only those who show an interest and prove to have some ability. Some people became traditional healers having received the knowledge of healing and herbs as a precious gift from their ancestral spirits.

When a man wishes to train as a traditional healer he pays one beast to an established *ngaka* as an indication of loosening the bag (*khunulla moraba*) of the divination set, but there is no payment required from a son or of grandson. After a while the initiate will acquire the ability to divine and the instructor will then test him in various ways. When the period of instruction is completed, the pupil will be initiated as a fully qualified witchdoctor who may practise on his own and receive fees for his work after he had returned to his home. One may also increase his knowledge by going to other doctors who have earned for themselves a reputation in curing certain specialised disease and will buy his knowledge from them. The author believes his grandfather was an instructor of those who wished to be trained as witchdoctor since he was a popular *ngaka* within the community.

Nowadays the *bongaka* profession like priesthood is much misused by unqualified people who induce their victims to pay for a bogus service. The quality of the profession is being downgraded as so many of the so-called *dingaka* use *bongaka* to cheat others to make a living for themselves. It is a shame that the revered profession, that is believed to act as the intermediary between living people and their ancestors, is today so often perverted. The traditional healer is believed to make the wishes of the ancestral spirits known, interprets their actions to living people and prescribes the sacrifice that the ancestor demands.

Traditional healers are highly respected and their power and influence in the community is second only to the Kgoshi and his close councilors (*magota*). They control supernatural forces and may turn their beneficial practice into a harmful one since there is only a slight difference between good and bad magic. The chief can delegate certain functions to any of the traditional healers in his area. He can appoint a *rathipana* to act during the tribal initiation school and a *moneśapula* to prepare the rain-medicine.

Traditional healers and prophets have existed in their thousands in every race, nation and country in the world. Churches accuse witchdoctors and *didupe* of working with demons and for demonising the ancestors, but many Christians might find themselves in a difficult situation when they face their ancestors after death. The doctrine of spiritual welfare holds that every person has the right to health and prosperity. According to this doctrine, illness, poverty and misery can be combated not only with biblical prayers but also with healings, positive confessions, exorcism and sacrificial.

NATURE vs RELIGION

Having discussed our belief in ancestral worship, we turn to the issue of Nature or the Unknown God and its miracles and how communities, in particular the Batubatse, are associated with it. The Batubatse people believed that everything that exists is the product of Nature – even the Ancestors, Biblical God, Quranic Allah, Camagu, Ganesha, Anu, Jah, Yahweh and all the deities that people believed in survive because Nature was on our side. Gods, goddesses and all the objects on Earth or elsewhere, including ourselves, unfold from the divine mystery, Nature (*Hlago/Tlhago*) or the "Unknown Creator-God and its miracles" (*mehlolo*). Nature has no beginning and ending, is omnipresent and omnipotent.

Tshimangadzo Benedict Daswa was a Venda man of Mbahe village who, because of his Christian faith, feared and respected the Biblical God. He was regarded by members of the Catholic Church, of which he was also a member, as a man of God. Today he is considered by his church as one of their ancestors, a saint, a holy person as having won by exceptional holiness a high place in heaven and veneration on Earth. He is still to be declared a saint if he qualifies. He refused to contribute five rand for a sangoma to identify the "dark forces" behind lightning strikes in his village that had caused several huts to burn down. On 2 February 1990 he was caught at a roadblock residents had erected and fled as they stoned him. He tried to hide in a hut, but was cornered. After begging his attackers to spare his life and not succeeding, he prayed before a steel knobkerrie landed on his head and killed him. His attackers continued pouring boiling water through his nostrils and ears despite the well-known belief that a powerful God is always there to protect his children, particularly those who believe in Him. Daswa's uncle Tshipenga Matshikiri was later accused of being behind the lightning stories. For this he was hacked with pangas and died in flames after his house was set alight with him inside. Why these gruesome and disgusting murders? It was the Unknown Creator God or Nature. Without Nature nothing was made that has been made. No prayer, wish or request can avoid what the Unknown Creator God or Nature provides.

Africans believed in this Unknown Creator-God popularly known as *Ptah*. Nature brought everything together. In general those things that have not been altered substantially by human intervention, or which persist despite human intervention, are considered as "the natural environment or wilderness".

This view might be a narrow interpretation but it was considered correct by the ancient Batubatse people; everything on Earth and other planets is the creation of the Unknown God or Nature (*Hlago/Tlhago*), which cannot be seen heard or felt. Nature cannot be compared with anything.

There are many stories about the creation. For instance the Akan people of Ghana also have a creation story with the word "In the beginning…" They say that in the beginning the heavens were closer to the earth. The first man and woman had to be careful when cultivating and grinding grain so that their hoes (*matjepe*) and pestles (*mese*) would not strike God, who lived in the sky. Death had not yet entered the world and God had provided enough for them. But the first woman became greedy and tried to pound more grain than she was allotted. To do this she had to use a longer pestle (*mose*). When she raised it up it hit the sky and God became angry and retreated further into the heavens. Since then there has been disease and death with no hope of an after-life. People believed that when they die they would rot; however their spirits would live in a world of Ancestors.

The Batubatse word for the Biblical God in earlier times was unknown, but with the passage of time they referred to the Biblical God as *Modimo*. But *Modimo* to them meant an ancestor; the word God did not describe the characteristics of the Supreme Being. The Supreme Being to them was the Unknown Creator-God or Nature, referred to as *Ptah* or *Anu*. The Batubatse pray to their ancestors through sacrifices, just as many other tribes who prayed to God, but they believed that Nature, which cannot be seen with the naked eye, was above all. The Batubatse regarded the name God as an assumption since it was inconceivable to them that an important man such as Him should have no wives or cattle.

To them Nature did not have a beginning or end. Nature alone was the creator, nourisher and sustainer of the whole Universe and of everything that was in it. Nature was present everywhere and was not made or born. We do not know of any partner, sons, daughters, wives and equals of Nature. None had rewritten and reinterpreted Nature or Ptah. Little more was known about the creation among the ancient Batubatse other than Nature. Certainly they could not be said to have a well-conceived creation myth. However, they had many other myths which were told, as were other fables, to children in the evenings when families were gathered around the fire.

Ancestors were closely associated with the elements of Nature such as wind, rain, hail and lightning. The Batubatse did not pray to God or Allah, neither of whom had any bearing on their daily life. As already indicated above, to them the Unknown God, Nature or *Ptah* was the Creator, the beginning of all, the Supreme Being and the cause of miracles.

The Batubatse recognised miracles as being the work of Nature brought to us either directly, or through prayers and intercessions of specific ancestors. They recognised certain events as miracles, some occurring in modern times. For instance it said that a young man's leg was miraculously restored to him after having been amputated two years earlier. It is also said that many generations ago members of the Batubatse community witnessed the sun dim, change colour, spin, dance in the sky, and appear to plummet to Earth, radiating great heat in the process.

Miracles did not conflict with the creation-order, since both usual and unusual events were the expression of Nature. A miracle set aside the natural order of things to allow for the impossible to happen. Nature was seen among the Batubatse as an independent order into which ancestors had to align with to work miracles.

The Batubatse had never believed in the existence of so-called supernatural things beyond Nature, hence the spirits of our ancestors and miracles remained the creatures of Nature. They claimed miraculous accounts of men and women who had the ability to become invisible and function independently of the physical body. They also declared that holy men were able to tame wild beasts and traverse long distance in a short time span. They could also produce food and rain in seasons of drought, heal the sick and help barren women conceive. Were these not miracles of Nature?

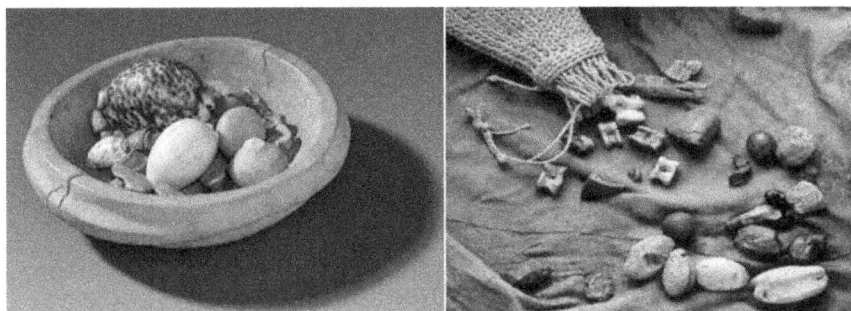

Sets of divination bones

The Batubatse believed that ancestors could work naturally to perform what people saw as miracles. They regarded miracles as transgressions of the law of Nature by a particular volition of the deity.

The influence of Christianity, Judaism, Hinduism and Islam upon the Batubatse meant that the concept of Nature has been practically lost. Unlike God, whose appearance is definitely male, there was no clear conception of the appearance of Nature. God is described by different persons in accordance with deities that our people believe in. Some have dreamed of having stood, sat or kneeled down next to a "Father God" and taken orders from him but none would describe him.

Some would say that they distinctly heard the God's voice telling them to kill and were ultimately locked up in jails for life for carrying out such orders. The Batubatse considered the Biblical God or Allah in the Quran as an ancestor of another tribe or community. Few if any of South African names are mentioned in the Bible or Quran, yet people say that these books speak for all nationalities at the expense of our unwritten beliefs. We view the existence of God or Allah as a myth.

In fact religion could be as an insult to natural history. What the Batubatse see in Nature is a magnificent structure that they can comprehend only imperfectly. The Batubatse did not believe in monotheism (a single God) without reference to their ancestors. They believed that reality was to be found on earth and that life after death was a pipedream. They never used the word "pagan" in a derogatory sense to undermine another's religion. The word "ancestor" was never used metaphorically to denote persons outside the bounds of the ancestral community.

However, like the Biblical God, the Devil was considered a male but did not have wives or cattle. The Batubatse, like pagan societies, knew no Devil with whom individuals could make a pact, and thus no torture and persecutions of false prophets and prophetesses took place among them, but witches (*baloi*) were put to death if identified. They also didn't recognise any central evil force or entity such as the Devil opposing ancestors (*Badimo*) or men, but they did recognise that some human beings and the departed ones could perform evil acts (wrongs), miracles and magic under the dominance of Nature and had caused worldly sufferings.

The origin of life was a mystery that bothered the ancients as much as it bothers moderns today. Our ancestors had no science or written history – just their imagination.

It is exciting to stand on the threshold of a concept: not to know where it originated but to guess and make predictions. How will these differ from one's preconceived notion and which of these predictions will stand up to one's own experiences and observations? You look up to the sky and see clouds, darkness, the moon, stars, other planets, unidentified objects, without reaching the end of it. You look down at the earth and see mountains, trees, rocks, water, animals and many other things. You dig down and go beneath the surface of land and sea to find many things without reaching the end. Some speak of the existence of a so-called heaven which no living being ever reached.

What was discussed in this sub-chapter might bring robust criticism, condemnation, censure, vigorous reactions and the like. This is because we understand things differently. But everyone has the right to freedom of speech and his or her views about life. Equally anyone can oppose these observations but any criticism will not dampen our determination to reveal the truth that can be proved with evidence. When and how our lineage dispersed out of Africa has long proven controversial but evidence had suggested that an exodus took place some 60,000 years ago. All the population groups outside Africa are descended from a small band of human beings that left Africa, probably 50,000 to 80,000 years ago. In a sense, therefore, we are all Africans. Modern man is two hundred thousand years old and the Christian religion only about two thousand years old. It was not until man garnered communication skills and the intellect that he asked the proverbial question of all time, "Why are we here?" Without the science and knowledge of the cosmos we have today, people only understood one answer.... creation. They then deemed there must be a creator... and God was born. If a creator existed, who created the creator? Nature.

Batubatse children, like any other children, grew up, procreated and, having learned from their own parents, taught their own children similar ideas. Children have a right not to be force-fed myths by anyone, even by parents who believe they have the right to teach them what they want. Because of the recent rights that Batubatse children have acquired and the emergence of biblical and other religions, some have lost the belief that Nature, not god, is the father of everything. Christian and Muslim religions were gross religious errors to many African children when they grew up. If this means we are going to be called heathens, then so be it.

There are many false prophets, priests, pastures, believers and teachers in our present day who will deceive many people about God, Ancestors, Devil and other deities. They will interpret their dreams wrongly in order to start new churches. Though these people might claim to know and communicate the truth, they will be spreading lies. They will inspire fear in our minds, making us to succumb to their false wishes, hoping that we will be saved on the unknown and non-existent last day. They will do everything available to them to defend their lies and point of view. These people are really hungry, dangerous, selfish and ferocious wolves dressed in sheep's skins. Many of them want to become rich. Many are very popular, good speakers and friendly.

Some can even produce miraculous signs and accurately predict an event. False prophets, priests, pastors, believers and teachers of religions speak with conviction sweating, since they expect their lying words to be fulfilled. Stories have been reported in some parts of Africa, South Africa included, about how religious leaders with names like Bishop, General Overseer, Daddy, Papa, Mummy and many others train young ministers, pay them good salaries and send them to establish branches of their churches in a foreign countries, not necessarily to spread gospel, but to generate income. These ministers are then asked by their churches to collect offerings and tithes and send this money to church headquarters. In most instances, these ministers or priests are sent to countries with a booming economy so they can send good returns back home. The river water only rolls where the stones sleep.

Such people have natural powers to predict success and victory in the name of the Biblical God at the expense of our ancestors. Of course it is acknowledged that certain religious practices can reduce stress or cure certain ailments. The world benefits much from different religious beliefs. The personification of the divine as the only God leads to the birth of a multiplicity of conflicting spiritual traditions. Let us not upset the ancestors. Belief in a single Biblical God is a delusion, an aggressively-held belief that is evidently false. A single Biblical God and Devil or Satan never existed among the Batubatse people. While the Batubatse mainstream contains no overt concept of a Devil, Christianity and other religions have variously regarded the Devil as a rebellious fallen angel or jinn that tempts humans to sin. As such, the Devil is seen as an allegory that represents a crisis of faith, individualism, free will, wisdom and enlightenment.

In mainstream Christianity and Islam, God and Devil are usually portrayed as fighting over the souls of humans. The Devil is believed to command a force of evil spirits, commonly known as demons. Whether these assertions are true or not, the Batubatse regard that as the work of Nature since both God and Devil are its products.

According to Wikipedia, Nature in the broadest sense is the natural, physical, or material world or universe. It can refer to the phenomena of the physical world, and also to life in general. It can also refer to the non-physical and non-material world. The study of Nature is a large part of science. Although human beings are part of Nature, human activity was and is still often understood as a separate category from other natural phenomena. Within the various uses of the word today Nature often refers to geology and wildlife: it encompasses the general realm of living plants, animals, people according to their different races and ethnicity, and also the processes associated with inanimate and non-living objects – the way that particular types of things exist and change of their own accord, such as weather and geology on the Earth and other planets discovered by human beings through Nature or *Ptah*.

"What you think of yourself is much more important than what others think of you."

- Seneca

5
RITES OF PASSAGE

Male initiates   Female circumcision candidates

BATUBATSE BIRTH AND NAME-GIVING

The origin of names is derived from a person's culture. Each culture has its own rules as to how these names are formed. In some cultures there are different forenames for male and female members of the family. Traditional African names given to a person often reflect the circumstances at the time of birth. Some names describe the parent's reaction to the birth, while others reflect the birth order of the newborn, and so on. People need names for identification purposes. People, places and other special references distinguish one person from another to avoid any confusion. Name indicates reputation, identity and family association. Naming can be further personalised as parents combine names of different ethnicity or include more than two individual names for the child. Parents may choose names that are popular in the country where their ancestors once lived.

Onomatopoeia, being the formation of words from sounds that resembles those associated with the object or action to be named, is also applicable in name-giving. African names often relate to languages spoken in Central Africa. The birth of a child among the Batubatse was an important event in the family. The rites connected with the birth centre on the mother and the child. The birth of a first child was and is still the most significant event in the life of a Motubatse woman. Barrenness was feared because it affected both the woman herself and the family group to which she belonged. It was for this reason that another woman would be married to bear children for the barren woman after everything was done to help her bear children, but had failed.

During the period of pregnancy various taboos were observed. A husband was not to have relations with other women as this would affect the expectant mother. The husband should in fact have relations with his wife during the first two to three months of the pregnancy to build up and strengthen the child. A pregnant woman should avoid other pregnant or menstruating women. She should not go out in the rain, quarrel with others or be angered as all these could adversely affect the child. Elderly women should be close to any expectant woman, particularly when she was about to give birth. When the first child was expected, a woman would go to her relatives for the confinement to take place in the hut of her mother.

During delivery two or three experienced midwives past child-bearing age would attend the woman. If delivery became difficult, the assistance of a traditional healer would be obtained. Other children to follow were born in the parturient woman's hut. Once the child was born the midwives would tie off the umbilical cord with a piece of sinew, making two knots, and the cord would then be cut between the knots with a special lancet. If the child did not cry immediately after birth it would be smacked lightly to cause it to cry. Afterwards the child would be washed with water containing certain healing and purifying medicines. In doing so, the midwives would stretch the child's limbs to change the foetal position (*kudupana*) of the body in the womb. Children were fed with a thin porridge shortly after birth.

The midwife would immediately emerge from the hut to make the joyful announcement. If the child was a boy the father would be informed of the happy event personally or through a messenger. If the child was a girl people would hear one of the midwives ululating. This was done because it was believed that a girl would bring cattle home upon her marriage. The mother would then be given medicines to clean the womb. The afterbirth would be placed in a clay pot filled with water which was then buried in the bank of a river.

A protective stick treated with medicines (*lepheko*) would be placed at the entrance of the hut to warn men and all impure women not to enter as this might endanger the mother and child. After two or three days the child would be suckled by the mother after her breasts had been treated with medicines. A woman would be appointed to attend to the mother and child during the period of seclusion, and other women would fetch water for them and sweep the courtyard.

The period of seclusion came to an end with the falling of the umbilical cord. A traditional healer would then be summoned to prepare the child (*go thusa ngwana*) by treating the child's head and shaving off the hair. Thereafter the child would be strengthened (*tiisetja*) by a medicine (*tshidi*) for protection against witchcraft. This was done by rubbing the medicine powder into small incisions on the ankles, knees, neck, shoulders, elbows, wrists and temples. The *lepheko* would then be removed and the father allowed to see his child.

Both parents had to be treated together with medicines before the father was allowed to have sex with his wife, otherwise his stomach and legs would swell, his feet would get hot and he would not able to walk properly anymore. After the parents had been treated old ladies would take the child out to a dry wood in the bush and apply medicines to prevent him or her from contacting head disease. When the child was brought back to the father a small feast would be held and the baby would get its first babyhood name for its formal introduction and acceptance into the family.

Names were frequently chosen from events occurring on the day of the child's birth. New names were given when a person achieved a new status such as on entry into the patrilineal group or at initiation into the tribe when the whole group of male initiates received a collective regimental name. Each name was often given a corresponding praise-name (*sereto*), which was commonly used when speaking to or about that person.

Names were never chosen without some meaning attached to them – from historical events such as triumphant wars won by our forefathers, or something that happened long ago in that particular family, or to commemorate a particular person. For instant the Baroka tribes gave the author the praise-name of *Sebolodi-a-Monare* because he was a leader in the development of Baroka communities. In all Baroka gatherings or elsewhere he is addressed by that name. New names were not invented, hence everyone was named after particular relatives by the family. Regularly name-giving ceremonies for all the children of a particular age were held. Such ceremonies have in them an element of sacrifice to the ancestral spirits and have the function of introducing the children to the communal forefathers of the patrilineal group. The Batubatse names have deep meaning. But there was more to their names.

Some names are derived from clan or sub-clan names. Some keep their ancestral names and some even carry their father's name, but a clan or sub-clan name was considered more important than having to carry another name. If a child's paternity was not known, or if the putative father denied paternity, the new-born child would have a name derived from his or her mother's side. When deciding on a name, one should be sure to consider the difficulty in usage and significance of the name. It helps to remember that one is choosing an early identity for the child. That is still the custom and law in many cultures and countries.

EARLY TRAINING FOR BOYS AND GIRLS

African customary education and training, a system which persists even now, was aimed, firstly, at preserving the cultural heritage – initiation, laws, language and values inherited from the past – and how it applied to the extended family, the clan and the tribe; secondly, at teaching members of the new generation how to adapt to their physical environment.

In the early years of childhood, education was largely in the hands of the biological mother, and as adolescence approached the community assumed the greater role. Language training was given by the mother and the extended family. Thus indigenous education and training met the requirements of the society at the time. If this heritage was not adequately understood, the Batubatse community would be faced with confusion, loss of identity, and a breakdown of intergenerational communication.

During the first years of its life, before undergoing initiation, a Motubatse child was treated with leniency and love. Parents would abstain from conjugal relations until the child was weaned. Thereafter the child, as it became more independent, would be subjected to harsher treatment. Play-groups would be formed among children of the same age. When they reached adolescence, boys would wear loin-cloths (*makgeswa*) or cruppers (*ditsiba*) to cover their private parts and young girls would wear short string aprons (*dithetho*) in front and triangular skin-aprons (*dimbepana*) to cover their buttocks.

Through both formal and informal processes, young people acquired knowledge, skills, ideas, attitudes and patterns of behaviour. Tribal legends, poems, proverbs and idioms were told and retold by the evening fireside, and thus much of the cultural heritage of the Batubatse tribe was kept alive. There were oral riddles to test children's judgments and myths to explain the origin of the tribe and genesis of man.

The names of the trees, plants, animals and insects, as well as the dangers and uses of each, were learnt. Boys learnt their role in society by being engaged in farming, house-building, herding and hunting, while girls did so through cooking, keeping the home clean and child-rearing. Imitative play, too, formed an important part of informal education. For instance, boys would stage mock battles, and make model huts and cattle pens, while girls made dolls, played with them as husband and wife, and cooked imaginary meals. Although there was no formal educational system for Batubatse children, basic education and training was imparted through succeeding stages of initiation, each stage accompanied by a sequence of ceremonies and rites.

Traditional cultural practices in which teenage boys and girls would be allowed to engage in sexual play that involves genital stimulation but not penetration was known as *go momelana* or *go kgomana*. These practices which encouraged the understanding of developing bodies are, however, no longer followed today. It is also worth mentioning that the Batubatse, as is the case with many other black Africans, did not have a kissing culture. From childhood to adulthood they did not kiss one another, even in the bedroom. But this is a thing of the past. Today, children and young adults' understanding of sex and kissing is largely influenced by media and pornography.

Play-groups play many games, but as the differentiation between the sexes develops many of the games become imitative of the activities of men and women. Among the Batubatse tribes, until you were ten years old or so you were counted as a small boy or girl with minimal social duties. Boys were expected to tend the livestock of the family from an early age. At first they looked after the calves that remained in the kraal, and then joined the other boys in herding the sheep and the goats and eventually cattle and donkeys. One was then expected to undergo initiation to manhood, a process lasting about six months punctuated by ritual examinations, social training and teaching by elders, the early activities largely controlled by the group of boys just older than young ones.

In these youthful activities lies a great deal of the enculturation of all children from the start. In the same way girls have to start at an early age to help their mothers to grind (*šila or setla*) corn and to fetch water and kindling-wood. These activities of the girls were performed commercially, and older girls also controlled the activities of those younger than themselves. They played traditional games. Apart from the traditional games, boys acquired the essential knowledge of pastoral skills and the girls that of agriculture. As youths they were taught etiquette, agricultural methods and other techniques that ensured the smooth running of the social entity of which they were an integral part. The boys observed and imitated their fathers' craft as they learned practical skills which they performed according to their capacities as they matured into manhood and became heads of their own households.

They learned the dances and the mysteries of their tribe. They were taught such essential qualities as generosity, respect for elders and courage. The older boys encouraged the younger ones to fight one another to choose a leader *(nkgwete)* of their group. In every fight, the loser had publicly to confess his defeat. The winner of the last fight among the bigger boys would be the overall leader, while the lowest loser would be the messenger of the group. Training and education of girls was different in that the leader (*malokwane*) was chosen for her ability to sing and dance, and she would lead the girls in the feasts at which they entertained guests with singing and dancing. Once the groups of boys and girls had become formalised functional units, they were no longer called a boy (*mošimane*) or girl (*mosetsana*) but uninitiated boy (*lešoboro*) and uninitiated girl (*lethumaša*). The *mašoboro* and *mathumaša* formed a transitional group over which their parents were no longer held liable for their deeds.

These uninitiated youths had a mode of life and a code of rules of their own. They conducted mock marriage among themselves. Every boy was expected to find himself a make-believe wife and, if he was unsuccessful, his friends would help him. In this popular game among Batubatse children, known as *manthwana,* youths built themselves play houses on the outskirt of the village. In the building process boys would do the work that was generally done by grown-up men in hut-building, going to the bush, cutting poles and constructing huts. The girls would undertake women's work, cutting grass for thatching the huts and preparing food for the working men. When the hut was complete, the boys would bring fire-wood and any small game they might have caught while herding cattle during the day and the girls would bring mealie-meal. They prepared food and had a feast of their own. At these *manthwana* all the pretended couples gathered in the evening. Usually in such plays older boys and girls were paired off as husband and wife, while the smaller ones took the role of their children. Most children were released by their mothers in the afternoon to play *manthwana.* In the pretended marriages, many of the normal relations between husband and wife were enacted. The "husband" had a measure of control over his pretended wife. These unions often lasted up to the time of initiation and, if the parents on both sides were agreeable, these might end in a formal marriage after initiation. The only restriction on the conduct of these pretended marriages was an absolute prohibition on sexual intercourse. The boys were taught to have sexual relations with girls without penetration to avoid pregnancy. Pregnancy was regarded as an extremely shameful occurrence and often led to an abortion.

Initiation ceremonies marked the transition from adolescence to adulthood. The young initiates were indoctrinated into tribal mythology and ancestral history. The rituals entailed circumcision for boys and clitoridectomy for girls, female circumcision being a deeply rooted rite of passage among the Batubatse, in which the young girls were formally initiated to womanhood. In the past young girls would be instructed at an early age through songs and dances as to the importance of female circumcision. However, it is now no longer a common practice.

The training prepared the youths for their proper role in society insofar as their responsibilities in a wide range of military, family, agricultural and cultural activities were concerned. It usually took several years before a boy passed from adolescences into adulthood, during which time every effort was made to ensure that even the most cowardly youngster went through the circumcision process. The most common methods employed were group instruction, group assignments, apprenticeships and age groupings to experience a particular significant event. Private instruction by one's brother or sister, or one of the parents was also provided. Among the Batubatse were people who had memorised the history and legends of the tribe and stories were handed down from one generation to the next to induct the youth into the moral, philosophical, and cultural values of the community.

Modern European-style education among the Batubatse tribe was provided by the missionaries in the eighteenth century and it was only after the First World War that colonial administrators in South Africa assumed greater responsibility for education. Because there were no permanent school structures for traditional African education and training, Europeans viewed African education as informal. Some went to the extent of saying that Africa had no culture, history, or civilization, which is patently untrue because African education dates back to ancient time in Egypt, to the establishment of Muslim mosques in the centuries following the death of Mohammed and to the University of Timbuktu in the sixteen century.

Yes, traditional education had its own weaknesses. Many families would withdraw their daughters from primary school as they approached puberty since they wanted them to get married. As a result few female members of this tribe received formal training and education. In the modern context and in the light of South Africa's economic, political, technical and cultural development, traditional education fell short of what was required. Traditional education failed to produce scientists as we know them today and did not produce great military men to fight successfully against colonial armies. Most Batubatse girls, rural scholars and poor children could not attend school. Even those who started school were often unable to complete their grades since their parents viewed primary schooling as a mostly foreign process that might change their daughter's ability to pass on culture.

TRADITIONAL DANCING FOR ADULT AND YOUNG MEN

Dance traditionally played an essential role in the culture of any tribe. Much more than entertainment, dances communicated emotions, celebrated rites of passage, and helped to strengthen the bonds between members of the tribe as a whole. It was performed by male and female, youths and adults. Most Batubatse villages had a "dancing master" who taught the members of the tribe from a young age how to perform the various dances. In all cases, the body movements were very precise, and the same dances we see today have most likely been danced in the same way for centuries. Dances demonstrated social patterns and values and enabled people to praise or criticise members of the community while celebrating.

Traditional dance was polyrhythmic and involved total body articulation, with spectators being part of the performance. With the exception of some rituals, religious or initiation dances, there were traditionally no barriers between dancers and onlookers.

Traditional dance in South Africa expressed the life of the community rather than that of an individual. Some dances were performed by only males or females, indicating strict taboos about interaction. Dances celebrated the rites of passage from childhood to adulthood or spiritual worship. Boys showed off their stamina in highly energetic dances, providing a means of judging physical health. Children would learn the dance exactly as taught without variation. Musical training among the Batubatse people began at birth with cradle songs, and continued on the backs of relatives both at work and other social events. Children would move their heads and limbs whilst on their mothers' backs, in unison with the tune which was playing.

The most widely-used musical instrument of this tribe was the human voice, *dinaka* being a traditional male dance while *sekgapa* was a traditional female dance among all the Northern Sotho people, Batubatse included. Among this community, coming together in response to the beating of the drum was an opportunity to give one another a sense of belonging and of solidarity, a time to connect with one another and be part of a collective rhythm of the life in which young and old, rich and poor, men and women were all invited to contribute to the society. In Batubatse dance, a drum or drums were instruments or tools to set the mood and bring everyone together as a community. However, many other instruments were used as well, such as the strung gourds. Music and dance were considered inseparable and two parts of the same activity.

Shoulders, chest, pelvis, arms etc, may move with different rhythms in the music. Jumping up and down in a dance has made the Batubatse tribe well known. Their striding dance known as *mohobelo* features striding, leaping, and in some cases sliding and almost slithering along the ground. Dancing together or separately in certain songs, they gyrate to the right, then to the left: left-left, right-right, arms stretched out like the wings of birds about to take flight, quivering with excitement. The energetic male or female would rush towards the centre of the circle of dancers and start to dance energetically. The spectators would explode into thunderous howls of approval at the recognition of their all-time favourite dancer.

Dancers would take the audience on a sentimental journey. There were three important reasons for dancing: to welcome and pay respect to a visitor; to demonstrate the talent of the tribe to the visitor; and to depict love in marriage ceremonies and tribal rituals. Dance was also a means to summon the spirits of the ancestors, to honour them, and to ask for guidance and for forgiveness in case the spirits were angry.

BATUBATSE SURNAMES

In many countries it is still common for ordinary people to have only one name. The concept of "surname" is a relatively recent development, evolving from a medieval naming practice (the "by-name"). Today a surname is a family name, a hereditary name shared with family members. Among the Batubatse and other African tribes it is usually placed after the forename, but in some cultures the surname is placed first.

Though there is no clear record regarding the first use of surnames, it provided an additional description to identify individuals. The Batubatse used to live in clans or sub-clans and later in colonies; hence it was import to have the surname of a particular ethnic group. Surnames should be combined with appropriate first names to ensure balance so that the child's name does not seem too out of place.

Children would always take the father's name unless paternity was not known or if the putative father denied paternity; then new-born child would have the surname of the mother. Like any other culture Motubatse women changed their surnames after getting married, but they would still belong to their fathers' clan or sub-clan surname and use this with a feminine prefix. That is still the custom in many cultures. Recently, however, there has been a trend towards equality whereby a married woman may use her maiden surname together with her husband's surname.

INITIATION FOR BOYS

Initiation in Northern Sotho is termed *koma*. Literally the word "circumcision" (*lebollo or modya)*, from the verb to hurt (*go bolla*), was applicable to boys only but in ancient Batubatse times it was also applicable to women. *lebollo or modya* to describe the excision of the foreskin which was similar to the Jewish or Mohammedan rite of spiritual purification. In the past, a practice which is not followed today, there were two sessions of initiation for boys, firstly the circumcision (*bodika*), then the *bogwera*, and this was followed by the initiation for girls, *byale*. From the outset it must be stressed that initiation/circumcision falls under cultural practices which are protected by section 31(1) of the Republic of South Africa Constitutional Act, Act 108 of 1996 which provides that persons belonging to a cultural, religious or linguistic community may not be denied the right to enjoy their cultural practices. However, this right is not limitless and a licence to operate needs to be obtained from the provincial authorities. Regulations require circumcision school operators to be qualified, to have a good track record and to refrain from admitting forced or abducted initiates or children under a certain age to their schools. The child's health must be checked before admission and if in doubt a government hospital must be referred to. Officials from the Department of Health must be allowed to inspect the circumcision schools; this is done because these schools, though part of our culture, are now being run for profit like any other business entity.

Uninitiated youths were considered insignificant individuals. As a group they were expected to render free service to the headman and members of their unit. It was a disgrace for men to have relations with an uninitiated girl. The erring boy and girl were ridiculed by others. As the time for initiation approached, the headman called on their services more frequently and the youths came into closer contact with the members of the community. As part of the ritual the young men purposely indulged in obnoxious behaviour, forcing their elders to request the headman to start a new initiation immediately. The inner council of the unit would then gather to decide on a suitable time, date and place, and to announce their decision for the ritual to commence. During this period the excitement in the community would rise to fever-pitch. The boys were allowed complete freedom and their behaviour would become increasingly shameless. They would take by force melons or sugarcane from the women returning from the land and would make lewd suggestions to them. In this manner the boys would create a situation where circumcision has to start to rid the community of their objectionable behaviour.

CIRCUMCISION LODGE AND OTHERS

The initiation of youths was, to the Shai/Shayi or Batubatse people and other groups, a sacred institution and one of the cornerstones of the whole social and political fabric undertaken by the whole community. This ceremony underlined the fact that initiation was not merely an educative institution, but an introduction of the candidates into the

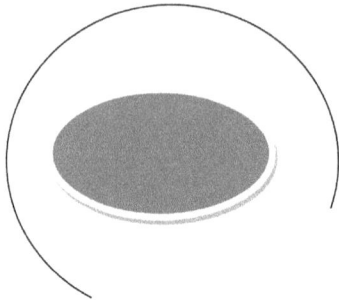

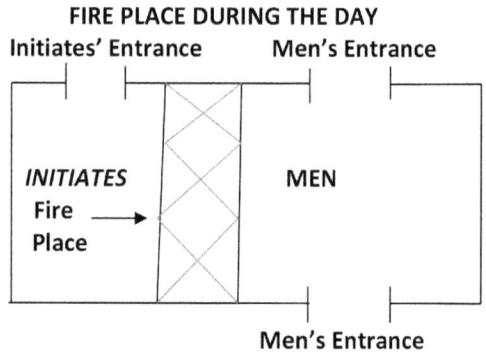

CIRCUMCISION STONE

FIRE PLACE DURING THE DAY

COOKING FIRE

Initiates' Entrance   Men's Entrance

INITIATES   MEN
Fire
Place

Men's Entrance

π π
π π
FOOD TABLE COVERED WITH   **CIRCUMCISION LODGE**
MAT OF LEAVES

social and political structure and organisation of the community. It took place under the personal direction and control of the headman with the approval by the chief of the tribe. The initiation of boys is taboo to all women and uninitiated children, and that of the girls is equally taboo to all men and uninitiated children. Everyone was extremely reticent in speaking about it, and so women knew very little about male initiation and vice versa.

In the past the attendance of circumcision school was compulsory for all youths of the appropriate age. The normal age of initiation was between twelve and sixteen years. Later, since many boys were away working, they could only attend initiation at a later age; and one may thus find young men between the ages seventeen and twenty-five attending the same initiation school. The normal period lapsing between the end of one initiation and the start of another was six to ten years, depending on various factors. For instance, it was never held during drought since a large quantity of food was required at the school to feed the initiates, and the death of a chief or headman would also cause delay.

Initiation tends to strengthen the chieftaincy of the tribe. All headmen or any person qualified to open a new circumcision school had first to obtain a permit (*sesa*) from the chief. Initiation is a transition process from boyhood to manhood; hence certain formalities would take place before the school could be opened. During this period one would hear elderly men saying "*Byato e ragile lekgeswa*" (boys are ripe for circumcision). A few days before the opening of the initiation school (*bodika*) the elders close to the headman would meet him to nominate an initiation master (*rabadia*) and his deputy (*moditiana*), who together would control and direct the activities of the school. The *rabadia* carried out his functions as the personal envoy of the headman under whose auspices the initiation took place (often the *rabadia* would indeed be a close relative of the headman.) A trained person, not a member of the headman's unit, would be elected as the traditional circumcision school doctor (*rathipana*) to perform the circumcision, usually being retained for successive initiations.

As soon as these functionaries were appointed, the circumcision doctor would produce a bag containing the foreskins of the previous initiates, which he would get from the Chief. This was known as a firebrand. The foreskins were then roasted and mixed with medicine (*tšhidi*), the usual preventive against witchcraft, and the site where the initiation lodge was to be built was also treated with this medicine. A headman or his spokesperson or the owner of the school would then announce the day on which the *bodika* would commence and invite neighbouring headmen and important people, including the Chief, to attend the opening ceremony (*go ntsha koma*). The next stage involved an assembly of the boys in the gathering place (*kgorong*) of the headman or school owner's *kgoro*, after the cattle had been driven out early in the morning by young men called *mediti* or *batape* who had been initiated in the previous school.

These young men would be largely responsible for the initiation of the boys under the direction of the *rabadia*. Upon arrival at the initiation centre the boys would be lashed with a circumcision stick before they enter the circumcision lodge. The boys would be instructed to go out into the forest for the day to collect fire-wood for the headman and tree-bark from which they, unknowingly, fashioned small rings to be used the following day to tie up their penis after circumcision, to protect their wounds. The boys and other men would remain at the headman's *kgoro* during the night, and no man was allowed to have relations with women. One important ceremony which was regularly repeated throughout the session was to be performed during the night.

On the night of the opening ceremony the initiates would be lined up in single file according to their seniority or rank. They would be made to bend over, and each would be lashed twice with a switch by the master down the line, striking them in descending order of rank. The same night a traditional healer would rub protective medicines into incisions caused on their bodies by lashes. Before dawn of the following morning, the war-horn (*phalafala*) would be blown, and by the order of the *rabadia*, they would all get up and move out of the gathering place closely packed together. The boys would be surrounded by the *mediti/batape*, and the procession, led by headman and/or the *rabadia*, would be followed by all the adult men of the unit, singing loudly. This parade would move towards a predetermined spot, usually near a river, far away from the village, where the boys would be circumcised according to their rank. They would be taken out one by one and led to a certain rock on which they sit facing the man who was tasked with circumcising them. The operation would be performed by the *rathipana*, each boy being held by a few men with one man collecting the foreskins.

The circumcised boys were led to the river and made to stand in the cold water to relieve the pain. All circumcisions were completed before sunrise regardless of the number of candidates. Circumcision is the final act of separation from the status of youth, and serves to remove the boy's insolence. Uncircumcised boys were always, disrespectfully, addressed as *mašob o ro* (singular *lešoboro*) and sometimes as *bashaa* (singular *moshaa*), meaning small boys or boy respectively. Having been circumcised initiates were *badikana*.

After being circumcised, the boys were made to lie on their backs in the shade for the rest of the day with their legs drawn up, a position in which they had to sleep for the duration of the bodika. They were provided with some protection for their wounds against being hurt by grass or bushes, but were to remain naked. After the circumcision the men returned home, singing joyfully to show others that something important had been achieved. In the meantime the *mediti/batape* built the initiation lodge where the boys would spend the nights for the duration of the school. The area was strictly taboo to all women, children and uninitiated men, any transgression being dealt with harshly.

The circumcision lodge differentiated between men and boys by having separate entrances as well as sleeping areas on opposite sides of the building for each respective group. The two areas were divided by a long fire pit which was kept alight for the duration of the *bodika*. They slept at night according to their seniority. One boy of lower standing was tasked with tending to the fire for the duration of the ceremony. When entering or leaving the lodge, the boys could only use their own entrance and they marched in the order in which they were lashed at the headman's kraal. In the past, for six to twelve months they moved around the forest during the day and returned to the lodge at night without being seen or coming into contact with any women or uninitiated children. The period was later reduced to three to six months. They would sing special songs loudly so that women and children could hear them approaching and get out of the way. The meanings of these songs were given to them.

Various customs were to be practised at circumcision school: initiates were taught a secret language which was used for the duration of the school. All the orders they received and the utensils used had special names, used only in this session, which an uninitiated person would not understand. For instant, if someone said something uncalled for one would say to him "*wena ga o tshabe maru*", meaning "you are not afraid to speak secrets". At the initiation school water (*meetse*) was known as *matshala;* to drink water (*go nwa meets*) one would say *tsalametsa,* fire (*mollo*) was known as *sesepe* (soap) and to make fire one would say *ba hlaba sesepe* (they stab the soap), when people called then *badika* (initiates), the called themselves *baloi* (witches); *bogobe* (porridge) was called *mogau* (thirsty) and so on.

Many of their normal daily activities were also performed in an unusual way. Great care was taken to guard against witchcraft, and food that was brought for the initiates in separate bowls would be mixed together, so that it would never be eaten by a particular initiate. The initiates were not allowed to touch the bowls handled by women, and porridge was served on a mat of leaves to prevent this. Most of their day-time was taken up by hunting and practising the craft of men, such as wood- and leather-work. The rest of the time was devoted to formal instructions and the singing of initiation songs. Whereas the leader (*nkgwete*) of the group still retained some functions in connection with the hunting activities during initiation, his authority was entirely subordinate to that of the leader of the initiation lodge (*moetapele wa mphatho*).

From childhood to manhood a male child passed through several stages of development, namely baby (*lesea*), boy (*mosimane*), youth (*leshoboro*), circumcised youth (*modikana*), member of a short transitional period (*sealoga*), initiate (*lealoga*), initiate undergoing the *bogwera* (*legwera*) and finally adult man (*monna*). The female stages were named differently but represented the same transitions except for the final legal adult phase. In all these stages they are taught the traditionally masculine attributes such as courage, endurance and obedience to their parents and adults, as well as tribal history, the genealogies of the royal house and other families, tribal laws and sex education. Formal instructions were usually given in an archaic form of language using traditional formulae and idioms that had to be learnt verbatim.

If they forget their phrases, they were harshly beaten by *mediti/batape*. Initiates who caused pregnancy among girls were dealt with more severely than others. Sticks would be placed between their fingers that were then crushed together. With this severe treatment and the harsh life they led, it did occasionally happen that boys, particularly young ones, died during initiation because they could not stand up to this treatment. This consequence was accepted within the tribe and it would be said that the deceased boy "has been eaten by the initiation" (*o lle ke koma*). These incidents were treated as taboo and no discussion on the matter was held. Everything was under the control of *rabadia* and under the direct attention of the *mediti/batape*.

Towards the end of the session the age-group would be given a group name and thus formally become a regiment (*mphatho*), with its own leadership and regimental name. Each initiate would be taught to formulate his own praise poem. (As an example read Masegare Isaac Shai's praise poem in the appendices.)

Few recognized individuals were sometimes allowed by the chief to open circumcision schools. Thatale Shai Seshai, a product of Batubatse under Kgoshi Maupa Maake, was one of them. The few known regiments emanating from circumcision school opened by Thatale Shai Seshai and others staying close to him under Kgoshi Maupa Maake are the following:-

Regiment	Owner	Year of initiation
Dikwete	Unknown	1895
Mashweni	Unknown	1903
Madikong	Thatale Seshai	1910
Matladi	Thatale Seshai	1921
Manala	Thatale Seshai	1931
Dithaha	Seripana Machete	1945
Dikwete	Ralekitima Selowa	1953

It is unknown to most of us as to when and where some of the Batubatse's previous many circumcisions took place and who led them. They could have took place along their way to Maakene or there. What is known is that the Batubatse used to open circumcision lodges at an interval of between six and ten years led by a boy from the royal family. The circumcision schools under the auspices and control of Kgoshi Mashishimale Shai of Batubatse near Phalaborwa, as far as the few that could be remembered, their respective leaders and dates are given as follows:

Name of Regiment	Initiation Year	Bogwera Year	Leader
Mahlakwana	-----	-----	-----
Mapulana	-----	-----	-----
Makwa	1865	1870	-----
Madima	1875	1880	Mabine, son of Lethamaha
Mankwe	1885	1890	Leshwene
Melau/Malau	1895	1900	Matela
Mahlalerwa	1903	1906	Mashabane, son of Molotole
Manala	1915	1920	Khashane, son of Leshwene
Madima	1925	1930	Mabine Johannes
Madisa	1935	1939	Morakane, son of Leshwene

Once the regiment has been formed, the villagers would be informed of the closing date of the session (*go swa ga koma*), and preparations for a feast would begin. Large quantities of beer and food would be prepared, and neighbouring headmen, important people and the chief would be invited to the feast. The boys were washed, their hair was cut and they were clothed with new loin-skins (*makgeswa*). Nowadays European cloths are used. Their bodies would be rubbed with a mixture of fat (*makhura*) and red-ochre (*letsoku*) which their mothers or relatives had prepared and sent along in a small container. While this was taking place, the men would break up the circumcision lodge and heap all the poles, branches and grass together. The boys would be lined up to receive their last ceremonial lashing and then march towards the village without looking back. Meanwhile the *rabadia* would set fire to the remains of their lodge. Upon arrival in the village the boys would be joyously greeted and a great village feast held in their honour. Any deaths that might have occurred during the session were announced by dropping the container of fat and ochre which has been sent for the deceased relative's hut. A short fasting period would be observed by the boys and the corresponding age-group. This would end when the boys, now referred to as *dialoga* (graduates), would take a ritual bath to cleanse themselves of their red decoration. Before arrival at the village a group of village elders and other parents would wait for the initiates at the gathering place, where they would be decorated with traditional beads. By then all the graduates would be wearing loin-skins (*makgeswa*, singular *lekgeswa*). During this process men would playfully strike each other with sticks in front of women and girls, who would also happily kick open their back aprons in front of men.

This was the occasion when the graduates (*dialoga*) would acquire new circumcision praise names, which they would boast about. Previously the initiates would remain at the gathering place for a period of two weeks, where they were lavishly entertained. For their part they were not allowed to show any emotion or raise their heads to acknowledge their families. All this signified respect by them. For this two-week period their faces or bodies would remain painted with red-ochre or red floor polish to signify that they had completed the initiation rituals. They were allowed to pay individual visits throughout the village and they were well received everywhere and given small gifts to make them talk to the people. A goat would be slaughtered for them on each homestead they visited. In this fashion they were finally introduced and incorporated into the community. At the end of this period all the initiates would be addressed by one of the elders who enumerated their duties and responsibilities. The elder would also preach that nothing short of respect and good behaviour would be tolerated. From here the initiates were allowed to go home to celebrate with their families.

They would dress in modern clothes before heading to their families to take up their roles as new men in their households. Some would, however, remain in their loin-skins for some time while at home before donning formal clothes.

Whereas boys were initiated to community status in the *bodika* session, the essence of which was repeated in the *bjale* session for girls which incorporated them into a similar status, the boys still had to undergo a further session. After the *bodika* session the boys were allowed to attend the informal council of men (*lekgotla la banna*), which was not compulsory. They were called to attend formal gatherings once fully initiated to the status of men during *bogwera* session. A period of between two to five years usually lapsed between the *bodika* and *bogwera* sessions. During this period the recent initiates resumed much of the activities of their youth. They were still, during this interim period, not allowed to have intercourse with girls.

When the boys completed their circumcision process, elderly people call them *magaola* (boys who underwent circumcision only). To remind *magaola* to undergo *bogwera,* people would embarrass them by spitting mucus (*mamina*) on their faces. The word *bogwera* means friendship, and apart from its political-legal significance its purpose is to cement a lasting bond. The outstanding difference in the conception of the roles of men and women appears with the *bogwera* session for boys. Circumcision (*bodika*) is a transitional state into full community status, while *bogwera* is a final state for boys. Members of the same regiment form a brotherhood in the *bogwera* session and, as real brothers, may not marry one another's daughters. A strong bond of solidarity and mutual co-operation is created for the life of its members. Once again the session was under the control of *rabadia* as assisted by the *mediti/batape*.

At the commencement of the *bogwera* session old men would gather outside the village to weave (*loga*) a mat (*hlokwa*) with a thread (*lenti*) of a *babi* tree which grows on the mountains. This tree produces a fine string and has fruits covered with a husk (*boya*) that causes inflammation on the body. The *pashaka* tree, which grows on river banks, can also be used to weave *hlokwa*. *Hlokwa* is also the name of a flexible grass used for thatching. The friends (*bagwera*) would bring a fowl to be slaughtered, skinned and consumed by the elderly men who were weaving *hlokwa*. The place where the mats were being weaved was known as *thimamong*.

On to the *hlokwa* would be stitched the skin and feathers of a fowl, and when the *hlokwa* was placed on the head of each *bagwera* the fowl would appear to be flying. Any woman would then able to know her friend by identifying his fowl. When the *bogwera* session was convened, the recently circumcised boys would gather in the mountain where they discarded their old clothes and donned new garments prepared for them by relatives. That *pashaka* would be tied around their hip. They would now be referred to as *magwera*.

While they were away in the mountain the men would build a special shelter in the gathering place, known as the *sedutung*, where they could sleep at night. Usually the *bagwera* meet at the *thimamong* in the morning, then went to gather woods to make fire at the *sedutung* in the evening. The routine of the *bogwera* was largely a repetition of that of the *bodika,* although it was not formal or strict as the former session since the lodge was built close to the village or chief's kraal, visible to women. As candidates the *magwera* again received formal instruction, sang and repeated formulae during the day, and only returned to the shelter at night to sleep. Among the Batubatse a *mogwera* was identified by being in possession of a long, thin stick (*kgati*).

Young girls (*makgarebe*) would bring food for *bagwera* at the *thimamong* in the morning and would kneel down when they delivered it. If a *mogwera* did not like the side dish he would mix the relish with ash, known as *phuphe*. If a *mogwera* nevertheless ate the relish which he did not like, he would beat the young girl who brought it when she came the following day. To have *hlokwa* was not a strict requirement, and a *mogwera* who had no *hlokwa* was allowed to participate in the *bogwera* practice on condition that he arrived at the *thimamong* early in the morning before the others and was the last to go home. Batubatse refer to *bagwera* as *dipafi*, hyenas. The *bogwera* schools ended with a lion hunt, the initiates' first task as a new regiment.

Bogwera sessions were shorter than *bodika*, lasting only one mouth. On the day before the closing ceremony a pole would be raised next to the lodge, on top of which a flat, woven grass object would be attached. This object was something like a flag, and indicated to the villagers that the session had come to a close. The length of this pole had to be such that the candidates, standing next to one another, and each grasping it with both hands, could completely cover it with their hands, so that no one could see it. The following morning the boys would bath ritually, put on new loin-skins or clothes and march towards the gathering place, taking along the pole. The remains of their lodge, their discarded clothing and the hair that was cut from them, was be burnt behind them. The headman decided what to do with the pole. Again, a feast would be held, and after a few days one of the senior elders formally pronounced them to be men. As new men they would formally greet the chief or his delegate before going to their individual homes.

The teaching received in the bush had nothing mysterious about it or unfit for other ears. The lessons that men had been taught were restricted to outlining what a man's conduct should be, to cultivating all the virtues that go to make an honest man, and to fulfilling his duties towards ancestors, parents, superiors and neighbours. The men must not tell anything of what they had learned to women or to the uninitiated, neither were they to reveal any of the secret rites of circumcision. Women, too, were not allowed to tell men anything about the rites of excision. That was the custom.

INITIATION FOR GIRLS

A day after the conclusion of the *bogwera* session for boys, the *byale* session for girls started. Only girls who had undergone a puberty ceremony were legible to be initiated in *byale*. Today this is no longer the case within the Batubatse tribes. Details of the *byale* are difficult to obtain for a male researcher as it is taboo for men to be party to the intimate details of the ceremony. The few details which are being narrated below are correct, but deal only with the essential features which were secretly overheard from women. Individual puberty ceremonies were held within each family for girls to mark their attainment of physical maturity. These puberty ceremonies for girls, although not part of the initiation ceremonies, were rites of passage underlining an important change of life. The ceremonies were held secretly by the mother of the girl and a few older female relatives.

Training and education of a girl takes a number of puberty ceremonies. Among these every girl must attend her own puberty ceremony (*khoba or khopa*). At the first sign of physical maturity a girl would be secluded in her hut. The control of this ceremony was in the hands of the elder girls who had been fully initiated. They would walk about with a great sense of their own importance and have to be royally entertained and provided with plentiful food. In time of scarcity and during the ploughing seasons, when people are busy all day in the field, a girl's puberty ceremony would be postponed or cancelled altogether. Although in charge of the ceremony, the elder girls were subject to the supervision of an old woman called the mother of the *khoba* who was chosen by the girl herself, but could not be her biological mother who had no real say in the proceedings. Sometimes her elder sisters or close relatives would take care of her.

The puberty ceremony was conducted in seclusion. Upon arrival in her hut of seclusion the girl would be supported (*go thuswa*) by the old woman. Ground herbs mixed with red ochre (*letsoku*) and some of the girl's own menstrual blood would be smeared in a circle round the wrist, on the head, nose, mouth, neck and arms to avert illness (*go khuma*). The *khoba* always had a companion with her and they would sit to one side of the doorway of the hut clad only in a loin cloth, talking in whispers. When a stranger approached the hut or when the elder girls enter the hut her companion would wail loudly to warn them. If she failed to do so she would be beaten. If the initiate wished to relieve herself, she would walk out completely covered in a large skin or blanket.

Every morning, before sunrise, the initiate would be taken to the river, walking in a stooping position, covered in a large skin or blanket and surrounded by girls uttering a high-pitched wail. In the stream a hole would be dug deep enough for her to sit in. A fire would be kindled on the bank for the other girls, at whose pleasure she remained in the water uttering her wailing. After the ritual bathing in the river to wash off the dust (go hlapa lerole) the novice and her khoba would return home for their midday meal and attempt to get some much-needed sleep because at night they had little chance to do so as the older girls terrorised her as part of the ceremony. The older girls would also return to their home and both parties would be allowed to drink light beer (mageu).

During this puberty ceremony the girl underwent harsh treatment at the hands of the older girls. She would be beaten up for going to sleep. At night she was regularly woken and beaten if found asleep; her blankets were taken away, leaving her exposed to the cold with no fire to warm her, and she was given food without relishes and sometimes even filth to eat. All this was regarded as good discipline. She was cautioned about the dangers of sexual relations with boys now that she had reached maturity, and how dangerous it could be to fall pregnant or have more than one lover as this might jeopardise her future.

The initiate would be taught the rules connected to the new stage of her life and would be informed of the behaviour expected of a menstruating woman. As mentioned earlier, menstruating was considered to be a condition of impurity (ditshila), hence she would be advised to eat and drink from separate utensils during such period, lest she contaminate others. She would be taught not to enter a sick person's room, not to enter a cattle kraal and not to sleep with men during her menses. She was scolded or punished if she did not enlarge her labia minora (go kweba) properly. (The stretching of the labia minora was said to ensure greater gratification for men.) In some instances the elder girls inserted a maize cob (sehokothi) in the initiate's vagina to show her the danger of intercourse, hurting her so badly that she would be unable to walk properly. The kgoba would be told to be respectful to her elders, and to honour and obey her mother. There would be dancing every night associated with the lessons of the puberty ceremony. Most of the teaching was done in the form of songs and miming, with no connection to marriage.

The last night of the ceremony was devoted to dancing (go pebela) and the explaining of many secret things (dikoma). One dance consists of movements in which the legs were held close together, and sometimes crossed, symbolic of the manner in which male advances can be prevented from becoming dangerous. Another dance was that of two girls, one with a cloth passed between the legs to represent the loin covering of a man, dance facing each other; the "man" dances with a lighted fire-brand between the legs, the girl wearing a cloth which makes her look pregnant. On the night of *dikoma* all the women of the area who wished to attend would gather either in the village, from which men were debarred, or at a secluded spot nearby, to hold a night vigil, bringing with them something to eat. It was referred to as the night when one sleeps while standing (*selalaoemi*). In reality there was no sleeping at all the whole of that night.

The most secret rituals (dikoma) were conducted after midnight when most people were beginning to doze around the fire, and continued until down, when disguised figures would come dancing in. Later in the morning, while the girls were at the river, the hut of seclusion would be swept and freshly smeared with wet mud or cattle dung (*boloko*). On her return, after having her head shaved along the sides and back, leaving a circular top, the girl would be anointed with fat and red ochre. She would be given three skins or cloths to wear, a frontal covering, a rear covering and one over the shoulder like a cloak. When dressed, the girl would respectfully salute the assembled company of women by lying down on one side, palms held together. She would then be taken around by the elder girl to greet various relations. A month after the ceremony a grand beer party would be given by the girl's parents for the women of the area to dance for *dikoma*. This signalled the end of the puberty ceremony.

Besides signifying the end of the girl's childhood, and marking her change of life, the puberty ceremony stressed the importance as well as the dangers of sexual maturity. Premarital chastity was emphasised in order to avoid the birth of an illegitimate child, which would offend the social structure. It did not preclude the satisfaction of sexual arousal since this was associated with fertility, upon which great value was placed. Like the *bodika* for boys, the initiation did not change girls to fully-fledged womanhood and she was regarded as a mature girl (*kgarebe/khoba/khopa*) or an uninitiated girl (*lethumaša*). The *kgarebe/khoba* became an unmarried bride. After the birth of her first child she became a young woman (*mothwana*). She would become a venerable old woman (*mokgekolo*) later or when her children got married. (The puberty ceremony seems to have disappeared in our midst nowadays and it is a forgotten practice among women of many tribes.) After the conclusion of the puberty ceremony a girl would be known as a mature girl (*kgarebe/khoba*). Theoretically she was now entitled to marry, but as she was not initiated to community status this was practically impossible. In the eyes of the society she would be referred to as an uninitiated girl (*lethumaša*), since her mature status was not recognised until she was initiated.

It was essential that all the girls attending *byale* should have concluded the ceremonies of maturity beforehand. As was the case with boys *byale* was a community institution, and attendance was compulsory for all uninitiated girls (*mathumaša*) of the appropriate age. The *byale* was always under the direction of the principal wife of the chief, but under the protection and authority of the Chief himself. As a man, the chief was not allowed to have knowledge of the secrets of the *byale*, and the arrangement were made by his principal wife, assisted by the older women of the tribe and by the girls who were initiated in the previous session.

On the appointed day, after the closing of *bogwera* session for boys, the girls were summoned to the chief's head kraal (*kgorong*) by the war-horn (*phalafala* or *lepatata*), from where they would move to a secluded spot in the bush or forest. Before this they were each given a front-apron (*mbepana/nthepana*) and a back-apron (*mbepa or nthepa*) to wear, and their bodies were smeared with a mixture of red ochre (*letsoku*) and fat (*makhura*). Just before sunrise of the following morning, they would be lined up according to rank, treated with protective medicines and be lashed one after the other, after which they march off to the secluded spot in the bush. Here a ritual would be performed which was similar to the circumcision of the boys. The girls would be told that an operation was to be performed to them. A knife would be sharpened in their presence and they would be taken, one by one, made to lie down, and covered with a large skin or blanket. The knife would then be pressed between their legs without injuring them, but the women who performed the 'operation' would emerge from the blanket with their hands reddened with plant-juices, causing terror among the girls still awaiting their turn. The fright and bewilderment of the girls would be equal to that of the boys while being circumcised. The senior high-ranking daughter of the chief or the most senior girl of the royal house would become leader of the age-group.

Their place of initiation was known as the *sebitlong*. After the "operation" they were no longer uninitiated girls (mathumaša*)* but were now initiates (*bale*, single *ngwale),* for a transitional period of about a month. During this time, they received formal education on the work and duties of women. They were told to respect men and were given education about sexual matters with men. They were also subjected to various endurance tests, for example being made to carry a clay doll, covered with thorns, bound tightly to their backs. Singing and dancing played a significant role in the initiation of girls.

At the end of the period of seclusion the girls went through the bathing ritual once more. The legs of each girl were tied together at the knees to ensure that they walked slowly. Each girl was provided with a large grass mat to cover her body from the neck to the ankle, after which she was allowed to return home. If a high-ranking man addressed her she could reply briefly in a soft voice. The *bale* girls remained in this transitional state for up to nine months, sleeping together in groups according to each *kgoro* (unit). They moved about the village during the day helping where they could, and during the night the girls of every *kgoro* would gather regularly in a special hut to be taught special initiation songs and formulae (*diema le dika*).

Towards the end of the session the girls had to be secluded in the bush for a period of less than ten days, during which time various secrets of the initiation (*dikomana*) were revealed to them. The exact nature of these secrets is unknown to me. At the end of seclusion the girls were formed into a regiment (*mphatho*), of which the senior initiate would be the leader. They would be smeared with red ochre and fat, after which they proceeded to the village to be introduced and incorporated into community status, no longer as *bale*, but initiated girls (*dialogana*), the same status which the boys had during the similar period at the conclusion of the *bodika* session. Two days later the girls would go to the river to bathe for the last time and get new clothes. In front they still had the stringed apron (*mbepana/ nthepana*) of the unmarried women, but at the back they now wore the long apron (*mbepa/ nthepa*) of married women which reached down to the ankles.

They were now allowed to change their hair-style to that worn by marriageable and married women alike. They would then return to their homes and introduce themselves to every person on receipt of a small gift. As they were now fully initiated into community status, they were referred to as mature girls (*dikgarebe*) and their physical maturity given full recognition. After the girl had undergone *byale,* she was entitled to marry. If a marriage had previously been agreed and arranged, it would take place soon after the girl had attained marriageable status.

Puberty ceremonies are rarely held nowadays and it has become a forgotten practice among women of many tribes. The same goes for the male rituals of *bodika, bogwera* and *byale* as they have largely fallen into disuse or have been restricted to school holidays due to the demands of formal education.

In Ghana, where the Shai people originated, initiation practices were similar to those of the Batubatse and to other tribes in Limpopo. These puberty rites followed after the child-naming ceremony and prepared the children for a new social status. The best-preserved puberty rites are those of the Dipo ethnic group, part of the Shai/Krobo people, and the Bragoro of the Ashantis. During the Dipo ceremony initiates wear beads of all colours of considerable value as well as an elaborate headdress called *Cheia* made of hoops of cane wrapped in blackened cord. The *Cheia* is constructed on the girl's head before the Dipo dancing ceremony starts. Suitors watching the dance would often approach a girl's family after the ceremony and make an offer of marriage. These Dipo ceremonies mark the entry of young women into adulthood.

In Ghana only a few tribes, mostly in the northern parts of the country, have initiation rites for men, and when they occur they are done in secret and not given as much prominence as that of young women. In the Shai and Akan cultures women represent the beauty, purity and dignity of society and are protected against corruption by traditional laws and regulations. The characters of children are built during their early years, which they spend mostly with their mothers. They believe that mothers with good morals and proper training are needed to bring up good children. It is therefore little wonder that the initiation of women into adulthood is given more prominence in the Akan society than that of men. Just like the Batubatse in Limpopo, the young Shai women, after their first menstruation, are secluded from the community for two or three weeks, during which time they are taught the secrets of womanhood and are given lessons in sex education and birth control.

Further, they are taught to relate to men properly so that they can maintain a good marriage in society with dignity. After the period of seclusion a function is held which is attended by the chief and most of the community. The newly initiated women dress up in their finery and adorn themselves with beautiful African beads and cosmetics to show off their vital statistics. Young men of marriageable age feast their eyes on the parade and select their prospective wives. The rituals are carried out amidst drumming and dancing, with the spirit of the departed ancestors invoked to bless the participants and ensure their protection, blessing and fertility.

According to traditional law, a woman in Ghana is not allowed to marry without having gone through the puberty rites and must remain a virgin prior to this. These laws ensure that young women grow up disciplined enough to control their sexuality and to prevent them from premature motherhood and unwanted babies. So important are these laws that any woman who falls pregnant or lose her virginity before the rites are performed is ostracised, as is the man responsible. On top of that a heavy fine is imposed on the guilty party, after which purification rites are performed to rid the society of the negative repercussions of this behaviour.

The culturally sanctioned sexual practice that facilitates female ejaculation, or what is called squirting in the West, among the old Batubatse was encouraged between partners for centuries. It is understood that the men in the Great Lakes nations of Uganda, Burundi, Congo and Tanzania had long been inducing female ejaculation. This was the type of sex education young girls would receive when they grew up, particularly after initiation. Only a few Batubatse people remember about this practice and are shy to explain how this was done. Yes, culture determines who we were, who we are and how we do things, but I believe that culture is a living thing that can be changed and adapted for the better. There is a clash between the law and culture, but we need to strike a balance between the two. We should not throw our culture away, but the law-makers of customary law should find ways in which we can influence the legislature to strike a balance.

The above practice was more or less similar to the one practised in Kenya whereby the initiation and coming-of-age ceremonies of young women of the indigenous tribe of Pokot in Baringo County mark their journey from girlhood to womanhood. More than 100 girls take part in initiations, which begin at night and last until the following day. During the ceremony the girls sing and remain standing throughout the night and during the next day. Before the ceremony the girls are secluded for more than a month, as Pokot tradition dictates, out of sight of men. After the ceremony the young women will be able to get married. For most of them their marriages have already been arranged.

In addition to the above the Batubatse practised female genital mutilation, also known as female circumcision. This was the ritual removal of some or all of the external female genitalia by a traditional circumciser using a sharpened white rock (*legakadima*). The age at which it was conducted varied from a few days after birth to puberty. There were basically three types of female circumcision practices; clitorodectomy, a partial or total amputation of the clitoris; the amputation of both clitoris and the inner lips; and the removal of the clitoris, some or all of the labia minora and incisions in the labia majora to create a raw surface. These raw surfaces were either stitched together or kept in contact until the skin healed as a hood covering the urethra and most of the vagina. The vagina would be left open for urine, menstrual fluid, intercourse and open further for childbirth.

This was done as an attempt to control women's sexuality. Female circumcision applied an equivalent in severity with male circumcision. The circumciser was usually an old woman. Most girls were cut by the age of between five and fourteen years to avoid them facing exclusion from the community. The Batubatse considered female circumcision as a necessary practice in terms of their ribal law, religion and morality. No proper Motubatse man or woman would marry or have sexual relation with someone who was not circumcised. This type of practice has long been abandoned, the reason being that the female body should not be subjected to so much abuse and indignity within the community.

DEATH AND BURIAL RITES

Ancestor belief was a component of faith and has been embraced in various forms and degrees by societies throughout the world. Like other aspects of faith it has no tangible form and is predicated on an abiding and firm acceptance of its existence, rooted deeply both in history and culture. It could hurt if preyed upon by persons seeking to exploit such beliefs to callously profit therefrom. The customs of the Batubatse emphasised that the death of an individual brought about a critical change of life for both the deceased and for the remaining relatives. The correct rituals had to be observed to ensure an orderly transition of the deceased from his or her previous life to the new existence, and to readjust the altered relationships of the relatives.

The burial rites were in principle the same for everyone. The death of a small child who had not yet initiated into the larger lineal or tribal group did not affect many relatives beyond the family group. The status of a deceased person was important because it determined the extent of the relatives' participation. The relatives were differently affected by the death of a man and a woman, since the status of woman was always inferior to that of a man. According to Batubatse tradition, as soon as the head of a family died his immediate kin and, in particular, his widows were expected to go into mourning. The purpose of this tradition was to suspend the everyday routine and to segregate affected kin from the community, so that they had time to adjust to their loss and cleanse themselves of the spiritual dangers associated with death.

The chief and/or the headman had to be informed and permission for burial be obtained, thereafter messages were sent to all relatives affected by the death. The burial usually took place on the following night and was only attended by those who lived near enough to come on such short notice. The other relatives might arrive on the day after the burial to join in the communal mourning. The more important a deceased's status happened to be, the more elaborate the burial and the longer the period of mourning. Traditional leaders, senior or junior, and family heads fell into this category. The death of a woman, the young and the unmarried could be dealt with in more or less perfunctory ways.

Immediately after death the body of the deceased is attended to by a close relative who will pull the arms and knees in towards the body, so that it lies in a drawn-up position. The eyes are closed; small stones are placed on the eye-lids (or sometimes soil is used); and the body is covered by a dry skin, cloth or blanket. Thereafter a stick (*lepheko*) is placed across the entrance to the hut to warn visitors against entering. As soon as the relatives have arrived for the burial the body is tightly bound with leather thongs up into the embryonic position (*kudupana*) to prevent witches from later making use of the body. A beast would be slaughtered and the deceased's body covered with its skin before being taken into the grave (*lebitla*).

In the case of a chief a black bull would be slaughtered; for poor people and children, a goat. The sister of the deceased would then indicate the site of the grave by beating on the spot with a hoe. The brothers and/or the father's brothers of the deceased would dig a shallow, round grave for the burial. Chiefs and heads of lineages, and their wives, and heads of households were buried in the kraal. Certain women were barred from entering the kraal for burial. Young men and women of less importance were buried in the private courtyard (*mafuri*) behind the house. Babies were buried inside the hut. Death in the Batubatse religion was the last transitional stage of life requiring passage rites. The deceased had to be detached from the living and the transition to the next life made as smooth as possible.

If the correct funeral rites were not observed, it was believed that the deceased might come back to trouble the living relatives. Personal belongings were often buried with the deceased to assist in the journey. The Batubatse used to have a custom of removing a dead body from the house through a hole in the wall, and not through the door. Alternatively they would open a new entrance to get the dead person out of the homestead yard to the graveyard or cattle kraal. This was believed to make it difficult or even impossible for the dead person to remember the way back to the living, as the hole in the wall or the new entrance would immediately closed. Sometimes the corpse was removed feet first, symbolically pointing away from the former place of residence. A zigzag path might be taken to the burial site or a barrier erected at the grave itself because the dead were also believed to strengthen the living.

Some dead were even buried under or next to their homes or in the cattle kraal. Various other rites follow the funeral itself. Only the nearest male relatives and the closest female relative, who pointed out the site of the grave, take part in the actual burial. The deceased's body in its skin covering will be placed in the grave, facing in the direction where the tribe originally came from, to establish contact with the ancestors of the past. The deceased's personal decorations and clothes are buried with the body. A few seeds of different plants cultivated by the Batubatse are also scattered inside the grave before it is filled with soil, to be used by the departed spirit in its future life. A goat's dung will also be sprinkled inside the grave. The grave will then be filled up with soil, and a stone is placed in the centre to indicate its position for future sacrifices.

Where the deceased was a chief, the person who was his most trusted servant who tended to the tribal fire would be secretly killed and buried with him as a cushion (*moseamelo*) to attend to his future needs. As soon as the grave was filled, all those who took part in the burial would cleanse themselves by washing their hands with water and purifying medicines contained in a clay pot and return to the courtyard. The men who officiated in the burial would be the last to return to the courtyard to join others in mourning throughout the night and the following day. Women would also lament throughout the night and the following day, and they were expected to renew their lament throughout the year on arrival of each relative who comes to sympathise. The grief at the death is obvious and a traditional healer would always be present to treat relatives against faintness. The day after the burial became a communal mourning day and none of the relatives would be allowed to work.

In the case of the death of a chief the communal tribal mourning lasts for about a week, whereafter every family is expected to grieve with the royal family by sending a mourning gift in the form of a goat, sheep or cattle. During the period of darkness (*lefifi*), which lasts for a full year on the death of a chief and widows, all those affected by the death are not allowed to start new buildings and to hold feasts. This is commonly known as the period of abstention in which the hair of all relatives is differently shaved. The widows wear special dresses during this period and are not allowed to engage in sexual intercourse lest men contract the disease *makhuma*. However, young who cannot abstain from intercourse for such a long period were given special medicine for men to chew which protected them from this disease.

The rituals of mourning and burial also function as rites of passage for the deceased because, on death, the spirit begins a journey from the world of the living to that of the ancestors (*Badimong*). Burial is often an emotionally and culturally charged issue. Disputes sometimes arise about where and how a deceased is to be buried or where the head of the deceased should face. These disputes arise in part because the person with the right to decide on burial usually stands to inherit the larger part of the estates. Mourning by members of Batubatse generally lasts for a year or from one planting season to the next. It ends with a ceremony of aggregation (*go hlobola*) whereby the deceased's spirit is laid to rest and united with the ancestors. At this ceremony the heir is identified, debts are discussed and settled, and the estate is distributed to family members. To restore the equilibrium in the family after mourning, usually a joyous feast with meat and beer will then follow.

VISITING THE GRAVES

South African history has many conflicts, giving rise to many heroes. A visit to famous graves throughout the country gives visitors a better appreciation of the people who have shaped South Africa's past and a better understanding of the country's turbulent history. However, a visit to our ancestors' graves had a different purpose and meaning for members of the Batubatse and the tribe as a whole. The ancestors are believed to exist in some usually undefined and unknown place to which the living have no access. There they look after their descendants' welfare and expect their cooperation. They have power to both help and harm their wards. They only passively bring harm, by withdrawing their protection when their instructions have not been carried out.

The ancestor cult was and is still a family affair; and members of a particular family usually observe the custom of visiting their ancestors' graves at least once annually. Ancestors reveal themselves through dreams, visions and diviners. They are also believed to visit their relatives through mediums such as snakes, hyenas or caterpillars or by direct possession. They can be angered, and thereby can bring calamity to their descendants, especially when their instructions are not carried out. The ancestors must be appeased with gifts, such as the ritual killing of a cow, a goat, a sheep or a fowl, a dish of porridge, the pouring out of a libation of sorghum beer and other rituals as demanded by the ancestors themselves.

The living are expected to look after the graves of their ancestors, to speak with the ancestors at the grave site, to ask for help when they are troubled, and to leave behind a gift of food. It was believed that the offer of tribute would bring peace and prosperity. For thousands of years various cultures across the globe have placed a high degree of importance on the veneration and worship of ancestors. Honouring the deceased has been seen as an essential part of ensuring the wellbeing of society and the family-clan-tribe. It was often believed that the soul of the dead had a profound influence on the lives of the living, and veneration of them was seen as necessary for the survival of the community.

The ancestor cult was the central feature of Batubatse belief system, the heart of their spiritual world. For them, the tradition of visiting the graves of the ancestors and praying for both the deceased and the living was an old and important demonstration of respect and remembrance.

The solemn atmosphere of the grave site required appropriate conduct from the visitors. The main purpose was to honour the deceased and to pray for his or her soul, to ask assistance in times of trouble or in decisive moment of life. During the visit it was a customary to recite a poem and to pour beer and sprinkle snuff on the ground next to the grave. Offerings of a bowl of food were placed on the grave so that the ancestor should not get hungry in the other world. African cultural thought is that, although a person has died, he or she still needs to be cared for in the spiritual world. The responsibility first lies with the closest family members of the deceased. They need to visit the grave frequently. Communication with the deceased was also possible through the traditional healers and traditional rituals.

In several cultures annual festivals are held to revere the dead, and to propitiate deceased spirits to keep them benevolent rather than malevolent. In Mexico City people erect private altars containing the favorite foods and beverages as well as photos and memorabilia of the departed. Traditional religion, like other religions, pervades life. It is not like clothes that one wears today and changes or discards tomorrow. It is like your skin. You take it wherever you go.

Practices also differ from sub-culture to sub-culture. All the Batubatse community members for instance approach the "great ancestors" during rain rites. Each year people in the tribe would be given permission by the senior traditional leader to clean the graves of his predecessors and beg them to intervene by sending rain to the area. The Royal House's traditional healer would attend and perform certain rituals. Women would sing at each of the graveside and a family leader would move to the foot of a nearby tree and speak to the "great ancestors", including those who had disappeared without trace, about the problems of the tribe. While he was speaking, people would place gifts at the tree and the gravesides. Sorghum beer was given to the head of each household, to be thrown on to the graves of the ancestors. Finally everyone would rise and the women would dance (*pepela*) while singing together before returning home to the accompaniment of the beating of a small drum. The "Great Ancestors" were only approached at a specific time.

The tribe, as a social unit, is made up of people who descend from a central ancestor, although the direct line of descend from the founding ancestor may not be known beyond three or four generations to all the community and tribe. The tribe or village would be largely made up of kin-related people. However, there were other people as well who were not related to the rest of the Royal House by blood. These include outsiders who had settled there for various reasons. Within the tribe or each village there were also a number of households. After the visit to the graves of the departed Senior Traditional Leaders, head-persons of each household, unit or family would be permitted to visit their relatives' graves.

When a person wished to visit the grave of a departed relative he would inform the head of the household, unit or family. Under the supervision of older persons, each household would contribute mealies, malt, cattle, sheep or goat for the process to succeed. It was the Batubatse custom that one should not do things alone. The eldest daughter (*kgadi*) was responsible for performing the rituals. If she was married her in-laws would be requested to release her from her duties do the job. If the *kgadi* was not available or deceased, her eldest daughter would replace her and perform the rituals. If she never had a daughter a male relative was used. She would inform the ancestors by pouring snuff and sorghum beer on the ground the day before the visit. The next day she would lead the group to the graves. Along the way they would kneel down from time to time and she would continue to pour snuff and beer on the ground to inform the ancestors that they were on the way. When they arrived at the graveyard they would place their offerings on the graves while being led in front by the *kgadi*.

Sacrificing to the ancestors and visiting the graves were considered one and the same thing for purpose of the ritual performance and enough sorghum beer would be brewed and consumed by all present at the grave sides.

In the Batubatse culture a visit to the grave of an ancestor, the offering of food and gifts, and the request for protection were important parts of traditional rituals, especially before the hunting season. This demonstrates the importance in their traditional religion of communication with ancestors. The livings are still struggling; they have to cope with the vicissitudes of life, to overcome temptations and obstacles in order to finally enter the world of the dead. The dead, on their part, would be doing everything possible to assist the living to observe faithfully the injunctions that they have left them as a lasting legacy. It is for this reason that one African scholar has called the ancestors "the living-dead". All this was carried out as a matter of course and it is a practice to be followed by generations to come.

"Cut the 'im' out of 'impossible',

leading that dynamic word standing out free and clear – possible." – Pearl Norman

6
ECONOMIC LIFE

Fields of millet and malt plants

TRADITIONAL AGRICULTURE AND SYMBOLISM

Among the Batubatse there was no exchange of goods. Each family unit operated on its own for itself and also for the benefit of the whole community. It was expected that families should share the products they produced from an allocated area. The chief as head of the tribe and symbol of its unity played a leading role. He was the one to start all economic activity within his tribe. Women enjoyed working on their land, even the old women who did nothing but pull out the weeds. During the time of leisure when there was not much to do one would find the people busy making some tool or utensil.

Wealth was fairly evenly distributed. The greatest incentive for work was to shine in the eyes of the community. Men who possessed more cattle than others acquired more wives to add personal prestige. Surplus which was accumulated in good years was given to the chief and during bad years the chief, as the richest person in the tribe, freely dispensed same to the community. The Batubatse can be traditionally classified as skilled agriculturists. They had a vast knowledge of plants and plant-life. The bulk of their material resources came from their agricultural activities and from what was gathered from the veld. Rain was the greatest single factor in determining their well-being. It follows naturally that their quest for rain dominated their whole relationship with the supernatural world.

The economy of the Batubatse depended completely on nature. Practically every adult person knew the names of the trees, shrubs, grasses and other plants in their environment, and the names of the insects, birds, animals, reptiles and other wild-life. They knew their habits and customs, how they grew and reproduced and what they could be used for. The Batubatse knew the stars and constellations by name, but did not differentiate between stars and planets, both being referred to as stars (*dinaledi*, single *naledi*). The appearance of the sun, moon and stars had a significant meaning in their life. They were observed carefully to discover whether their signs were favourable or unfavourable.

The appearance of a comet was believed to be a bad omen predicting the coming of war, and the eclipse of the sun or the moon was believed to predict the death of a chief. Certain phases of the moon were associated with particular seasons of the year. As a result much of the agricultural activity was therefore defined by the four different seasons, namely spring (*seruthwane*), winter (*marega*), autumn (*lehlabula*) and summer (*selemo*).

It would seem that the first season started with the appearance of the seven Pleiades (cluster of small stars in Taurus) or circumpolar stars (Selemela) at the end of September or beginning of October when rain starts. Thus, this period was called "*selemo*". During October the Batubatse held rain-making ceremonies to thank their ancestors, including the greatest Royal Ancestor, for the rain and fertility of the soil. Usually in November the seed sown the previous months germinated and grew. The new moon in December enjoined the community to begin preparations for the yearly "first fruit celebrations".

The tribe distinguished some seven types of soil known to them by the particular trees, shrubs and grass which habitually grow there. They knew the fertility of each type and the crops that grew well under various conditions and were best suited to each type. The types of soil known were *Sekuba* – a dark-grey soil; *Mashu* – a grey soil on which all crops grew quickly; *Seloko* – a heavy black soil; *Makuru* – blackish soil, good only for grazing; *Mahlabane* – a sandy, loam soil good for sorghum; *Lehlwahlwa* – a sandy soil for all types of crops; and *Sehlaba* – a red soil where few crops do well. These soil types did not all occur in each tribal area and some needed more rain while others need less rain to crops.

Traditionally the oldest and most important crops cultivated were sorghum (*mabelethoro*), green millet (*leotja*), millet (*mabele*), malt (*makhaga*), pumpkin (*marotse*), gourds or another type of pumpkin (*maraka*), watermelon (*magapu*), cow-peas (*dinawa*), ground nuts or njugo beans (*ditloo-marapo*), sweet potatoes (*merepha/dikgokgokgo*) mung-beans (*dihlodi*), sweet-reeds or sugar cane (*moba/dinyoba/metote*) and tobacco(*metsoko/lefola*).

The season of agricultural activity usually started with rain-making rites in which the chief played the prominent role. When sufficient rain had fallen, the men would approach the chief to open the season officially with seed rituals and ploughing ceremonies which had to be concluded before anyone could begin to plough. Ploughing the chief's land was the first task to be completed before each household was entitled to plough its individual land. Ploughing was done by men and the sowing by women.

If there were not enough women in the family it was customary a working-party (*letjema*) to be assembled. The chief was informed accordingly and was sent a pot of beer as tribute. Sowing was done by women placing seed into holes made by the finger, or dropped and trodden into the soil by foot, or scattered by hand, followed by a line of women who covered the seeds with hoes. All types of seeds were sown together in the same land. Fertilisation of the soil was unknown to Batubatse but cattle manure and ash from weeds, brushwood and trees burnt down in clearing the field certainly must have had some favourable effect on the land. The task of weeding, harvesting and chasing of birds when the cereal came into seed was left completely to the women and children. Weeding was done three times during the season and it was a task which was performed co-operatively by working parties. Weeding always started at the chief's land, but this was not a working party since no beer was supplied for the occasion.

Crops were protected from marauding livestock by erecting fences of thorny brush on the borders of the lands. There was a specific process (*go upa*) by which medicines, obtained from traditional healers, would be placed all over the lands by young boys to protect the crops from birds, baboons and worms. Harvesting was also initiated by the chief with a first-fruits ritual to his ancestors in the presence of heads of units (*kgoros*) and the tribal diviners. Thereafter everybody was free to start harvesting any crops that ripen. The fruits, heads or cobs were broken off by hand and carried home by baskets. Perishable fruit was eaten shortly after harvesting and those that last longer were placed in storage huts (*dithathase*, single *sethathase*) and large baskets. Crops such as beans, sorghum and millet were dried, pounded with a long wooden threshing stick and winnowed with flat baskets. The agricultural year would come to an end after harvesting and threshing was completed.

PASTORALISM

Pastoralism, the branch of agriculture concerned with the raising of livestock (goats, sheep, cattle and donkeys), was practised by the Batubatse in regions with little arable land, as they moved from place to place over an area with a radius of a hundred to five hundred kilometres. Fire was used to revitalise pastureland and to prevent forest re-growth. The ownership of traditional African cattle conveyed a sense of pride. The Batubatse carried out mixed farming: both livestock and crops. There were many factors that were taken into account to decide what type of farming should take place on a certain area of land; these included topography, altitude, exposure and rainfall. Soil played a big role in determining how land could be used for pastoral or arable farming.

Although the Batubatse took pride in their stock they could not be regarded as good pastoralists, for their main desire was quantity of stock rather than quality. The tribe distinguished between domesticated animals (*diphoofolo tša gae*) and wild animals (*diphoofolo tša naga*). Excluding the pigs (*dikolobe*) and fowls (*dikgogo*), the herded animals were cattle (*dikgomo*), sheep (*dinku*), goats (*dipudi*) and donkeys (*dipokolo*). Unherded animals were never included in marriage goods and they were never offered for payment of fines or sacrificed. They were kept only for their economic value.

Fowls were reared for their flesh, which was eaten regularly. Unherded domestic animals included pets such as dogs (*dimpya*) and cats (*dikatse*); the former helped men to herd livestock while the latter were useful for protecting grain from rats and mice. Given the vital role played by livestock in the social and economic system, pasture was an essential community resource. All members of a unit were entitled to graze their stock on the ward's commonage, to which everyone had equal access, and individuals could not appropriate particular areas to their exclusive use. Individuals were not allowed to move from one ward to another in search of grazing. In arid and mountainous areas villages were located at a considerable distance from grazing land. The Batubatse stock-owners would therefore maintain cattle posts (*maraka*) at the pastures so that they could keep a watch over their herds. Usually boys were sent to these cattle posts as soon as they started showing interest in girls and would remain there until they were initiated or married. A temporary home was built where they might live for a number of years under the control of an adult man, who lived with them. A large cattle kraal would be built adjoining the hut and the cattle would be driven out to graze every day.

Although the person who built a cattle post at the pasture had full rights to it, he could not take up permanent residence there. The stock-owners had to keep a careful watch over their herds to prevent any damage to crops for which they would be liable. In order to keep grazing and farming rights separate the two types of lands were always distinguished. Livestock was confined to the commonage until the harvest had been brought in and was then allowed to roam freely through the fields to graze on the stubble. Goats and sheep used to graze near the village and return to their kraal at sunset every day. Overstocking was prevented by distinguishing between controlled and open pastures, the latter being available to everyone as were natural water resources.

Cattle were important for their economic value, and also for their social and religious

---

During their pastoral movement the Batubatse did, however, experience droughts and water shortage. Wizened men would sit forlornly in the river bed without fear of drowning since the river was dry, as were the dams and fountains nearby. Their emaciated cattle and dogs would lie on the sand probably hoping that their human owners would perform miracles and bring back water to the once swiftly flowing river. An offensive smell would emanate from the nearby bush where the carcass of a cow would be rotting just a stone's throw away. Another cow would be lying on the river bank gasping for breath. Meat was rarely available as a side dish. In those drought days the cattle became friends to hug and talk to. When its owner took a stone knife and approached a tree, the cattle would follow because they knew he would be chopping down branches so that they could eat the leaves. In drought times the land became a desert. Animals would lick the dry soil to find morsels to feed on. Some of the thorny shrubs and trees on the river banks would survive, fed by underground water. Men would dig pits in the sand to get underground water for their cattle and for their households. They would put large hollow clay-pots or calabashes to keep the animals away from the pits they had dug, so that when villagers came to collect water, it would not be polluted by animals. Subsistence stock farmers would be ruined because drought was literally killing their livelihood. Women would abandon their gardens because the vegetables were dying without water. Poor crop production became a reality. There were no modern machines to dig deep pits to extract more underground water. Water tankers that supply schools, hospitals, clinics and households today were not available in those olden days. Reservoirs, boreholes and water taps were completely unknown then. People and animals finally died of hunger and many trees disappeared for good even after rains had fallen. All this was testimony to the devastating droughts that hit the Batubatse people during their travels from place to place. The cause of these droughts might well have been the so-called El Niño, a phenomenon that affects weather conditions around the world and curtails summer rainfall.

significance. They were acquired through natural increase and through exchange, principally by way of marriage goods. The head of the household was in control of family cattle and he would be assigned cattle to individual household, whereas cattle acquired from the marriage of a daughter were assigned to the household of her mother. The *maf i ša* custom whereby a man places some of his cattle under the care of another largely reduced the unequal distribution of cattle. Should the herd increase greatly during the tenure of his care it was customary for the owner to reward him with one or two calves. Units pastured their cattle in common and everyone had to assist in the herding. This was an important factor in group solidarity.

For sacrificial purposes, tribal ceremonies and wedding feasts one beast would be slaughtered, cooked and eaten by all present or otherwise divided in such a manner that the owner gets a small portion. The Batubatse did not own many sheep and goats since these came second in importance to cattle. They were used mainly for ceremonial and ritual purposes. Unlike cattle, sheep and goats were not individually named and were herded and kraaled separate from cattle. Like cattle they were sometimes sterilised by crushing the testicles between two stones.

Through the passage of time it would seem that donkeys became increasingly popular as draught- and pack-animals within the Batubatse communities because of their resistance to adverse conditions. They were not used for any ceremonial or ritual purpose, but rather for ploughing and transporting bags of grain. Their milk, meat or hides were also not used and when dead the animals were simply left to rot. The Batubatse used the skins of cattle and animals for making clothes and shields; their horns were used as receptacles; switches were made of their tails and the tail-skins were used for binding axe and assegai shafts. The dung was used to smear the building in decorative patterns. The hides of the sheep and goats were used to make clothes. The Batubatse had a good knowledge of stock diseases and treated their cattle with medicated water against ticks.

Although the situation was critical during these droughts, the Batubatse people persevered. They would argue that drought was a natural occurrence and played an important role in the ecosystem, a regulatory process that reduced animal populations but never wiped them out, notwithstanding the crippling effect it had on farming. Diseased and old animals would be eliminated by predators and scavengers, and the strong ones would migrate to wet areas in search of water and would survive to face many other setbacks.

HUNTING AND GATHERING

A hunter-gatherer or forage society was one in which most or all food was obtained from wild plants and animals, in contrast to agricultural societies which relied mainly on domesticated species. Research shows that hunting and gathering was the ancestral subsistence mode of Homo, *and all modern humans were hunter-gatherers until around 10,000 years ago. Hunting and gathering was humanity's first and most successful adaptation. Following the invention of agriculture, hunter-gatherers were displaced by farming or pastoral groups in most parts of the world. Only a few contemporary societies were classified as hunter-gatherers, and many of them supplemented their foraging activity with farming and keeping animals. The Hadze were one of the few contemporary African societies that lived primarily by foraging. The earliest humans probably lived mainly on scavenging, not hunting. Early humans in the Lower Paleolithic era seemed to have lived in mixed habitats which allowed them to collect seafood, eggs, nuts and fruits besides scavenging. Rather than killing large animals for meat, they fed on carcasses of animals killed by other predators or those that died from natural causes.*

Hunting and gathering was the subsistence strategy employed by human societies beginning some 1.8 million years ago by Homo erectus, *and from its appearance some 0.2 million years ago by* Homo sapiens. *It remained the only mode of subsistence until the end of the Mesolithic period some 10,000 years ago and thereafter this was replaced only gradually with the spread of the Neolithic Revolution. During the transition between the Middle to Upper Paleolithic period, some 80,000 years ago, hunter-gatherers began to specialise in a smaller selection of game and gather a smaller selection of food. This involved creating specialised tools such as fishing-nets and hooks and bone harpoons. Agriculture originated and spread in several different areas as early as 10,000 years ago.*

One of the longest surviving traditions in southern Africa is that of the Bushmen, who have lived for tens of thousands of years in the natural setting of the continental wilderness. This indigenous people whose territory spans most Southern Africa are variously referred to also as San, Sho, Barwa, Kung or Khwe. Their way of life has continued in its original status of hunting and gathering and has resisted the enculturation that has affected most lifestyles in the sub-continent. Bushmen are now confined largely to the central parts of Botswana, presently called the Central Kalahari Game Reserve.

These Bushmen, who are related to the pastoral Khoikhoi, switched to farming as a result of government-mandated modernisation programmes and technological development. Hunting (go tsoma)*, the art of approaching an animal silently, was not only for food. Spoils of the hunt, the skins, hair and feathers of the prey, were used for clothing and decoration. Horns were used as musical instruments, while fat and other body parts were mixed with medicines. Hunting was an activity solely for men and boys but* *there are some documented exceptions to this general pattern. For instance about 85 per cent of Philippine Aeta women hunt the same quarry as men. It was also found among the Ju'/hoansi people of Namibia that women helped the men during hunting by tracking down quarry. In the early days game was abundant but today many species have become extinct. Previously men would spend weeks and months hunting large and dangerous game but now it is only an occasional pastime.*

The Batubatse hunters used hand signals to let each other know which animal they had sighted. The Shai group of people, as part of Batubatse tribe, classified their fauna into various categories; animals of the bush (*diphoofolo tša naga*), birds (*dinonyana*), crawling creatures (*digagabi*) and creatures that swim (*dihlapi*). These categories were further classified into edible and non-edible fauna. For our part hunting of animals and birds was solely the activity of young men and boys. Hunting of crawling creatures and fishing was rarely undertaken. Up and until recently there were still a number of game species to hunt, including impala (*diphala*), duikers/red duikers (*diphuti*), small antelope (*dipudibudu*), reedbuck (*matlabo*), bushbuck (*dishosho*), leopard (*mapogo*), hyena (*diphukubye*), hares (*mebutla*), porcupines (*dinoko*), rock-rabbits (*dipela*), small carnivorous animals (*dibata*) and others.

Hunting of totem animals was taboo. It was also taboo to kill the "big five", which had a special meaning in the community. The elephant never forgets; hence a person should always be mindful of what is going on; the male lion stays behind and when the lioness brings down the quarry, the male eat first; the leopard is pursues its target relentlessly and will not be distracted by anything; the rhino charges head on against any threat or danger, and we need to do likewise when tackling any problem; and the buffalo has strength in numbers, a practice that we should follow.

There were certain protocols in hunting; for instance, a leopard had to be taken to the chief, who would reward the hunter with a sheep or goat. Leopard skins were for the sole use of the chief and headmen, and they could not be worn by any other tribesman. Snakes were taken to witchdoctors for use in their medicines. If a hare was killed by a herd-boy it was to taken home and enjoyed by his family. If he was assisted by someone's dog he would share the hare with the owner of the dog. Traditional Motubatse men grew up using a bow and poisoned arrow (*bora le mosebe wa mpolo*) for hunting. They also hunted with specially trained dogs. They used traps (*metheo*) and snares (*melaba* or *difu*) and arranged hunting parties which consisted in most cases of the initiates during sessions. Group hunting was also undertaken by so-called regiments (*mephato*), Anyone could hunt whenever he liked in the tribal area. The knowledge of hunting was extensive, multiple techniques were employed in hunting and the products of hunting were diverse. Some of these hunts produced large numbers of game animal, which were processed and portions of which were made available to members of the hunting group for food. Skins, horns, feathers and other products would go to their senior traditional leaders and other high-status individuals. Hunting techniques included ambush hunting and the use of spears.

The Batubatse mobile hunting communities typically constructed shelters using temporary building materials, or they occupied caves when these were available. The hunters often grouped together based on kinship, band or sub-clan membership. Among the Batubatse the women did most of the gathering, while men concentrated on big-game hunting. In all hunter-gatherer society, women prepared the meat brought back to camp.

When hunting large animals such as gemsbok, wildebeest and hartebeest with bow and arrow, the arrows were tipped with various poisons made from beetles, plants, snakes or spiders. Pitfall traps covered with branches, up to twenty metres deep and thirty metres square, were also used in hunting. The group of hunters would surround large numbers of the game and drive them towards the pit, into which they fell. The throwing of "bones" was a common strategy used by the hunters to ensure success. The meat from animals slaughtered in the veld would be dried in strips for transport home together with the skin. Generally speaking, hunting had a social and symbolic importance and contributed to the Batubatse sense of well-being.

Gathering was an important activity and, apart from food, practically all medicines, clothing and housing material were made from objects gathered in the bush. Vegetables consisted largely of wild plants. Although most of the gathered foodstuff could not be preserved, certain fruits and insects could be kept for some time.

The gathering activities did not involve any special rites or ceremonies. The ancestor spirits were not approached or thanked for these. Phrases used to describe various ways of gathering included to pick up (*go topa*), which was the term used for picking up fruits up from the ground, particularly marulas; to pluck (*go fula*) which describes the plucking of fruits off trees or shrubs; to dig (*go epa*) for roots; to cut (*go sega* or *go ripa*) for grass; to hew or chop (*go rema*) for chopping trees; and to collect (*go gola*) for gathering of insects such as locusts and flying ants (*ditšie, makeke, dinhlwa,*) which were used as side-dishes etc. To gather *dinhlwa* a hole would be dug next to the anthill (seolo) and during the night these insects would fall in.

The Batubatse people like other communities had extensive knowledge of edible plants and insects. They knew which poisonous plants to avoid and which type of grass was best for basket making or utensils. There were very few taboos (*diila*) concerning the use of natural objects. Some grasses could not be cut during the agricultural seasons, and the red mite, which was regarded as God (*Modimo*), could not be killed. Breaches of these taboos would result in supernatural punishment. Families had the sole rights to whatever is grown on their cultivated lands and were entitled to gather insects or to collect beehives on the lands. However, common lands which were lying fallow were open to everyone. Should someone disturbs a marked beehive, the owner could demand compensation. Gathering was largely a daily activity for women and children. Women were expected to provide a regular supply of vegetables and firewood. When certain fruits ripened or certain insects appeared women and children spent the whole day out gathering.

Herd-boys while herding gathered whatever they could in the bush. Most of the edible fruit, leaves and insects appear from August to April each year. The most popular edible leaves used as vegetables were *leroto, theepe, letelele, sereperepe, bolotse, moshitši*, etc. These are eaten or served as traditional vegetable side-dishes with maize or cereal porridge. Some leaves of plants were used as herbs and added to vegetable dishes, for example blackjack (*monkgankgane*). Extensive use was also made of the leaves and male flowers of crop plants like pears and pumpkins. Some leaves were dried up (*mokhuse*) and preserved for a long period to be used later as side dishes.

Fruits provided a valuable source of food. These included fruits from trees like plum (*mohlatswa*), wild medlar (*mmilo*) and sour plum (*motshidi*), all of which were eaten fresh from the trees. The *motshidi* was also used in the tanning of hides. By far the most important fruit was that of the marula tree (*morula*). These trees bear fruit profusely for a short season – the fruits are still used for making a pleasant tasting beer, of which Ba-Seshai were fond. The fruits were also eaten fresh and the dried kernels used as nuts. Beers of different flavours and potency were made from the marula fruit, namely the sweet one (*letotho*), the sour one (*mokgope*) and the most bitter one (*lephoko*). The first one does not cause drunkenness, the second one makes one slowly drunk, while the third one is the most potent and causes almost instant inebriation.

Goats, unlike other domestic animals, are also fond of morula fruit. For most people the morula season is the most joyous period of the year even today. In Limpopo province a

"Morula Festival" is held at Mashishimale village near Phalaborwa once a year. Anyone free, including the Limpopo Cabinet, chiefs and politicians, attend the occasion itself and enjoy the morula beer. Other fruit trees such as peaches, oranges, paw-paws and avocados were also planted by the Batubatse people. Bees provided honey. Many of the edible insects were preserved and formed a very important part of the Batubatse diet. These insects could be classified into locusts and grasshoppers, ants, termites, caterpillars and beetles. Other insects were not eaten. Locusts and grasshoppers were gathered day and night, roasted or stewed and then dried so they could be enjoyed for months afterwards as a side dish with porridge. Ants and termites were used in the same manner. Flying ants (*dintlwa*) were gathered as they emerged from the ground.

The most important and regular seasonal caterpillar was the mopani worm (*mašotja*, "soldier"). Even today these caterpillars appear once a season in great quantities. Their stomach contents are squeezed out between the fingers and the worms are roasted or stewed and then left to dry in the sun. In this manner they may be preserved for a fairly long time and are eaten, as a great delicacy, as a side-dish. At the height of their season young boys were given the task of collecting these worms.

FOOD CONSUMPTION

It would seem that before the Batubatse people and other tribes began farming, hunters and gatherers ate mainly wild vegetables such as roots and leaves of trees, with some meat, fish and eggs as well. Depending on where they lived, they ate different foods. Each area or region where they lived had a major staple crop that formed the bulk of their diet. They harvested some wild grain to eat. When they began herding cattle they milked the cows and fermented fresh milk to turn it into thick sour milk. Around the same time they acquired sheep and goats which, together with other wild animals, provided meat. As the climate change gradually dried up the grassland, it got harder to get food. They then began to farm their foodstuff.

In general European explorers and traders introduced several important food staples in Africa which did not escape the Batubatse. Maize, beans, groundnuts, tomatoes, sweet potatoes and many others were thus introduced. As time went by the principal food crops for Batubatse were maize, green millet and wheat. Roots crop such as sweet potatoes (*merepha*/ *dikgokgokgo*) were also important. Perennial cash crops included groundnuts and beans. Groundnuts were mostly cooked and pureed into a thick, rich source while sweet potatoes could be boiled, roasted or baked in their skin.

Thick maize or cereal porridge (*bogobe/bouswa*) made from the different types of grain, and which was cooked in various manners, formed the staple food of the Batubatse group of people. They made underground storage pits (*seletese*) for grain that were continually opened and closed and the grain taken out when the need arose. Wheat was most commonly baked into bread. There were also several thin porridges as well as sour or fermented porridges (*pelle/ting*). Apart from these there were several methods of boiling or stewing whole grain into a stamp (*dikgobe*). A thick porridge made of a mixture of pumpkins and thin rough meal-meal (*thopi*) had a fine, clean texture. These dishes were generally cooked by women. The large variety of traditional side-dishes (*dišebo*) was made from seeds, meats, vegetables, beans, fruit-juices, milk, insects, etc, and their texture varied from thick to sauce-like.

A few non-intoxicating liquids such as light beers (*motogo* and *mapoto/mageu*) made of fermented cereal bases were enjoyed between meals. All meals consisted of cereal porridge and a side-dish (*sešebo*). The thick porridge was either made of green sorghum (*leotša*), malt/ millet (*makhaha/mabele*) or maize (*mabelethoro*) and the side-dish was either one of the above or from another source. Traditional African or sorghum beer *byalwa/byala*) and water, kept cool inside clay pots, played an important role in the Batubatse diet.

Normally there were three meals a day. The first meal (*molatša*) was referred to as breakfast (*borakane*), taken in the morning before cattle were driven out to the grazing field. Then there were lunch (*matena*) and supper/dinner (*dijo tša mantšiboga*). In those days there were no wrist-watches and time was measured by shadows of trees or mountains, or the moon and stars at night.

There were always two fireplaces for each household of Batubatse, one in the courtyard of the homestead and one inside the kitchen hut (*setlhaka*). Women used to grind (*šila*) corn for meals on a grinding-stone (*tshilo le lwala*) or pound maize with a heavy pestle (*mosé*) inside a mortar (*lehudu*) to make mealie-meal. Every woman prepared the meals for her own household, while each wife of a polygamist prepared a full meal for her husband. The husband would choose which meal to eat.

The fruit of a tree known as *mogwagwa or mowawa* growing in the bush would be ground and mixed with maize meal. This lasted for days or months without deterioration. The dry gourds of *dikoko* or *ditshedu* trees would be broken and the seeds inside mixed with maize.

This was known as *bokomo* and would last for months before going off. *Sekgwa* or *senkgwa* was another food made from ground maize or wheat, cooked with sugar or honey. This "bread" was the carried along during long journeys.

The technique of grinding by women was attractive to watch. Two grinding-stones, *tshilo* and *lwala*, were used to grind grains into meal or dried fruit seeds into powder. *Tshilo* was a smaller, roundish, flat stone pushed back and forth with both hands or on top of a bigger stone, *lwala*, resting on the ground. The woman would seem to be dancing while kneeling down on the ground. The resulting meal was deposited on to a mat or a large shallow bowl *(leselo)* placed in front. All types of grains and dried fruit seeds could be ground in that way. However, the grains commonly processed by Batubatse tribes in that fashion were malt or millet (*makhaha* or *mabele*) and sorghum (*mabelethoro*).

Men ate separately from women and children, usually in their gathering place. A large amount of porridge was made for the evening meals, and what was left over was eaten in the morning. When men or boys were going to herd cattle far from home they would take with them a dish of cold porridge left over from the evening meal and some milk. Herd-boys roasted birds or other small game during the day, or milked the cows and goats directly into their mouths. Some food regarded as a delicacy was only consumed on Christmas day; such food included bread, sugar, tea and coffee. Canned fruits, meats and fish were often eaten by hand in the same way as porridge and side-dishes. Of all the prepared food-staff, traditional African beer was by far the most important for its ceremonial and social value.

Beer played a central role in all social intercourse and in all feasts offered to the guests. Traditional beer was consumed by adults more or less daily. Social beer-drinking was usually accompanied by singing and dancing. Wherever people gathered socially one was sure to find a pot of beer among them. Herd-boys and children were not permitted to consume beer.

"Motivation is what gets you started. Habit is what keeps you going."

– Jim Ryun

7
SOCIAL ORGANISATION

Shai initiated Dipo girls - Ghana   *Shai girl with Dipo Cheia headdress*

BATUBATSE MARRIAGE REQUIREMENTS

Within the Batubatse people, marriage was a legal act entered into between the two groups of the relatives of the bride and of the groom, and the presence of the bride was essential only in the final act of transferring her to the family of the groom. In some cases the ceremonial connected with marriage was concluded when the future bride was very young or even before she was born. Today this practice has disappeared completely. The relatives on both sides participate in the marriage negotiations and in the enactment of certain ceremonies including the delivery of marriage goods (*magadi*) which established the relationship between the two parties. Correctly speaking, *magadi* was and still is the foundation upon which the Batubatse customary marriage was founded. There is, therefore, justification for the view that a *magadi* contract has a greater binding force than a marriage in common law. If the marriage goods included the transfer of cattle or their equivalent, this was regarded **as** an act of great significance. Previously the marriage goods were gathered from among the relatives of the groom, and their distribution among the relatives of the bride established the relationship between the two groups or families. Nowadays the groom must provide the marriage goods himself to be delivered to the bride's family. It is no longer compulsory for other relatives of the groom to assist in contributing marriage goods, but they are not prevented from doing so. The transfer of *magadi* defined the powers of the husband and father, **as** well as those powers, duties and obligations of the two family groups of relatives involved. This tradition has been weakened by European influence and there are no longer the same obligations attached to the family groups. Once the bride and the groom decide to stay together as husband and wife the two family groups are obliged to recognise the new structure created by their new relationship. Marriage negotiations may even start and end with the bride and groom already living together. Sometimes the *magadi* are not even delivered.

Among the Batubatse people there were few restrictions on the choice of a partner in marriage but there was no limit to the number of wives a man could have. A man could have a principal wife and a number of secondary wives (mistresses or concubines) in his household. The most basic prohibition affects men and women related to the direct line of descent. A man may not marry or have sexual intercourse with his mother, his sister or his daughter from both paternal and maternal side. Marriage was and is still prohibited between a man and his parent's sisters, the daughters of his brothers and sisters, and his half-brothers and half-sisters. A man also may not marry his step-daughter, his step-sister or their daughters, or his parent's step-sisters. Finally, a man may not marry the daughter of his mother's sister or of his mother's step-sister. In addition it was and is still expected that a man should not marry the divorced wife of his father, or of his father's brother or of his brother or of his sons or of his father-in-law.

The mother's sisters are potentially preferred spouses of his father, and their daughters are thus his potential sisters. A man may, however, marry the daughter of his paternal aunt (*rakgadi*) – his cousin (*motswala*), but not the daughter of his younger maternal aunt (*mmane or mmangwane*). This type of marriage was referred to as "cattle return to the cattle-kraal" (*dikgomo di boela šakeng*); the daughter was going to grind mealie-meal for her paternal aunt (*o ya go setlela rakgadi*). Thus Batubatse culture allows marriage between the son of a maternal uncle (*malome*) and the daughter of a paternal aunt (*rakgadi*), but does not allow the same marriage between the son of a younger paternal uncle (*rangwane*) and the daughter of a younger maternal aunt (*mmane/mmangwane*). The latter marriage, which includes children of an elder paternal uncle *(ramogolo)* and an elder maternal aunt (*mmamoglo*), is prohibited.

Another significant instance occurs when a man, according to the levirate custom, begets a child by the widow of his deceased brother. A son or daughter born from such a secondary union is regarded, sociologically, as the child of the deceased father in the primary marriage, and he is not entitled to marry the daughter or son of this father's brother because such a spouse will be a half-brother or half-sister. Unlike other groups of people, according to the Batubatse culture men who have initiated together and belong to the same regiment are not regarded as brothers, and are thus allowed to marry the daughter of one another.

Should a man marry or have sexual intercourse with his mother, sister, daughter, paternal aunts or daughter of brothers and sisters, this would be regarded as incest (*bohlola*) and disastrous results would be expected. The term incest refers to any action which was or is completely unnatural and evil. It was believed that a child born from an incestuous marriage or relationship or act will be a cripple, malformed, imbecile or in some other way abnormal. Marriage with the wife of a man's father or brother was not regarded as incest, but it was prohibited because it would lead to quarrels among paternal relatives, and accusations that such a man broke up his father's or brother's home. In the past, transgression of the rules prohibiting marriages seldom occurred, and although incest took place on many occasions, no disastrous results came about. Our understanding is that incest is an unnatural and evil thing and it must be strongly discouraged within our communities.

Among people with such strong marital conventions the Batubatse people generally regarded extramarital relationships as normal and natural within their culture, provided that such affairs were conduct discreetly. Not to behave discreetly showed disrespect to the parties to a proper and valid marriage. Married men and women who indulged in this risky pursuit used a secret signal or talk/speech (*sephiri*) by which these affairs were arranged. If the lover approached a woman's hut at night, under such an arrangement, while her husband was present, she would make some warning noise on hearing him approach. Of course if the husband discovered this affair, which was considered a serious breach of the law, the guilty man might be fined a beast or two at the tribal court. If two, one beast was for the woman's husband and one was for the tribal court members who deliberated on the matter, the meat of which was referred to as the jaw-hardener (*mangangahlaga*).

On the other hand the man would be advised, on marriage, never to go to his wife's hut without first notifying her. A well-mannered man would whistle when he approached his wife's hut at night, so that any strange visitor would know that he should leave by the back entrance (*mafuri*) before the husband arrives. Also, if the man had been away for some time, he should not go to his wife's hut immediately, but should first visits his parents or relatives who might sent a message to his wife to expel the strange man or visitor. This practice was somewhat incongruous since the Batubatse people had a strong moral code, with strict rules of etiquette and demeanour, transgressions of which are strongly disapproved.

Marriage was a union of two family groups, rather than of two people, and it was contracted largely to create and to perpetuate relations and alliance between groups of people. Such alliances ensured the easier and more equal distributions of marriage goods (*magadi*). The reciprocal relationship between relatives among whom perpetual marriage links exist was basic to the social structure of the Batubatse people. Every man had certain basic obligations towards his uncles and aunts and they also had the same obligations towards him. When a young man married, these relatives had to attend the meeting of the kin when the marriage goods for his marriage were being collected. They were expected to contribute something towards his marriage goods, but it was not compulsory to do so. The marriage goods thus transferred to the relatives of the bride might well return at the marriage of the groom's sister.

A marriage with the maternal cross-cousin was always favoured because it was believed that the mother-in-law was assured of being taken care of in her old age by a relative, and the daughter-in-law would be less inclined to quarrel with her. This view was also expressed in the rule that says "One is expected to marry one's cross-cousin" (*O swanetše go nyala motswala wa gagwe*). This rule applied to the father's sister's daughter. A young girl, and her parents, could not lightly refuse a request for marriage from the son of her father's sister. In practice such requests were mostly instigated by the mothers of the prospective grooms. The marriage goods received for a girl at her marriage, previously, was used to acquire a wife for her linked brother – but nowadays this does not happen. The groom must himself provide marriage goods; others may assist at their pleasure.

The marriage of two sisters to the same husband was much favoured among the Batubatse people because this led to close unity of family ties. Children of full sisters married to the same husband were regarded as full brothers and sisters, and not as half-brothers and half-sisters as was in the case with children of unrelated wives in a compound family. However, the children of the younger sister would be ranked below the children of the elder sister, irrespective of the relative age of the children. For this reason a man could never marry, as a second wife, an elder sister of his existing wife.

Two sisters married to the same husband are recognised as independent wives, and each is entitled to her homestead. Usually the man gives more marriage goods (*magadi*) for the second sister than the first, to indicate that the second union results from satisfaction with the first marriage. There are many of these types of marriages among the Batubatse people. One of the objects of the marriage alliance between two groups of relatives is the procreation of children. One group of relatives delivers *magadi*, which entitles it to the paternity of all children born by that woman delivered in return by the other group.

When a man fathers and raises children with the widow of a deceased relative it was referred to as "to enter into the hut" (*go tsenela ntlong*) and a woman married as a substitute for her deceased sister was referred to as "to go into the hut" (*seantlo*). *Seantlo* had no independent status or homestead of her own. If, after some years of marriage, a woman had no children due to barrenness, her parents would be approached and ask them to give her younger sister to help her as an ancillary. The man could just claim such a sister, but he had to marry her, although the *magadi* offered need not be as much as that for the primary marriage. If a younger sister was not available, relatives would be approached until all avenues had been exhausted and the matter would be left there. Such ancillary wife was referred to as "the cleanser of the thighs" (*hlatswa dirope*). It was said that she comes to "clean the thighs" of her sister by bearing children for her. Marriages of the two sisters to the same husband and the customs of *go tsenela, seantlo* and *hlatswa dirope* were more favoured because they led to close unity of family ties.

An ancillary wife was not a substitute wife and had no independent status of her own. She was not entitled to her homestead like other wives, but she had to live in the homestead of her barren sister as barrenness was not seen as a legitimate reason to dissolve a marriage. The children born from this secondary union would be regarded as the children of the primary marriage, and would inherit that homestead. A woman who bore daughters only could also request for an ancillary wife to bear a son who would inherit and perpetuate the name of his father. Should the primary marriage produce a son later, the ancillary marriage will become an independent primary marriage with a separate homestead build for the second wife. All her children will rank after those of the first marriage.

Sterility and impotence among men was also recognised. According to Batubatse custom a sterile man may secretly approach a younger brother with the request that he look after (*hlapetša/hlokomela*) his wife. There was no manifestation of this custom. It was merely an arrangement which was secretly discussed between brothers. This differs with the practice of "to enter into the hut" where a younger brother was allowed to have a relationship with his deceased elder brother's wife. The elder brother could perform this function as this might lead to status problems. In both instances, if a younger brother or half-brother of the deceased was not available, some other junior relative would be looked for. In practice a widow will abide by the choice of a man presented to her, but such man must perform the juridical/legal activities for and in the name of the household. Some of these customs, cultures, practices and traditions have been fallen into disuse. Polyandry, a practice whereby a woman had many husbands, was unknown to the Batubatse people.

THE FAMILY

This subject was comprehensively discussed under 3.5 above. A family is a group of people affiliated by consanguinity or recognised birth, affinity through marriage or coincidence. In most societies the family is the principal institution for the socialisation of children and the formation of an economically and productive households. A household consists of two or more people who live in the same dwelling and so share meals and living accommodation. It may well consist of a single family or some other grouping of people. A single dwelling could contain a multiple of households even if meals or living space are not shared. In addition there is the extended family, covering grandparents, uncles, aunts and cousins all living nearby or in the same household. The Batubatse did not have a specific word for a family. They would say "those of your house" (*ba ntlo ya gago*) or "those of your village" (*ba motse was gago*).

To them a family was a basic and fundamental social unit, and represented a prominent *nexus* in their social life. Of considerable importance was the respect given to elders and ancestors. The major characteristic of the Batubatse household was that it was mostly rural, patriarchal and hierarchal, polygamous and open to kinship networks and lineage continuation. These patriarchal and hierarchal systems precluded the possibility of women making deliberate choice on the number of children they wanted to bear. The Batubatse women were in this respect voiceless and powerless. Male supremacy had a prominent strong hold in the society. The interest of the family as a group was subject to the interest of the larger kin group.

Traditional family relationships are under threat from modern ones. However, a popular trend is the merging of traditional and modern marriage norms, values and practices. But fertility control is not practised in limiting family size since the extended family remains the norm: the married couple and their children togetherer with uncles, aunts and grandparents. Family was considered a basic cell of the Batubatse society. All social and cultural practices revolve around the notion of family, either supporting or distorting it. The extended family provided an individual with a personal and corporate identity. The cultural and moral norms of the community that were applied within the extended family helped an individual to grow into a productive and respected member of the community. Members of the extended family supported each other mutually, psychologically and practically, in farming, the rearing of children, and the support of elder persons and the sick.

In the days of Batubatse's glory a woman considered herself nothing without a man to defend her, and a man was nothing without a woman and family to defend. Polygamy was adopted by African women to ensure that every woman in the society had access to a man whose primary role was to be a protector, guide, provider and keeper of the realm. This was the usual way of life in those wonderful, golden days. As we review the great benefits of polygamy to our ancient societies, we humbly suggest that this way of life should be revived and redeveloped correctly and in harmony with good principles.

THE KGORO AND LINEAGE

The word *kgoro* (unit) had a number of different meanings in our group, all of which referred by extension either to the dwelling unit (*motse*) or to the people living in the unit. In the first place the word specifically meants the enclosed, circular gathering-place behind which the homesteads of the dwelling unit were arranged in a semi-circle. It could also refer to the entrance of this gathering-place, and further also to the area surrounding the fire-place (*sebeśo*) within the gathering-place. This gathering-place was the area referred to when it was said that the men were in the *kgoro/kgorong* (court), by which it was implied that they were occupied with their political and juridical activities. The word was also used to indicate the whole dwelling unit (*motse*) including the gathering-place and all the households comprising the unit. Lastly it could also be used to describe the people living in the unit, for example *Kgoro/kgorong ya Shai/Seshai* meaning the people belonging to the Shai/Seshai group/unit. When the term was used by men in court it implied that they were occupied with their political and juridical activities. The *kgoro* performed, on a smaller scale, similar functions within its own group to those performed by the tribe for the whole community. It functioned as a social group and as apolitical unit. It performed juridical activities within the group and guided the economic activities of the group. It also operated as a religious unit in the performance of communal rites and ceremonies. As a social group a *kgoro* consisted of a core of agnate-related men together with their wives and children. In this book when we talk of *kgoro* we refer to the people belonging to the unit.

With regard to the history of Batubatse two or three generations ago, the Seshai sub-clan belonged to the Matome Shai unit. The surname Seshai originated when Thatale Shai, a man of some status, always said *Rena batho ba Shai re dira dilo tša rena Seshai*, meaning "We Shai people do our things Shai's way". Both Thatale and his brother, Matome Booyi Shai, were at the time members of the Bakgaga Ba-Maupa regiment that fought bravely during the Maupa-Makhoba wars. Thus under Bakgaga Ba-Maupa the Seshai unit was established and included men not only related to Shai or Seshai but belonging to the parent tribe of Bakgaga Ba-Maupa.

Other men who apparently had no association with the Shai or Seshai group, including Nyaunyau Lebepe and Ratshwene Sekgota and a few others, were accepted into the unit as senior citizens as a reward for their brave conduct during the war against the white settlers. At the moment the unit is still in existence, but its members are scattered all over the country due to forced removals. This was a typical example of the formation of a new unit in a newly established tribe, but the normal method of establishing a new unit was through subdivision of the tribe, which was accompanied by custom and certain rituals.

The originators of *dikgoro* were usually important sons of the chief; they were also likely to have been leaders of the regiments formed during initiation sessions. Thatale Shai was not the son of a Chief Maupa but was allowed to establish a *kgoro* since his maximal lineage (*leloko*) comprised minimal extended families (*lešika*). Thatale's wife Maafbyana was the daughter of Matebete Maake, a member of the Bakgaga Ba-Maupa inner circle. Thus Matebete was a maximal lineage of Chief Maupa while his daughter Maafbjana was a minimal and maximal lineage or extended family to Chief Maupa. Through marriage to Maafbjana, Thatale became both maximal and minimal lineage to both Matebete and Chief Maupa, hence there was nothing to bar him from setting up his *kgoro*. Apart from that his father was from Shai royal family.

Thus Seshai *kgoro* did not form a single lineage, and in fact the descendants of other members of the *kgoro* belonged to separate lineage groups (*masika or meloko*). The difference between a *lesika* and *leloko* is slight and frequently vague, as there is no accepted standard for the span which each should comprise and there is no formal system of segmentation. The *lesika*, as a segment of *leloko,* formed a more cohesive group and functioned more actively; *leloko* featured in more serious situations. All the descendants of Matome Booyi and/or Thatale and/or Mokhokolo now belong to more than one lineage, hence the different number of both maximal and minimal lineages. However, the children all belong to the same lineage.

At the heart of the Seshai unit was Thatale Seshai and to a lesser extent, Matome Booyi Seshai. They were the greatest and most powerful ancestors to whom homage is paid and to whom communal sacrifices are made. Thatale's extended family accepted his surname and sought protection from him through his supernatural power. The Seshai people cannot use the name Thatale as a surname because he was the originator of the surname Seshai/Seshayi. It is important to the Seshai people to commemorate his spirit so that he is not disturbed.

The lineage and the *kgoro* have separate functions. The lineage was a kin-group with social and religious functions. The *kgoro* was a sort of corporate body, with political, juridical and economic functions as well as social and religious functions. For this reason a woman belonged to the lineage of her birth, but politically and jurally she fell under the jurisdiction of the *kgoro* of the husband. Socially and economically she participated in the activities of her husband's *kgoro*, and religiously she joined in the proprietorship of the founding ancestors who guarded the well-being of that *kgoro*. She belonged to the unit which delivered the marriage goods (*magadi*) for her marriage or the unit which accepted her as daughter-in-law (*ngwetši*), even though *magadi* were not delivered for her. She retained, however, her membership to the *lesika* and *leloko* of her birth. In all social ceremonies, such as marriage, the lineage of her birth could call on her and they retained their rights to her services in all these functions.

THE KINSHIP SYSTEM

In anthropology, kinship is the web of social relationships that forms an important part of the lives of most people in most societies, although its exact meaning, even within this discipline, is often debated. Kinship can refer to the patterns of social relationship themselves, or it can refer to the patterns of social relationships in one or more human cultures. Broadly, kinship patterns may be considered to include people related by both descent and by marriage. Kinship can also refer to a principle by which individual or a group of individuals are organised into social groups, roles, categories and genealogy by means of kinship terminologies. In biology, "kinship" typically refers to the degree of genetic relatedness or coefficient of relationship between individual members of a species.

The Seshai people recognised their relationship with all people with whom genealogical connections could be established: a wide network of kinsmen scattered over a large area. Since a marriage was regarded as a group affair, the entire group linked through a marriage was similarly related. In other words the group from which a son was born from regarded him as a son-in-law *(ba bogwe)*. A male parent-in-law was referred to as *ratswale*, while the female was *mmatswale*. *Ratswale* could mean his wife's father or his husband's father and his male relatives, while *mmatswale* could mean her wife's mother or her husband's mother and her relatives. The sons-in-law could also refer to a wife's and husband's brothers and sisters *(balamo/molamo)*. Children regarded all the members of the group whence their mother stems as their maternal kin.

Kinship groups fell into three categories, namely male ancestral relatives *(bešo or bana bešo)*, maternal relatives *(ba ga malome)* and affinity relatives. The last mentioned was subdivided into male *(ba bogwe bjaka)* and female *(ba bogadi bjaka)* groups. The closest unity was between those descended from one father or one mother. The children of one mother, full brothers and sisters, were grouped together in one category as children of one breast *(bana ba letswele)*. The elder brother was regarded as superior to his younger siblings and was entitled to their respect and in return was expected to protect and advise them. Similar relationships existed between older and younger sisters. The eldest brother was expected to look after his sister's well-being and to protect her against her husband. Whereas male ancestral relation-ships were usually based on mutual respect, the relationship of maternal kin was usually of a friendlier nature. There was greater mutual affection and children looked to their mother's brother *(malome)* to resolve their problems, to advise and console them. Although no formalised system existed of a "joking relationship", the one between cousins most closely approached this. They used words amongst themselves which in any other relationship would be regarded as swearing or in extremely bad taste. The close relationship from youth frequently resulted in marriage between preferred partners.

Affinity relationship was one of mutual respect and friendliness. Where a person married a preferential partner, the relationship remained the same as before. If a man married the daughters of his maternal uncle, his father-in-law (*ratswale*) remained the close friend that he always was, and the mother-in-law (*matswale*) of the bride would be overjoyed to receive her niece into the group at her residence. A mutual exchange of gifts and regular visits were expected between these affinity relatives.

In the kinship, terminology sisters were called *kgaitšedi*, irrespective of their age or status, while brothers were *warra/ngwanarra*, as were half-sisters and half-brothers. Of the brothers of one's father the elder paternal uncles were called *ramogolo*, and the younger paternal uncles, *rangwane*. The brothers of one's mother, one's maternal uncles, were known as *bomalome* irrespective of relative age or status. One's father's sisters, or paternal aunts, were called *borakgadi*, and one's mother's sisters were either elder maternal aunts (*bommamogolo*) or younger maternal aunts (*bommane* or *bommangwane*). The children of a father's elder brother or mother's elder sister were all referred to as *mogolle* and of a father's younger brother or mother's younger sisters as *samme*, while all the children of a father's sisters and mother's brother were grouped together as cousins (*batswala*), disregarding age and status.

Status did not only depend on the relationship between full siblings. For this reason co-wives were regarded as if they were sisters, and were referred to as *mmamogolo* or *mmane*, as were a mother's older or younger sister, depending on their status within the family. Their children between them were regarded as half-brothers and half-sisters. Taken as whole, the kinship terminology classified those relatives who were superior or inferior to someone, and the behaviour would correspondingly be respectful or expecting respect. That was the motto of the Batubatse people.

THE VILLAGE AND THE TRIBE

The biggest unit of Batubatse was the tribe (*setshaba*) headed by the chief, whose position was hereditary. The tribe shared a common name and territory, managed its own affairs, and acted as one unit in defending its territory, rights and its members. In fact a tribe was a political unit. A tribe was a large group of people gathered in a given area. The original type of Batubatse tribe as a group of people under its lineal head was extended to include unrelated groups which became connected to the tribe through conquest and negotiation.

The Batubatse of Shai, who entered South Africa as a single group, have since been divided into different tribes such as Mmanyaba, Balebye, Mohlabe, Mmola and Mampa. The tribes which seceded from the parent group called themselves with other names which were not tribal names. These names were used to distinguish themselves from the parent tribe. They were, however, ranked according to the status of leaders within the parent tribe at the time of secession. Each of these was formed around a core of Batubatse, all with elephant as their totem, but into which a number of unrelated groups, with different totems, had been incorporated. All the members of these tribes would refer to themselves, and consider themselves to be, Batubatse. A good number of the Batubatse had also been incorporated into other tribes, and regarded themselves as belonging to those tribes. They no longer called themselves Batubatse but their association could be traced historically.

Formally the Batubatse of Shai always lived together in one village (*motse*) on land that extended as far as the eye could see when standing on top of a mountain, without having well-defined boundaries. Rigid lines of territorial partition were foreign to them. The ideal of living in one village was the order of the day. For example the tribe of Masetla Maenetja all lived in one village and the tribe of Mashabane Mmanyaba occupied a far-distant village. Each village had its own name. That of Masetla Maenetja was Bolebye, and that of Mashabane Mmanyaba was Modubeng, both having been established after they left Maakene/Tsubye. The name of the village was usually derived from the name of a mountain against which it was built, as in the case of Bolebye, or from a nearby river which decided the siting of the village, as in the case of Modubeng. Villages were also named after the leader of the group who built it or after an event, as in the case of Mohlabe.

Villages were built at the foot of a mountain for reasons of defence, thus leaving the valleys free for agriculture. Sometimes larger villages were spread over a wide area, with smaller hills and valleys included therein, or around a mountain as barriers between people living in the same village. Villages were permanent and would only move to a new site on secession of a new group or on threat of war in search of a more defensive position. Once a new site had been identified the whole tribe moved to a new one in a single migration.

Upon arrival at the new site one man from each unit (*kgoro*) would be chosen to help erecting a temporary hut (*mošašana*) for the chief and his principal wife. Thereafter each unit would erect its own similar temporary hut. The units were placed according to rank.

That, having been done, would pave the way for a traditional healer of the tribe to proceed with the magical protection of the new village, just as when a new homestead was being started. It was only when all these preliminary measures have been completed that the actual building of a new village would begin. The unit of the chief was and is still known as the capital (*mošate*). *Mošate* was the hub of all tribal life, controlling all the activities of the tribe as a whole and of each individual in it.

TOTEMISM

A totem was an emblem of a tribe. It was held in high esteem and revered by all within the tribe. The word for a totem in North Sotho was *moano*, derived from the verb *go ana,* meaning to honour, venerate or respect, or to swear an oath or take an affirmation. A totem could be traced back genealogically to the founders of the original group of people. The totem group could be considered as an extension of the lineage (*leloko*) group, and it was in no way associated with marriage requirements. It was a fairly loose association of descendants from a male ancestor and the only other sexual grouping based on kinship. Totemism was, therefore, the belief that there was a relationship between people or groups of people on the one hand and creatures of the animal and vegetable kingdom on the other.

The totem group was not a clan because a clan was a group of people united by actual or perceived kinship and descent. Even if lineage details were unknown, clan members could be organised around a founding member or apical ancestor. The kinship-based bond could be symbolic, whereby the clan shared a stipulated common ancestor who was a symbol of the clan's unity. When this "ancestor" was non-human it was referred to as a totem, which was frequently an animal. A clan was a smaller part of a larger society such as a tribe, chiefdom, or a state.

People with the same totem were expected to render assistance and mutual aid. For instance, if two people at work or employment found that they had the same totem they would immediately join one another and share their resources. Two people who were complete strangers felt happy when they discovered that they had both the same totem and recognised the bond existing between them, although they might be unable to trace any direct relationship. Within the *kgoro* itself, which might include groups of different totems, the related groups associated more closely, and a person would ask assistance from those with the same totem rather than other members of the *kgoro*.

The totem of a group could be changed under certain circumstances. The acceptance of a new totem frequently followed on group succession when the new group wished to distinguish itself from the parent group. Such a change could naturally occur when the new group was a homogeneous one. The present Seshayi/Seshai group is heterogeneous and includes several totem groups although historically they are unrelated. To establish the totem of a person the normal question asked between strangers was, "What do you dance to?" (*o bina eng or o binang?*), to which the reply was "I dance to such a totem". The totem dance is rarely done these days. These dances represented solidarity, and were mainly performed by women dancing around a wooden effigy of the totem which was placed on a raised platform made of clay specially prepared for the occasion. Change of a totem, like the change of a tribal name and surname, was sometime done for security reason to hide the identity of the tribe against enemy elements.

One could change one's totem if a significant event justified it. An example of this was when Thatale Shai opened an initiation school with the permission of Kgoshi Maupa. At this particular initiation, while the initiates had gone hunting, one of them was attacked by a lion. A boy from Shai's family, probably Thatale's son, rescued the other boy by stabbing the lion in the mouth with a stick and causing it to retreat. At that stage other initiates joined the attack on the lion and ultimately killed it. Shai's son was showered with praise for his bravery and honoured as a hero of their regiment even after the closing of the initiation school. This event marked a turning point in Thatale's life.

When he closed the school he decided to change his totem from elephant (*tlou*) to lion (*tau*), the king of beasts, in honour of his son who bravely attacked the lion with a stick. He reached this decision after consultation with other members of the Shai clan in the area. One of his elder brothers and a key figure in the Shai clan, Matome Booyi Shai, approved the change. There were, however, some who tried to discourage him from altering the totem, but they were a minority. In terms of Batubatse custom, the Shai ancestors were accordingly and formally informed of the decisions at a secret family ceremony where offerings were made to them. Important figures within the Bakgaga Ba-Maupa community, including the chief of the tribe, were invited to attend, and during this celebration Thatale announced the change of totem. Meat of slaughtered beasts and traditional beer were enjoyed, and dancing, singing and other cultural activities took place throughout the day and the night that followed.

Changing to a new totem did not mean a complete abandonment of the old. The Seshai/Seshayi proper still retain in their culture some traces of their former totem. One of the main objectives of assuming a new totem was to confuse a rival group, particularly during war-time. But this was not the case with the Seshai group. That is why, even at the time of writing this book, these people do not form a group large enough to be called a tribe. They came down into the Lowveld with others originally as Transvaal Ndebele from the south and are probably of Sotho origin. At the time of migration all the Batubatse's totem had been an elephant (*tlou*) and they had respected an elephant as their only totem, although a few sections of them changed to other totems. The new totem would always become their secondary totem while the original became the primary totem.

One was not allowed to kill and eat the totem animal as this would invoke natural sanctions, and to swear on the name of the totem, which was considered to be the breaking of a promise, would result in similar sanctions. However, the totem was not associated with any rituals nor did it have great religious importance. It had natural qualities which existed and acted independently, but not actively. The totem had significance mostly in the social sphere. Once the head of a family had changed a totem all family members had to honour that decision and could not contradict him. This happened many times in the world before, based on various reasons.

An appeal was always made to those that were still committed to the old surname or totem to remain as such, and not to regard those who had adopted the new surname or totem as a breakaway faction or to discredit them. They were still one tribe or family with one common ancestor, no matter where one lived. They were expected to remain united as one because they still owed their allegiance to the same secret place of their common ancestor.

The totem of Batubatse is still an elephant (*tlou*), the origin of which could be traced to a story that, on their way from Ghana or Central Africa southward, a group of Batubatse hunters came across another unknown party of hunters. A hit-and-run fight ensued, with neither group gaining the upper hand. While running away and looking for a place to hide, the Batubatse hunters came across an injured elephant in a dense forest. It was the first time they had seen such a huge animal. Initially they thought it was a big black rock.

The forest was so dense that it was difficult to go through it. The big animal, on hearing noises, started pulling down branches thus providing an opening which allowed them to pass through the forest and hide on the other side. Suspecting nothing, their opponents, in pursuit, followed through in order to attack them. The Batubatse hunters, well hidden, were able to attack their opponents and massacre them to the last man, emerging victorious.

They returned home to inform the elders of what happened. A group of strong men was selected to accompany the hunters to the scene to verify their story. Upon arrival at the scene they found the big animal nipping leaves above the trees. Having verified the story, they returned home to inform their leader and the whole tribe about this big animal. The leader of the tribe gave instructions that they should give the animal the highest respect for saving his men, and indicated that anyone who defied the instruction would be killed. Since then the whole tribe started to honour an elephant as their totem. Such is the story.

"To exist is to change; to change is to mature; to mature is to create one self endlessly."

– Henry Bergson

8
POLITICAL STRUCTURES AND ORGANISATION

A political structure is one in which an authoritative leader or small group commands the support of a corps of supporters. Hierarchy and discipline are the hallmarks of such a structure.

The Batubatse community was organised in many respects like that of an army, It was characterised by a central authority, the chief *(Kgoshi)*, assisted by trusted and able lieutenants, the royal councillors, who communicated with different district headmen whom they alternately bullied and assisted. These district bosses in turn had a number of subordinates, district councillors who further chose the captains, leaders or family heads to help them maintain contact with the community.

The traditional leadership structure of Batubatse was thus a hierarchy. At the base was the community consisting of households headed by the family heads. Above them were the village headmen and their councillors, some forming units (*dikgoro*). Above these were royal councillors under the control of the chief. There was no recognition of someone as King or Paramount Chief in this hierarchical structure. Upon the chief's person centred the administrative and judicial functions. The entire system of controlling tribal life was based on the institution of chieftainship, which permeates from the chief downwards through the tribal structure. The political organisation of the tribe was directly related to the ties of kinship which united the various units in the tribe, clearly distinguishing the political role of the two sexes, and found the sanction for its authority in the organised force deriving from the system of age grading.

The chief enjoyed ties of kinship with all the units in the tribe. In this manner the groups of people who attached themselves to the tribe became related to the homogeneous core of Batubatse who traditionally produced the chief. As a result the whole tribe was united not only through their common subordination to the chief but also through their mutual relationship to the ruling group. This plexus of kinship ties was the basis for all power and authority. The most important political unit within the tribe was the *kgoro* composed around a core of kin. The political hierarchy in the tribe ascended to the senior units of the tribe, where it attained its summit in the position of the chief.

Succession to all political office in the tribe, including that of the chief, was hereditary in the male line according to the normal principles of the kinship system. No woman had any independent political status or could perform any political role in her own right. All political activities and offices were reserved for men who were entitled to perform their roles by initiation during *bogwera* sessions. The chief commanded all the structures of the tribe which enabled him to rule unilaterally in a time of outside threats for the defence of the community and the maintenance of the order. To the Batubatse their chief was not merely someone who could enforce his will on them. As their hereditary ruler his position was derived from antiquity and was confirmed by divine authority. His authority was based mainly on his ritual power as the only link between the tribe and their highest ancestors. He was considered to be the father of his tribe, its executive head, the commander-in-chief of its army, its legislator and supreme judge and ritual head.

All the chief's functions and duties were united as a single whole in the chieftainship. As head of the tribe he was supposed to be informed of all occurrences of importance such as births, deaths, marriages, foreign visitors, new settlers and individuals who wished to leave his tribe. As commander-in-chief of the army it was his duty to decide on war, to plan the strategy and frequently to lead his regiment, and to negotiate for peace. He would protect or punish and provide justice to all. In all these varied functions he was assisted by numerous functionaries and councils. No other person in the tribe had such intimate and first-hand knowledge of all tribal affairs. A chief was their living God, who ruled by the divine right. He was supposed to be thanked for rain, for good crops and for general prosperity. He was unique and irreplaceable. Upon his death and during the period of mourning there was no recognised link with the royal ancestors until the issue of his successor to the chieftainship had been concluded by the royal descent group.

A Batubatse chief was addressed by various honorific titles such as *sebata* (wild animal), *tau* (lion) or *tlou* (elephant). His heritage and position was acknowledged by greeting him as Tubatse or Umtubatzi, a name of one of the first Batubatse chiefs. In the presence of the chief women would kneel down and men would clap their hands softly and continuously, calling his praise-name (*sereto*) and ancestors. The praise-poems composed for every chief reflected the history of the tribe and were recited at a feast when the chief made his appearance and after war when victory was celebrated. These praise-poems usually embodied all that was great in the tribe's history and would describe also those characteristics of their life and culture which they valued.

Councillors, headmen and lineage heads had great strength of spirit (*seriti*), as did witchdoctors, wealthy men or men with some other valuable ability, which enabled them to perform the roles accompanying their high status. In the formal manner of greeting all persons of higher status had to be greeted by softly clapping hands while addressing the person respectfully by his praise-name. Through their various rites of incorporation women were assigned the eventual statue of mothers, which defined their economic, social and ceremonial roles, other than political functions. It was compulsory for each chief to have a royal bead (*pheta ya thaga*)

BATUBATSE CHIEFTAINSHIP

There was one great central boss-the Chief, assisted by some trusted and able lieutenants-the Royal Councilors, who communicate with different district bosses- the headmen who they alternately bully and assist. Districts bosses in turn had a number of subordinates-district councilors who further chose the captains- leaders or family heads to help them come into contact with the common healers- the community.

SKELETON GENEALOGY OF SHAYI/SHAI DYNASTY
TOTEM: TLOU (ELEPHANT)

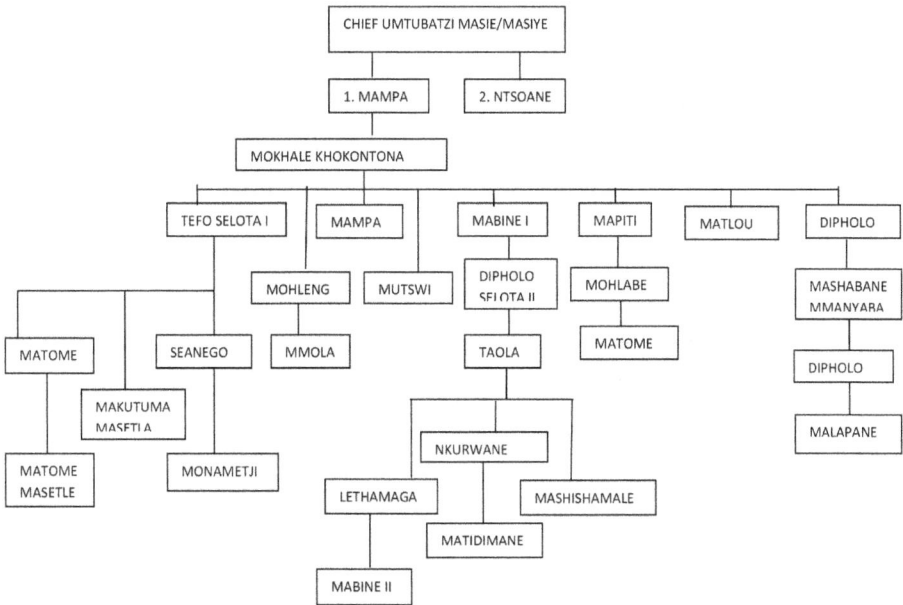

The first Kgoshi or Chief of all Batubatse communities, with their senior house being Shai, is still remembered as Umtubatdzi Masie or Masiye. He ruled the tribe until they settled in the Tubatse area which covered the present district of Mashishing, and this is where he died. The tribe lived there as an independent people until the Pedi came from Bokgatla and occupied the country. When he passed away, he left two influential and powerful sons, Mampa and Ntsoane. Mampa Shayi, who was also known by his praise name of Thelo or Rathelo, became the next Kgoshi. After a lapse of time he left Tubatse and migrated to what is now Ga-Mampa together with a large group of followers. Little is known of the other son, Ntsoane, except that at some stage he moved to Manoge with his family and a small group of followers. They proceeded later to Mphanama and to Ntsoaneng, named after him. It was reported that he later re-united with his brother, Mampa. But some of his subjects remained there.

When Kgoshi Thelo Mampa died his son, Mokhale Khokontona, succeeded him and ruled the tribe for a long period. During his reign several attempts to conquer the Batubatse were made by Kgoshi Sekhukhune but without success. Nevertheless Kgoshi Khokontona decided to leave the area, but he died there before he could move away. He too had several powerful sons, among them Tefo (Selota I), who succeeded to the throne and was given the praise-name of Mashishimale after his great-grandfather; he was known as Mashishimale I. Owing to a famine and finding the rule of the Pedi irksome, and also because of rumours that Chief Sekhukhune was still determined to defeat him, Kgoshi Mashishimale Tefo was prompted to depart. While a small group, known as the Batubatse of Mampa, remained behind, he, together with his trusted brother Mabine and some of his half-brothers, jointly led the tribe away from Ga-Mampa over the mountains to look for greener pastures across the Olifants River.

From Ga-Mampa they arrived at a place suitable for agriculture called Lekgwareng-La-Malatji. Mashishimale Tefo settled there, ploughing the land, while Mabine proceeded onward, leading a group of his circumcision regiment. Rumours that Kgoshi Sekhukhune was after him reached Tefo again, and as they had produced enough mealies to live on during a journey they believed it wise to move on. One family member had, however, erected a unique structure in which to store his mealies and did not wish to make the journey. The reason for his remaining is mentioned under the heading "Matlou Unit".

Mabine was always moving in front, leading members of his circumcision regiment that was ready to fight anyone they came across, while his brother, Mashishimale Tefo, became a follower (Selota) behind him with the tribe. Along the way Mabine's younger brother, Nakampe, broke off with another small section and settled at Leboeng. At the time berries (*mahlatswa*) were ripe. He said he would remain there feeding the section and himself with berries. He referred to himself as Mahlakwana. He was later joined by Mphage unit. After a while a section of this group proceeded towards the present Mapulaneng district and other places such as Modubeng near Burgersfort.

The name Mahlakwana was derived from the seasonal berries (*mahlatswanyana*) they sustained themselves on during this time. Tefo and the tribe crossed the high mountains and the Olifants River before settling near Makhutšwe, now Ga-Sekororo, where the houses of Mampa and Mohlaba/Mohlabe's sections were the first to break off. Each of the identified units with regard to their experiences, life, situations and the conditions which affected them throughout the past generations is set out in Chapter 11. BATUBATSE HOUSES / UNITS. Some of the units emanating from the Shayi Royal House are not indicated in the skeleton genealogy of the tribe due to the loss of connecting information concerning the earlier generations and stem (*thito or kutu*) of the tribe.

Elephant: The Batubatse Totem

RANK AND STATUS

The status of each person in the Batubatse community depended on his blood relationship and his ranking in the social structure. This also prescribed the role that he was expected to play in the community. Rank was acquired patrilineally. Children of one man were considered to be of the same blood, regardless of having different mothers. The rank that children acquired from their father was applied to other families of the same group. They were classified by ranking them above or below his group. Those of an elder paternal uncle (*ba ramogolo*) would be superior while those of a younger paternal uncle (*ba rangwane*) were inferior groups.

The individual within his rank acquired his status through initiation into his age and sex group. Full brothers were not allowed to attend the same initiation sessions; the same applied to full sisters. During initiation sessions boys were assigned the relative status which defined the various roles that they would perform. The elder brother would always assume the superior status that he was entitled to by his rank. Marriage also entitled him to the roles of husband and father.

The status of women was inferior to that of men. A Motubatse woman was a perpetual minor. However, if a woman married a man of higher rank and status she would be awarded the status of such a man. In polygamous marriage the status of a wife was passed down to her children, and children of an inferior wife were regarded as younger and thus of inferior status even when they were older than the superior wife's children. Slaves (*makgoba*) and captives from war (*mathopya*) or their descendants were classified as the lowest and were required to do all menial tasks. They were under the protection of the chief. Other people who were incorporated into the tribe were classified as foreigners (*bafaladi*) and considered as commoners.

All people belonging to the royal lineage were of royal blood. Full and half-brothers of this class were assigned the rank of senior and junior councillors (*bakgoma le bakgomana*) respectively. Sometimes these were referred to as *magota*. Their status was second and third below that of a chief who belonged to his own class together with his wife or wives and his heirs. The special class of the chief was also accorded to his half-brothers but their rank and status would be that of *bakgoma* or *bakgomana*. A half-brother, supported by some councillors and senior men of the tribe, might usurp the chieftainship or leadership of a unit. Although inferior in rank (*ka madi*) a man could acquire the superior status (*ka boemo*) because of his new office.

A superior status could also be acquired by a person through prestige following the acquisition of wealth and ability within the tribe. Such a man was valued because he could frequently give gifts as tribute to the chief. Men with sound knowledge of tribal law would attain high status because they were valuable to the chief at the tribal court. A man proficient in crafts or having some particular knowledge could acquire a higher status than the one he was entitled to by rank. Certain traditional healers, but not all, together with senior councillors, were considered second below the chief. A Motubatse chief, as the principal traditional healer, would stand at the head, and they fell directly under him. Women had their own class below that of men; however, upon marriage they assumed the class, rank and status of their husbands. The status of certain men could be enhanced by their marriage to women of high rank such as the chief's daughter. At wedding feasts women of low status were expected to help in the preparations. Women who excelled at pottery-making or had knowledge of tribal lore would also attain a high status.

The chief was regarded as having the strongest ancestor's spirit of the tribe. When greeting him, men would bow slightly without facing him directly, while women would kneel down. People of lower status would first greet superiors with respect and women would greet men first too. People of the same status and rank greeted each other in a friendly and jocular manner. Where someone wished to make a formal request from a superior person an intermediary was always used who would then pass the greeting to the superior. As already indicated, children derive their rank by blood from their fathers and would acquire status through rites of passage. The children of a commoner could enhance their status through marriage to a woman of royal blood. All children from any rank or status, being a boy or girl, followed the directions of their elders within the tribe.

CATEGORY OF AUTHORITY

Traditional Africans share the basic instinct of gregariousness. Families and members of kin-groups from minimal to maximal lineage generally lived together and formed a community. There were communal farmlands, fruit trees, streams, barns and markets. There were also communal shrines, ritual objects and festivals for recreational activity and for social, economic and religious purposes. Someone had to have authority over all these and such authority had to be legitimate.

The term "authority" refers to an abstract concept with both sociological and psychological components. No easy definition exists. It is a right given to a person to achieve the object of the organisation or tribe. It always flows downwards from top to bottom. Of particular concern throughout the literature on the topic is the entanglement of the concepts authority, power and legitimacy. Power is a broader concept than authority. It is the ability, whether personal or social, to get things done: either to enforce one's own will or to enforce the collective will of some group over others. It is the ability of a person or a group to influence the beliefs and actions of other people. It is the ability to influence events.

Power can be from his personality or from his expert knowledge. Power can flow in any direction and can be seen as evil or unjust. Legitimate power is formal authority delegated to the holder of the position. Apart from legitimate power there are other bases of power such as referent, expert, reward and coercive powers. Legitimacy is a socially constructed and psychologically accepted right to exercise power. A person can have legitimacy but no actual power; for instance, the legitimate king might reside in exile, destitute and forgotten. A person can have actual power but no legitimacy; for instance, the usurper who exiled the king and appropriates the symbol of office.

In all social situations a person is treated as an authority only when he has both power and legitimacy. If someone says to a person "You have no authority here", it might mean that the person had no legitimate claim to be heard or heeded. It might mean that the person has no social power; he has not the ability to enforce his will over the objections of others. Or it might be both. In any event, both must be present for authority to exist and be acknowledged. When a person has authority over others it means something more than simply that they have a right to exercise existing power. If I have authority over you, I can expect that when I make a decision you will accept that decision, even if I don't take the time to explain it to you and persuade you that it is indeed right. In turn, your acceptance of me as an authority implies that you have already agreed to be persuaded.

The supreme status of the chief is bolstered by various factors which enforce the centralised power that he exerts in his various roles. The restriction of succession to a single prince also emphasises the uniqueness of his position, which is further strengthened by his ruling by divine authority. Sometimes these factors tend to show a system of legitimate autocracy which would ultimately lend itself to authoritarian rule. An abuse of power has occurred only rarely in the history of Batubatse. Even a prince such as Lethamaga, who claimed the chieftainship from his father, Mashishimale ll, by force, did not succeed as he was killed before he could assume the position, and he did not alter the character of the political organisation with his rebellion. The political system of the Batubatse of Shai presents a balance of forces which sustains effectively the diverging interests of all groups and individuals.

While certain senior traditional leaders, through the power of their personality or the energy of their activities, may strongly exert themselves and wield great influence, even the rule of outstanding personalities like the senior traditional leader Tefo Mashishimale was described as democratic and was supported by public acclaim. A senior traditional leader or any other person who holds political office has responsibilities towards the general welfare of those over whom their office grants them authority. Their power and authority is balanced by their obligations and responsibilities. A senior traditional leader was, by virtue of his position, entitled to receive tribute in various form from his people.

He was expected to dispense freely his accumulated wealth to the poor, the aged and the disabled. It was his responsibility to entertain guests, and to provide food and drink at tribal festivals and the sacrificial animal at tribal rituals. He was expected to protect the tribe as a whole with his army, as well as protect the rights of the individual. Much of his time must be spent in court to ensure equal justice to all his tribesmen. As the religious leader of his people a senior traditional leader has to perform a series of rites to ensure that he is accountable to his ancestors, to those who partake in the rites and through them to all the lineages and groups they represent.

The tribe must also check its senior traditional leader. Like the ancestors he should be appeased. The tribute that the Batubatse brought to him had the effect of keeping him well disposed to them. In this manner they blunt the force of his power which might otherwise be applied contrary to their desires. The customary tribute of a pot of beer for every quantity of beer brewed ensured that a senior traditional leader was always well supplied with this sought-after beverage. The custom of men to offer a daughter in marriage to him, and in return to marry his daughters, resulted in a number of families representing a large section of the tribal population obtaining influence within the households of the senior traditional leader.

This led to his having many wives and sons and, despite the fact that there was a designated single prince, maneuverings for power among the royal sons frequently occurred. This tends to keep the chief occupied in maintaining order within his own family, and it forces each party to rely on the support of its tribesmen. The status that the chief holds makes him a very inaccessible person. Only if one was very close to him could the chief be formally approached without an intermediary, and he could not move around unless accompanied by one or more of his tribesmen. The institution of senior traditional leader was well suited to the Batubatse way of life and they jealously protected their chieftainship.

The most effective control of the power and authority of the chief was the balance between central authority and group autonomy, which led to the distribution of power. He should be assisted by other office-holders whose co-operation was necessary for the effective exercise of that central power. The central authority of the chief was severely restricted by institutions such as councils and hereditary offices held by other members of the tribe. The whole network of the political structure works for the protection of law and the control of all possible abuse of power. On all levels there were men who had to be consulted before any measure would have any force. Failure to co-operate with these advisers of the chief and other office holders would lead to intrigue. If the chief was incompetent or a waster, the private advisers, who were his close relatives, would always uphold his power.

In the execution of his central authority the senior traditional leader would be assisted by a number of functionaries who were entitled to them by virtue of their birth, their rank and their status. Of these officials, the highest noble or chief councillor (*mokgoma e mogolo*) was the foremost and the man who, by virtue of his being senior in rank and status, was the leader of the class of nobles or councillors (*bakgoma*). This man, subject to the overriding authority of the senior traditional leader, was the leader of the tribe. The incumbent hold this position for the whole of his life. The *mokgoma* may be regarded as the deputy senior traditional leader, although in reality that was not the position because chieftainship was an office held by only one man. But during the illness or absence of the senior traditional leader, the *mokgoma* acted on his behalf. He also ruled with full power and authority in the interregnum period of mourning for a departed senior traditional leader, and he would act as a regent until the installation of the new senior traditional leader.

The *mokgoma* had to be consulted and kept informed by all officials. His influence in all tribal matters was considerable but he could be substituted during his illness or absence by the next man in rank and status. The *mokgoma* was assisted by a messenger, who was not a noble, whose function was to procure the services of a rain-maker during a period of drought. Together with the *mokgoma* he would point out to the rain-maker the special places in the tribal area where protective medicines (*pheko*) should be placed. A noble man (*mokgomana*) of considerable seniority was also appointed to control the agricultural activities of the tribe, with the assistance of someone to act on his behalf in case of illness or absence. The incumbent was always the half-brother of the chief or his father. Other important positions were that of the master (*rabadia*) of the chief's initiations for boys, and his deputy.

Authority is the right given to a person to achieve the objective of the organisation or tribe. It is the right to get things done through others. As leader of the army the senior traditional leader was assisted by the commander of the army and war (*molaodi wa masole le ntwa*). The *molaodi* always led the army in war if the senior traditional leader did not. Authority flows downwards from top to bottom and is legitimate. Below the senior traditional leader and the above-discussed functionaries there were indeed high-ranking men termed servants. One of these men was the servant of the household responsible for the control of the households, maintenance of household properties and entertainment of guests in the royal households.

In addition to household servants there was also a servant of the unit (*kgoro*), a position always offered to a lifelong associate of the senior traditional leader and a member of his regiment. He was regarded as the third most important man in the tribe, subordinate only to the chief and *mokgoma*. He should always be with the chief and assist the chief in all his functions. Through him as a messenger and his co-operation the chief executes his power and authority well.

He received visitors and arranged all meetings and assembles the court. His position could be inherited by his son upon his death. Under him was a minor official called "blower of the war-horn" (*moletša-phalafala*) who went into the mountain behind the village and blew the war horn which called the men to tribal meetings. Upon the death of the senior traditional leader, a new *kgoro* servant would assume office. All servants were frequently referred to as messengers or emissaries (*batseta*).

The strong centralised authority was counterbalanced by the most important political structure in the tribe referred to as the unit (*kgoro*) or village (*motse*), which was completely autonomous. It controlled the social, economic, religious, political and juridical activities of its members. Only in situations affecting all members of the tribe would the central authority exercise its power. The central authority had the power of intervention in the affairs of any individual *kgoro*, in cases of mismanagement from the norms accepted by the central authority. On the whole each unit or village maintained its own internal control, which was balanced by the independent management of their own affairs by families and extended families. In this manner a hierarchy of political power and authority existed within the tribe and the whole system would be well integrated. As matter of fact the unit or village, like the tribal structure, was basically a group of agnatically related people, to which some other families might have become attached.

At the head of each unit was a senior male member or headman who stood as head and representative of the unit or village within the tribe. In exercising his power and authority he was assisted by a number of his close kinsmen. The set-up of his assistance was on much the same line as with the chief but there were no appointed servants, intermediary or messenger. He made use of junior men in his unit or village for any messages. The various dwelling units in the main unit were functionally an integral part in it and were subordinate to the main dwelling unit. The affairs within a unit or village were concluded on the level of extended families. In every compound family the rule of *patria potestas* obtained and the father was responsible for the orderly conduct of family affairs.

In some important matters of a confidential nature the senior traditional leader and the inner council would consult a wider body of councillors known as a private council which confirmed policy decisions taken by the inner council. The private council, therefore, sanctioned policy or law, and might be described as the ruling nucleus of the tribe. This private council provided possibly the greatest check on the behaviour of the senior traditional leader and other political officials. All men of the inner council and heads of other units were part of this council. All matters of public concern were finally dealt with before a formal general assembly of initiated men known as the council of men (*lekgotla la banna*) or a tribal gathering (*pitšo*) assembled by the senior traditional leader.

Attendance by all adult men who have been incorporated into the full status of men was compulsory and those who failed to attend without a good reason would be fined. The senior traditional leader presided at such tribal gatherings and was considered as the holder of the axe (*moswara selepe*), as his function was seen as the cutting of the proceedings and reaching a decision. During the process the *motseta* would ensure that the discussion proceeded in an orderly manner. He would indicate when each man should speak and when to stop speaking. Any man might take part in the ensuing debate of any matter. The senior traditional leader usually took no part in the general discussions. However, he was the one who closed the discussion and gave his final decision. In essence the system was very democratic, as an attempt to gauge majority opinion was made on every issue of importance.

Authority is a right to take decisions. It is a right to give orders to the subordinates and get obedience from them. A person cannot do his or her work without authority, which he or she gets from his or her position, post, rank or status. The principal wife of the chief held political office as the leader of female activity. She decided and directed the initiation sessions of girls (*byale*) and arranged the free labour of the women who had to weed and harvest the chief's land. In all tribal rites and ceremonies she had the authority and power to arrange for the brewing of sorghum beer. She would always be assisted or accompanied by one or two other wives of the chief in the execution of her functions. The senior wife had all the time to accompany the principal wife wherever she went and had to act as an intermediary for any person who wished to approach her. She also informed other women about tasks that the principal wife ordered them to do. The principal wife of the head of the unit (kgoro) or village (motse) had the corresponding powers and authority in her unit or village.

TRIBUTE AND FREE LABOUR

Labour in the varied economic activities was divided between sexes. Because of ritual significant all the work connected with cattle, sheep and goats was undertaken by men, and women were not allowed to handle these animals. Pigs and fowls were excluded. The herding, milking and slaughtering of cattle, sheep and goats and the washing of the milking utensils were carried out by men only. Men were also responsible for hunting. The feeding and tending of pigs was done by the women, although they were slaughtered by men. All the housework was done by women. They were responsible for fetching water and firewood, for grinding corn, for preparing food and making beer, for washing the cooking and eating utensils and for keeping the huts and courtyards clean and in good repair. Women also gathered edible plants and insects, although men also did this when they were out in the veld.

In agriculture the sexes had separate activities. Men would clear new fields of bush and grass and would break up the soil. The rest of the agricultural activities was done by women, though men were not prohibited from taking part occasionally. The position of a woman as the economic mainstay of her household was clearly recognised by the Batubatse. When a woman died they would say "the fire has died at your house" (*mollo o timile ka geno*) or "this house has fallen in" (*o wetše ke ntlo*)". There was no division of labour in terms of age. However, certain of the duties were assigned to the children of each sex. For instance young boys would herd sheep and goats and youths the cattle, while young girls would fetch water, grind corn, sweep the courtyards and later assist in the agricultural activities. As a results women, girls and boys were kept busy throughout the day whereas men had a considerable freedom.

Women would make pottery, sleeping mats, beadworks and prepare gourds. They would also make the floors and walls of huts and courtyards as well as decorating the walls. In house-building the two sexes worked together. Men would do all woodwork, basket-making, carpentry, leather- and metal-work and thatching. Certain functions were performed by the tribe for the chief and his principal wife. The sons and daughters of the chief were not excused from boys' and girls' duties. In most cases servants who were responsible for attending to the men's fire and for performing other menial tasks were captives of war from other tribes or their descendants.

During ploughing time not every household possessed hoes, ploughs or a span of draught oxen, and this was the occasion for co-operation in which families assisted one another in ploughing their lands. The ploughing was done by men, and the sowing by women. It was customary to arrange a working party (*letjema*) whereby a group of people would come together and help each other during ploughing, harvesting and reaping time if there were not enough people in a family. Working parties were frequently arranged for all phases of the agricultural labour. This was done by brewing a quantity of beer, and inviting all who wished to co-operate to come and assist in the work and be rewarded by a beer drink. The chief would be informed of the formation of working parties and would be sent a pot of beer as tribute.

"Sometimes the poorest man leaves his children the richest inheritance."

– Ruth E Renkel

9
LAW

A typical gathering place (kgoro) under a tree

THE BATUBATSE LAW AND CUSTOM

The foundation of South African law is Roman-Dutch law, which is itself a blend of indigenous Dutch customary law and Roman law. It was this legal system that prevailed in Holland during the 17th and 18th centuries and was introduced into and applied in South Africa after the Cape was settled by the Dutch in 1653. When, at the end of the 18th century, the Cape was occupied by the British, Roman-Dutch law was retained and confirmed as the common law of the country. The common law was augmented by statutory law.

Among most African tribes, including the Batubatse, laws were based on unwritten ancient indigenous law. Indigenous or customary legal systems originated from African societies as part of the culture of particular tribe. South Africa customary law refers to that usually uncodified legal system developed and practised by the indigenous communities of South Africa. It has been defined as "an established system of immemorial rules evolved from the way of life and natural wants of the people, the general context of which was a matter of common knowledge, coupled with precedents applying to special cases, which were retained in the memories of the chief and his councillors, their sons and their sons' sons until forgotten or until they became part of the immemorial rule."

Customary law may also mean "the custom and usages traditionally observed among the indigenous African people of South Africa and that form part of the culture of those people". It is derived from social practices that the community concerned accepts as obligatory. Normative systems of this nature are never directly accessible to the outsider.

They must be discovered by questioning informants and on-the-spot observation. There is no distinction, then, between the religion, the culture and the law of such people. In some matters tribalised Africans can claim to be judged by their tribal law and custom, provided that these are consonant with the Constitution. In most cases this applies mainly to customary marriages, succession, guardianship and land tenure.

Before the advent of white rule in South Africa, customary law was the legal system that sustained the people. It was without challenge or competition and it met the needs of the people in those days. When European rule was introduced, the customary law as a legal system was no longer applicable to blacks. However, South Africa's democratic Constitution improved the position of customary law in two ways. Firstly it obliged all courts to apply customary law, when that law is applicable, subject to limitation by the Constitution and specific legislation dealing with customary law. Secondly it also gave every person the right to participate in a culture of choice. This dispensation allowed members of a minority culture to invoke cultural defence to secure acquittal or at least mitigate culpability, on the ground that their cultural norms were the reason for criminal conduct.

COURT AND PROCEDURE

Court (*kgoro*) refers to a venue for unit or tribal hearings which are attended by all adult men in the unit or tribe. There were two types of courts within the Batubatse tribe, the lower or headman's and the higher or chief's courts. The headman's court was a branch court of the chief's court. At both courts cases were heard near the homestead of headman or chief at a special place designated for this purpose, always in the open, under the shade of an accommodating tree, and usually at a time when members of the community were free to attend. The proceedings were quite casual. No rules prescribed who could attend and who could address the court. All adult males were free to participate, including male strangers. The Batubatse Customary Courts operated on the understanding that all adult males knew the law and court procedure of their people; hence the principle of representation was not available, allowed or practised. At the headman's homestead the court was presided over by the headmen on the lower scale, and at the Chief's homestead the tribal court was presided over by the chief on a large scale. In their absence there was always a deputy to act on their behalf. The headman of the unit was assisted by his advisors, who were knowledgeable on the law of the tribe. The unit consisted of a number of known large homesteads headed by their family heads and few other unknown villages or families. All adult men of the unit were expected to attend the session, and as the court hearing was done in public other men from other units were not barred from attending the hearing. All village members of the unit held their branch tribal court at the headman's home, which was a gathering place. The Batubatse branch or headman's court's jurisdiction was limited to minor cases affecting the members of the dwelling unit.

The verdicts of these branch tribal courts were limited and all could be taken on appeal to the court of the main stem (*kutu*) of the kgoro, chief's court or tribal court. Neither of these courts drew distinctions between civil and criminal cases in their proceedings and could try both, whether the bases of litigation have the characteristics of crimes or of delicts. In this lower court, as in the higher court, the binding decision is taken by the council (*lekgotla*) at a gathering place (*kgorong*). The headman's court is, in all cases, a court of the first instance. Among the Batubatse there were cases which were directly transferred to the Chief's Court without even entertaining them. Such cases included incest, some cases of witchcraft, setting fire to the grazing lands, the pollution or poisoning water resources and a few others.

When one individual wanted to lodge a complaint against another he would first take up the matter with his senior male relatives; his father, his paternal uncles and brothers. If they felt there was sufficient cause to pursue the matter, a message was sent to the family of the individual against whom they wished to act. These, in turn, consulted the case with their relatives and eventually sent back a message in which they either admitted or denied liability. Both parties might also meet together to discuss the matter, usually at the homestead of the senior male relative of the alleged wrongdoer. The issue could be settled in a friendly atmosphere to the satisfaction of all or, if still in dispute, would be taken to the headman.

Any litigant who wished to bring a case (*molato*) before the headman's court had first to advise the messenger (*motseta*) of his intention and provide details of the litigation. On receipt of approval from the headman, the messenger would supervise the correct presentation of the case, and the proper conduct and orderly procedure of the *kgoro*. Everyone in attendance could participate in the deliberations, although young men with little knowledge of the law were silenced by the elders unless they were involved in the case.

Whenever legal proceedings were instituted at the headman's court, the senior relative of the complainant (*molli*) would inform the *kgoro* of their complaint (*sello*) and the accused or defendant (*molliši or mosekišwa*) would be given the opportunity to respond. No attempt was made to segregate his witnesses from the accused or defendant's or one witness from another. When the complainant or plaintiff had completed his case, the accused or defendant (*molliši or mosekišwa*) would be given the opportunity to respond to the allegations against him or her. Customarily the accused or defendant was presumed guilty and had to prove his innocence by convincing the court otherwise. This assumption was used to test the credibility, not to prejudice the accused or defendant. Incidental details about the background to the case were admitted as they might be useful in finding a solution.

Thereafter the matter would be thrown open to general debate. All men in attendance were then allowed to participate in the deliberations, cast their opinions and question the parties and their witnesses. Any man was entitled to question the parties, their witnesses and to give his opinion of the case. The headman is the intermediary or messenger (*motseta*) of the chief's or royal unit and would intervene only when all views had been fully canvassed. Both parties had to accept the verdict the headman handed down in order for the trial to be brought to a close. If consensus could not be reached, it was referred to the Chief's Court.

There were no fixed sessions of the headman's court and it was convened as the need arose. The only time the *kgoro* could not be called upon was during the initiation sessions, as the headman and his men were occupied elsewhere. Cases were generally tried soon after being reported, and time was allowed only to enable all interested parties to assemble. This was not difficult as people lived close to each other. If the wrongdoer or any of the witnesses (*dihlatse*) failed to appear before the kgoro they would be brought to the court, by force if necessary. When all had gathered at the *kgorong*, the messenger of the court (motseta wa kgoro), would fetch the headman. When the latter appeared, all persons in attendance would stand up to honour and greet him with praise words such as *mminašoro* or *tau ya mariri*. Before the surname of Shai was changed, Thatale was greeted by the praise words of *Motubatse or Mmina Tlou* or *Tlou ya Bolebye*. Despite the change of the surname the Seshai people are still generally greeted by the same praise words of *Motubatse* or *Tlou ya Bolebye*, or simply *Tlou* and sometimes as *Motsubye*.

The headman and his advisors sat in front while the two parties sat facing them, each surrounded by his witnesses and relatives. All others attending the case sat in a semicircle behind them. Male witnesses were allowed to be present during the whole session but female witnesses remained outside until called in to make their statements. Women were normally barred from attending the *kgoro* unless they were the complainants. During the proceedings the men stood when addressing the *kgoro*, but women remained seated. Only the headman at his unit and the chief could address the gathering while seated. The headman was known as the holder of the axe (*moswara-selepe*) as his hands were viewed as a tool that "cut" the case. He did not normally partake in the deliberations but gave his judgments when the matter had been sufficiently discussed and when a majority opinion had become apparent. At that stage he "cut" the case and gave his verdict.

Oaths were not taken by either party or their witnesses, nor would they be punished if it appeared that they were not being truthful. The wrongdoer was not asked to plea because it was accepted that he considered himself not guilty, otherwise the case would have been settled privately. Inadmissibility of evidence was unknown and any man was entitled to lead the questioning in whatever direction he wished. He who deviated from the matter under discussion would be quickly silenced by the messenger of the court or the headman would instruct him to sit down.

In order to reconcile the parties the court would go back to the history of the case and bring the parties' entire relationship into the open. The Batubatse customary law system had no specific rules governing bias. The chief or headman were not obliged to recuse themselves if they were related to litigants or if they had personal knowledge of the case coming before them. Based on the opinion prevailed at the gathering, the presiding officer would consult his advisors without interrupting the proceedings, sum up the issues and general sentiments and deliver his judgment, which always included the payment of compensation (*tsenyegelo*) to the complainant as well as *mangangahlaga*. For the people of the headman's unit, the tribunal was generally considered to be a court of first instance.

The payment of *mangangahlaga* was done as a court fee to remunerate the *kgoro* and its officials for their labour. Where the parties had reached agreement between them and only went to the *kgoro* to formally notify the headman of their arrangements and to make them known publicly, there was no payment of the *mangangahlaga* fee. If a case went on appeal to the Chief's *kgoro* this fee was not paid to the headman's *kgoro*. Compensation and fines were always expressed in terms of livestock. The development of paying these fees in money is a recent development, since whites introduced monetary currency into African society.

The Batubatse people had no rules regulating the type of evidence that could be admitted. The parties could present whatever information they thought was appropriate and no other category of evidence was excluded as being irrelevant and unreliable. There was no strict separation fact and law. Through a belief in the power of ancestors, spirits and witches to influence events in the physical world they would sometimes attribute a misfortune to an individual's breach of rules of good conduct, without any specific evidence of factual causation. A belief in witchcraft did not only provide an explanation for the occurrence of natural but also allowed for special redress. Thus witchcraft was usually relevant to a dispute only if an extraordinary misfortune had occurred and was preceded by bad relationships within a small, close-knit community.

Circumstantial evidence was acceptable. There was also no law of prescription. The Batubatse law knew of no technical grounds for dismissal of a case. The court sessions were very informal. With the exception of the parties concerned and their witnesses, men used to come and go as they wished. Even the presiding officer might temporarily leave without stopping the procedure.

When the case had been tried and the headman had given his decision, both parties had to indicate whether they accepted the verdict or not. The case was obviously settled if they agreed, but if not it was referred to the Chief's Court for further trial. In all cases both the complainant or plaintiff and accused or defendant had to be present at the gathering place (*kgorong*) when the case was tried, as Batubatse law knew of no judgment by default because in olden days people were seldom away from their home. This is described by a legal proverb which says "a case cannot become rotten" (*molato ga o bole*). If the wrongdoer absconded after his deed, the complainant or plaintiff would have to wait his return before instigating his case. If the wrongdoer died his relatives might be held liable. In both instances the headman had to inform the Chief of the wrongdoer who absconded and the death of the wrongdoer.

If a case were too complicated to be settled by the headman, or if the headman's court was unsuccessful in its trial of the case or one of the litigants was unhappy about the verdict or punishment meted out, the case would be transferred to the next court in the hierarchy: the chief's court, which would give a final judgment. Here the chief was also assisted by his senior counsellors. Court procedure at the higher court was similar to that of the lower court. If a case from the lower court went on appeal to a higher court, the lower court was not entitled to any fee from either litigant. The same applied when an unsuccessful case was transferred from the headman's court to the chief's court. But if the decision of the lower court on appeal was accepted the verdict usually included the payment of *mangangahlaga* for the lower court.

Mangangahlaga literally means "the place where the cheek is pulled out". The term refers to the men who took part in the court proceedings and had to "work with their mouths and cheeks" in the deliberations of the *kgoro*. The payment of *mangangahlaga* was seen as a type of court fee to remunerate the *kgoro* and its officials for their labour. Where the parties had reached agreement beforehand, and only went to *kgoro* to formally notify the headman of their arrangements and to make them known publicly, there was no payment of *mangangahlaga*, for it did not discuss the case. That the *mangangahlaga* was not only a fee but also remuneration appears from the fact that if a court decision was not accepted, but goes on appeal to the Chief's *kgoro*, this fee was not paid to the headman's *kgoro*. The *mangangahlaga*, furthermore, has the overriding element of punishment. Compensation and fines were always expressed in terms of livestock; the equivalent of money is something of recent origin after Europeans had introduced money in our domains.

If the verdict was against the complainant or plaintiff, he would be ordered to pay a court fee referred to as "to close the court" (*tswalelakgoro*) as he was responsible for opening the *kgoro*._Trials were generally completed in one session unless an appeal was called for. The chief's order was final. Anyone who refused to obey the chief's order would be "eaten up"; in other words his stock could be confiscated and his crops destroyed. This could also involve death or banishment. Because of a member of the Batubatse community would sometimes ask for time to comply with the chief's order; however, within few days he would depart at night with his family and stock to a remote area to start his new life away from his own people and tribe.

For minor cases involving women only, if both parties were willing, they could appear before the superior wife of their *kgoro* or before the principal wife of the headman. This would occur only where the rights of a woman were affected or in cases affecting women only, such as cases forthcoming from the female initiation or the free labour of women organised by the chief or headman's wife. If both parties were agreeable they might order the payment of the accepted amount of compensation. In the case of women obstinately refusing to appear for free labour or to apply compensation, the case might be referred to the headman. Where a daughter-in-law had committed an offence she would be warned. But if she persisted in committing the same wrongdoing, the go-between (*mmaditsela*) who was sent to deliver the marriage goods for this daughter-in-law would be called and requested to accompany her to her parents to be admonished.

The principal vehicle for settling disputes outside the *kgoro* was the mediation within or between family groups. According to the informant, and what we know, most disputes were settled amicably in this way. Disputes of civil wrongs were also dealt with or at least attempted on this level. But even minor assaults might still be settled thus even today. The mediation cases, when tried on the family level, wee called little wrongs (*melatwana*) and only become wrongs (*melato*) when they were brought before the official headman's court, in other words, when they became too involved for the family groups to settle. Usually this happened where the dispute reached such proportions that either party would not accept the compensation decided upon as a compromise. With less serious wrongs committed by boys and girls, the solution was to lash the wrongdoer with a stick or cattle-skin sjambok (*setoropo*).

The judicial process of the customary court did not distinguish clearly between civil and criminal matters. Sessions were held weekly and there were no pleadings. The circumstances under which an offence was committed were not always canvassed. Previous wrongs committed by any member of the wrongdoer's family were taken into account when punishment was being considered against the offender even if those previous wrongs were not committed by him. Thus children often had to suffer for the wrongs of their parents. Accordingly there were many shortcomings in the legal status of customary courts. Although some call for the abolition of these customary courts, it would be preferable to address these shortcomings; reforms should be made instead of simply shutting down the customary courts. This alternative would be supported by many jurists.

WRONGS

In law a wrong can be a legal injury, i.e. any damage from the violation of a legal right. It can also be contrary to the principle of justice and law: contrary to conscience and morality and the unjust treating of others. A wrong involves the violation or invasion of a legal right of another. The Batubatse recognized the concept of wrongness before they recognised the distinction between civil and criminal wrongs. The term "wrong" will here be used for delicts as well as for crimes.

In accordance with the Batubatse's unwritten law the father or guardian was liable for the wrong actions of all his dependent, which included his wife or wives, all his unmarried children and foster-children as well as widows of the deceased allocated to him. Any incorrect, untrue, unsuitable, undesirable, unjust, dishonest and immoral actions were regarded as wrongs. He was responsible for paying debts, fines or compensation ordered against his dependents, but if corporal punishment was ordered it was inflicted on the actual offender. If the loss caused by a wrong was little enough, there was no compensation, otherwise damage or punishment would apply. If a man stole an object of small value, he would rarely be taken to court. All unmarried children were considered minors irrespective of their age. Whatever property they possessed was held under the guardianship of the father as head of the family or used by him to pay damages or compensation incurred by him or his dependents. In general the best way was to settle smaller complaints against minors outside the court. In fact the father would thrash his children or berate his wife or wives rather than go to court.

Legal wrongs were usually quite clearly defined in the unwritten law. These could be civil wrongs and crimes, such as assault, rape, murder, defamation, abduction, seduction or adultery. Dependents were not allowed to apply for legal action in the tribal court unless they were represented their fathers or guardians. Women, with the assistance of their husband, were entitled to sue in cases such as assault, rape or defamation, but any compensation awarded would be controlled by the husband. In cases like abduction, seduction or adultery it was the father or husband who would sue. If a woman was assaulted by her husband or guardian, she could turn to her father or close relative if the father was no longer alive. The principle of collective liability was not recognised under Batubatse law. A man had simply to pay the amount he was ordered to pay by the tribal court. If he had to ask for assistance from his relatives to advance payment it would be on the understanding that such amount would be paid back.

An owner or keeper of livestock was liable for any damage caused by them. Under the *maf i ša* custom of placing livestock under the care of another, the keeper was liable for the damage, but the owner could help to pay the damage. The question of intent in the legal action was considered, reasonable attitude being adopted. In cases of defamation the malicious intent of the accused had to be shown. Because of the principle of reasonableness actions of younger children hardly led to litigation unless excessive damage was caused. Negligence might lead to legal action if proper care was not taken. Moral wrong was an underlying concept for legal wrong, and some moral wrongs were punishable by law.

Other moral wrongs had nothing to do with law. Pure accidents were mostly excused. Motive in some offences such as abduction, seduction and adultery was never taken into consideration. Provocation was taken as an extenuating circumstance. Batubatse law only considered wrongs which had actually been perpetrated. Attempted murder was treated as assault.

In criminal matters the conduct of an accused was taken into account. Insolent persons who tried to mislead the tribal court were deal with more harshly and first offenders were treated lightly than habitual offenders. Members of the royal family, whether first offenders or not, were treated more harshly than others because they were expected to uphold the custom and law of the tribe. In the cases of defamation, the situation was more serious if a commoner had insulted a member of royal family. The court also considered the ability of the offender to pay. If the offender had sufficient means, that would influence the court to increase the amount of fine or compensation.

The principles of self-defence (*go ke tshireletša*), self-help (*go ke thuša*) and emergency (*go ke hlaganela*) were recognised by the courts of Batubatse tribes. Any member of the tribe was entitled to defend himself or his properties by the use of the force. If a man was threatened with murder he could kill his attacker. He might take the same action if a woman or a child was being attacked in his presence. When people were fighting or quarrelling, anyone had the right to stop them. If they didn't stop fighting this would be reported to the chief. If the chief assaulted or insulted an elderly tribesman and failed to apologise despite pleas from the tribe to do so, he could be deposed as chief, because old men who knew the laws and customs of the tribe should be respected by all, including the chief. The phrase "to take out of danger" was used in connection with emergency acts. For example, if a man saw a house on fire he could break down the burning section and extinguish the fire by any means possible. The principle of justification was also followed by the Batubatse. For instance, a man was entitled to punish with a severe thrashing anyone caught in the act of raping, adultery or stealing which affected his rights. However, the principle of revenge was not acknowledged.

Homicide, adultery, rape, theft, assault, witchcraft, etc. were viewed in traditional law as crimes or delicts against persons. In civil law a delict is an intentional or negligent act which gives rise to a legal obligation between parties even though there has been no contract between them. The law of delict deals with civil wrongs as opposed to criminal wrongs. One and the same act may be a crime and delict, and may also be a delict and a breach of contract. Cases of trespass usually arose from encroachment on the lands allotted to individual families for cultivation. But strangers who accidentally enter a person's fields were generally excused. However, because of suspicion of witchcraft, unless such persons had a reasonable explanation for their presence in the fields their trespasses might lead to a formal complaint before the tribal court. Incidents where a person ploughed over the border of his land into that of another were usually settled privately between the parties concerned.

Injury to property, defamation and seduction were regarded as similar and were classified as damages (*tsenyo*). Wilful injury to property was considered a serious offence calling for compensation to be claimed and awarded beyond the actual damage done. Damage done by animals was always excused because people were expected to keep their homesteads and property protected, such as keeping food out of reach of stray dogs. But goats could possibly cause damage to thatching by jumping on to the roofs of houses from the surrounding walls. When an animal was caught causing damage and was impounded, the owner would be invited to send an intermediary to plead (*khumela*) for the return of his animal. Compensation for impounded livestock was granted in accordance with the extent of the damage caused. If an animal killed another, such as a dog killing a goat, the owner of the goat would normally take its carcass to the owner of the dog, and the latter would have to replace the goat and keep the carcass. If the dog was incited by its owner, the owner might be forced to replace the carcass with more than one goat. If a man set fire to someone's crops he would be forced to give his own crops as compensation. A man who set fire to the house of another would be forced to rebuild it or pay more than the value of the house, plus the usual court fine.

For defamation, if the accusation was true, there were no grounds for complaint, unless it could be shown that the accusation harmed the plaintiff. The plaintiff had to show an element of persecution and intent to harm on the part of the wrongdoer. But unfounded accusations of witchcraft and the insulting of people of high status could lead to litigation. Cases of defamation between women were dealt with by chief's wife or the wife of the head of the unit (*kgoro*). Seduction, abduction and adultery were seen as wrongs against the father, husband and guardian. In the case of adultery the rights of the husband and guardian were infringed, while in abduction and seduction it was the rights of the father that were affected. The injury suffered by the father was similar to that caused by trespassing in that his consent was not obtained.

The wrong caused by seduction (*foraforetša mosetsana*) was not considered serious because if the seducer was acceptable to the father he could marry the seduced girl by payment of marriage goods. If the girl was pregnant the seducer might be asked to pay extra beasts on top of the required marriage goods. But if marriage did not take place the father could claim compensation. Seduction could not be sued more than once for the same daughter. Abduction (*go tshaba le mosetsana*) was considered to be a serious wrong because the father's consent was a requirement unless the consent to marriage was unreasonably refused. A beast in compensation for abduction was the order of the day. If a married woman was the subject of abduction more than one beast in compensation was a must.

The Batubatse viewed adultery (*bohlotlolo*) as a legal wrong. Although it was expected that extramarital relations might occur, these still had to be conducted with the necessary decorum. A woman could not disgrace her husband openly by having affairs with other men. In the same breath the husband was expected to warn his wife of his intention to visit her at night, more so if he had many wives. The mere fact that a husband found another man with his wife at night in the house was a clear proof of adultery. The husband would then take something from the man as exhibit and sue him in court for more than one beast in compensation. Adultery with a widow was not considered a wrong. In the case of rape (*kata/panya*), where there was sufficient evidence that a woman or girl has really been ravished against her will, usually with some injuries as proof, it was taken as a serious offence. The woman should inform her guardian or husband immediately after the deed, otherwise it would be assumed that she was a willing partner. She could sue for compensation with the assistance of her father or husband. Compensation of more than one beast was always ordered for rape.

Theft (*bohodu*) was regarded as a serious offence and was heavily punished. A thief, if found guilty, was usually ordered to pay more than double the value of the stolen object in compensation. If the thief was previously convicted of a similar offence he might be ordered pay even more in compensation. Ordinary fights or assaults that had caused minor injuries rarely led to litigation. If the matter happened to go to court consideration was given as to whether the wrongdoer was seriously injured or provoked, although this was not taken as an excuse but merely to decide the extent of the punishment. The court generally ordered young men who were wrongdoers to be lashed rather than to pay pay any compensation. Where the extent of injury was serious, compensation varied from five goats to a beast or more, depending on the degree of injury.

Formerly, when the Batubatse had jurisdiction in all wrongs, the concept of "a corpse for a corpse" (*setopo ka setopo*) for murder (*go bolaya*) seemed to be the applicable rule. Murderers were put to death by clubbing or some other means. For instance, at Maakene murderers and conquered enemies or prisoners of war (*mathopya*) were thrown from a wide flat stone (*lwala*) at the top of the mountain, from which they would fall headlong to their death. People found guilty of practising witchcraft (*boloi*) were generally fined and thereafter banished from the tribal area. In any accusation of witchcraft a number of diviners were consulted to agree unanimously before any action could be taken against the suspect (*mmelaelwa*). Incest (*bohlola*) was regarded as something unnatural and abhorred by the Batubatse tribes. Such complaints were rarely made formally because an accusation was usually made by a woman against her father or guardian.

In all cases that ended at the tribal court the wrongdoer would be fined an extra beast to be slaughtered for men at the court who were present during the deliberation of the case as *mangangahlaga*, the wrongdoer being entitled to one hindquarter (*serope*). In this connection it was said the brave man was being thanked (*mogale o a lebogišwa*). This gift was similar to that given by the chief to the man from the hunting party who had killed the leopard, the skin of which was brought to him, and a beast was slaughtered. By rewarding the man accused of say, assault, the court, though punishing him, indirectly praised him for being brave, recognising his potential fighting ability as a warrior like the man who killed the leopard during huntingThe Batubatse did not differentiate between civil wrongs and crimes. On the one hand the law of delict, as we know it, is a branch of private law falling under the law of defamation. It affords a civil remedy, usually by way of compensation, for wrongful conduct that has caused harm to others. On the other hand offences such as rape, theft, abduction, incest, injury to property and a few others are understood to be criminal offences, but when it comes to compensation they were treated like civil matters where fines were imposed against the wrongdoers. Compensation that could either ameliorate the damages done or forestall a more severe punishment was applicable to both civil and criminal wrongs.

Minor offences such as temporary injuries or negligence that resulted in damage or loss of property were treated the same as other wrongs. Grave offences against individuals that called for certain sanctions, minor or major, such as unintentional homicide in causing harm to a pregnant woman and/or her fetus, and other forms of personal injury related to sexual rights, were handled in much the same way. Included here were perjury, false witness and slander. Thankfully the Batubatse law has now been developed to suit present circumstances.

PROPERTY

In pre-colonial times the indigenous people of South had abundant land, with farming and herding being the predominant economic activities. African indigenous law on property was more concerned with people's obligations towards one another in respect of property, than with the rights of people who might own property. The concept of "ownership" was problematic, since all things were held in common, with everybody having equal rights. Land was common to all people.

The Batubatse distinguished categories of property, namely house, family and personal property. Although they were categorised in this fashion the chief and/or the kraal head was the main controller of these properties. The general understanding was that a woman, irrespective of her age, was a perpetual minor and had no proprietary capacity. Hence it was assumed, on the basis of male authority being an African tradition, that all property except for personal property vested in the husband.

It has been mentioned elsewhere that tribes acquired land by occupation or by conquest. By virtue of his position the chief, as advised by his councillors, administered this land and allotted areas to the heads of groups, who would again allot portions to all the heads of households in their individual units. In those days control over land was, subject to the power of the chief, entirely in the hands of the heads of households. The legal concept "communal" can mean that a right is held by a group jointly or it can mean that it is held by a group in common. It could also mean for or by a group rather than an individual. It is when something is shared in common by everyone in a group that one can talk about communal relationship.

Communal land generally referred to the property held communally by the tribe. It was a territory in possession of a community rather than individual or company. The chief officially owned the land but allowed members of the tribe to work on it. The control or access to land should be viewed in the context of a social relationship. Since the senior traditional leaders derived their legitimacy from the founding fathers and were seen as a direct channel of communication with the ancestors, they had power to allot the land, to regulate the use of common resources, and to expropriate and confiscate land in certain circumstances. The senior traditional leader not only allotted land to families but also allocated certain land for grazing and agriculture. In doing so he had a duty to "act like a father" in ensuring that the land was distributed fairly among the households. Traditionally the allocation of land was free. The right to residential sites and arable fields usually implied that a member of the community would have two plots, one for housing and kraals for livestock and the other for the cultivation of crops for domestic consumption. As far as the commonage was concerned, no individual could claim exclusive use of the land. The head of the unit controlled the kraals, including deserted kraals where ancestors of the unit lay buried.

Each married woman was entitled to a separate homestead. The elder sons were assigned sites for the homesteads of their wives by the head of the unit. Farming-land of a family usually consisted of a plot for every woman. The father would assign one or more plots to each of his wives as well as the wives of his sons for their exclusive use. The residential land was allotted as household property to each wife. Family groups enjoyed all rights to such land with the exception of the right of sale. The land could not be alienated for whatever reason. A family only forfeited rights over the land when it left the tribal area permanently. If the family failed to use the land for a considerable period, it could be allotted to another family if there was shortage of land. A man could loan land to another if he had more than his family could use. The tribe, as a legal community, had the right to exchange a plot of land administered by the senior traditional leader for a similar plot controlled by a family. Once again, if any portion of the tribal land controlled by a family was required for the general tribal benefit the tribal leader might by virtue of his position claim this land in exchange for an equal potion of land elsewhere in the tribal area.

Grazing lands and the right to make use of the natural resources such as water, reeds or clay were held communally under the administrative control of the chief A man could graze his cattle on virgin arable land or lands lying fallow belonging to another family. When all harvesting had been done the cultivated lands were opened for cattle to graze on the stubble without restrictions. Any tribal member could freely use any of the natural resources in the tribal area. The basic principle in Batubatse law was that all movable property owned by a family was controlled by the father. House property consisted of any assets that a husband had specifically allotted to a house. Another significant source of house property was the assets that automatically accrued to the house or any of its inmates. Domestic effects that a woman acquired during marriage formed part and parcel of house property. Household property included the homestead, all domestic utensils used in the homestead and all property obtained by or for any member of the household through appropriation. The household property was also controlled by the husband. The Batubatse considered the woman to be in charge of the property in the homestead, such as harvested crops, pots and baskets, while the husband was principally in charge of the property outside the homestead, mainly the household livestock. As owner of house property, the husband had general powers of administration and control. In his discretion he could use the same property for his personal wants and necessities, or for general family purposes. The husband's right of ownership was subject to the general obligation to use house property for the good of members of the house concerned. He was not permitted to move assets from one house to anther house without good reason. This was done because of the need to preserve the integrity of houses in a polygamous family.

Family property consisted of the husband's assets. Because the husband was not an inmate of any particular house, his property did not fall into a particular house as it was presumed that ownership in all cattle within the kraal vested in him until the contrary was proved. Any property owned by the husband formed part of a general family estate until allocated to a specific house. Upon his death his general heir inherited the family property together with property in houses without heirs, and house heirs inherited the house assets. A woman could use at her discretion any family property within the homestead, but could not sell or otherwise dispose of it without the consent of the husband. A husband could use the livestock assigned to a homestead at his own discretion. When a pot was stolen from a homestead, it was the woman who sued in the tribal court, being assisted by her husband; if livestock were stolen it was the husband who sued. Any assets obtained by a married woman through her efforts which were brought into the household were considered to be household property over which the husband had control.

Personal property served the interests of a particular individual, and as such it could be used and disposed of without reference to anyone else. Thus gifts or allocations made by the husband for personal use were considered individual property; however, the principle applied that all property accruing to any member of the family went into a common pool and was administered by the kraal head. A woman could exchange or make a gift of any object created by her, such as a clay pot, without consulting her husband because such items were considered personal assets. When a son married, he obtained guardianship over his wife, and the control over the property of their household. However, the whole conception of personal property has now been altered.

PERSONS, THE FAMILY AND SUCCESSION

The law of persons regulated the birth, private status and the death of natural persons. It determined the requirements and qualifications for legal personhood and the rights and responsibilities that attached to it. In jurisprudence a natural person is a real human being. Human rights are implicitly granted to natural persons, not juristic persons. To have a legal personality means to be capable of having rights and obligations within a certain legal system. Slavery (*bokgoba*) was a legal and economic system under which people were treated as property. Slaves (*makgoba*) had no rights or duties or capacities, and were treated merely as objects until slavery was abolished in 1834. Although the Batubatse knew of slavery they did not have slaves. However, prisoners of war they had taken were to a lesser extent treated as slaves for a short duration and thereafter they became part of the Batubatse tribes if they were not killed. Slavery has now been outlawed in all countries. A juristic person is a social entity, a community or an association of people which has an independent right of existence under the law. The so-called juristic person was unknown to Batubatse community members. The position of a person within the tribe depended upon his rank and status and how he was related to the royal house.

Before Batubatse youth were fully initiated and until their marriage they could not marry and they remained under the tutelage of their father or guardian. For a period before initiation young men acquired temporary independence but were rigorously controlled by their leader (*nkgwete*). Their fathers could not be sued for damages that they caused. They too could not be sued as they had no assets. Any adult man was permitted to thrash them if he found them doing something wrong. For more serious behaviour they would be brought to the tribal court to be lashed on the order of the senior traditional leader. Generally, girls did not act offensively during this period. After initiation the young men again fell under their fathers. They remained under this tutelage until they attained adulthood through marriage. A married man had the power to control his wife, children and possessions but his senior male relatives retained power over him.

Women never attained independence and through various phases of life they remained under the perpetual tutelage of their father, then their husband or guardian. Girls could not refuse partners chosen for them by their parents. Married women had certain powers over their homestead and the property assigned to them by their husband, but could not dispose of any property without the consent of her husband or guardian. A widow was allowed to attain some temporary powers of her late husband if his heir was still not married or when a suitable male relative was not available, but her powers were subject to the advice of the relative of her husband and other male advisors. A widow could also not inherit any property from her late husband's estate. Her son could not dispose of his inheritance without the consent of his mother. If a guardian was assigned to a widow she would be under his tutelage as long as this guardian was still alive. The son could become the guardian of his widowed mother only in her old age. Mentally retarded men remained permanent minors under the tutelage of their closest male relatives.

According to Batubatse law the whole community in the village took responsibility for the control of children and could lash them with a light switch upon finding them doing something wrong. When a girl who has been betrothed wished to terminate the betrothal, her family had to return all those gifts that they had already received. But if a prospective groom wished to terminate the betrothal, he and his family forfeited all gifts delivered. If a betrothed girl died before the conclusion of the marriage it was customary that a sister be given to replace her. If a suitable sister was not available, another female relative of the deceased might be offered, or the gifts had to be returned to the relative of the prospective groom. If the groom died before the conclusion of the marriage, the marriage would proceed as a ghost union.

When a bride was finally transferred, one of her relatives would convey a message to the groom that he should not ill-treat her under any circumstances and that her relatives retained the power to protect her against misconduct by the groom and his relatives. The groom might also be informed that "marriage with a woman is never ended" (*mosadi ga a fele go nyalwa*) since the husband could keep on paying his father-in-law. Marriage was dissolved by the death (*lehu*) of both partners or by divorce (*hlalo*). If the husband was impotent there were ways of ensuring sociological parenthood, and if a wife was sterile an ancillary wife would be married to conclude the duties of her relatives.

The Batubatse did not encourage divorce within their community. If divorce was imminent the relatives would do their utmost to remove the cause of the complaint and reconcile the partners through consultation between the two family groups of relatives. If divorce took place the guardianship over a woman was transferred from her husband and his group to her father and his group. Divorce was effected by the abandonment by the wife and her group of all rights in the marriage or by forfeiture by the husband and his group of all their rights. It was implied that if a man or woman no longer wanted to continue a marriage, he or she could not want anything from their partner.

The children born from the marriage, all possessions assigned to the household and the marriage goods delivered at the marriage were awarded either to the husband or to the father of the wife. There was never any sharing of the possessions or of the children. If the parties decided to go through with the divorce, this had to be witnessed by the chief in the presence of his customary or tribal court, as the chief had obviously been notified about the marriage. The Batubatse regarded witchcraft on the part of either party to be suitable grounds for divorce. Infidelity was not regarded as such. If a man repeatedly punished his wife excessively she could sue for divorce. If both parties no longer wished to continue the marriage and wanted to dissolve it, with or without good reason, after all attempts were made to save the marriage, divorce would be granted.

The Batubatse rules of succession were designed to perpetuate a bloodline and transmit a deceased's rights and duties to selected member of his close kin. This system could be described as intestate, universal and onerous; intestate because individuals were not free to decide to whom their estate would devolve; universal in that an heir succeeded to the deceased's rights and duties to maintain all surviving dependents; and an onerous responsibility in that it could not be declined or passed on to another. During the private administration of the deceased estate no outside authority was required. Although only the oldest son could be heir, other sons were not necessarily ignored because the family head might have given gifts during his lifetime. In practice, therefore, property was continually devolving from one generation to the next.

Because of the universal nature of succession in customary law, the heir succeeded to both assets and debts in the estate. Even if the debts exceed the assets, the heir was still liable to pay debts incurred by the deceased out of his own pocket. Among the Batubatse there was no hard and fast rule for specifying the time at which outstanding debts should be claimed. Usually claims could be lodged with the heir at the ceremony for laying the deceased's spirit to rest.

The Batubatse system of succession was patrilineal. If the deceased had only one wife the rules of succession were the same as the systems of customary law of other tribes in South Africa. The principle of primogeniture in the male line was always followed. The rules in terms of this principle were straightforward and formed part and parcel of their system of family law. Under the principle of primogeniture the eldest son succeeded in preference to younger sons. If the deceased had no descendant the whole range of male ascendants would be considered in order of seniority. Each family home was a separate establishment. This was done because only males were considered to have the legal power necessary to run the family's affairs, and the bloodline was traced through males. Movable assets acquired by the husband accrued to, or were allotted by him to, the different houses. The eldest son of each house would succeed to the assets of that house, whereupon he would be responsible for the widow and children. Thus the eldest son of each household would obtain control over the livestock assigned to the house, while the eldest son of the principal household obtained additional control over livestock which was not assigned to a particular household as well as other personal property of the father. The system of succession covered land as well.

Because propagation of the bloodline was one of the key purposes of succession, the preferred heirs were sons procreated by the deceased with his lawful married wife. However, other male descendants such as a son born of a levirate union, or a son born out of wedlock as the result of an adulterous liaison or relationship with an unmarried woman, were considered. For instance, if the deceased died with no male descendants, the first wife's second son was the heir. Failing any sons or their male descendants in the first house, the next in order of succession was the eldest son of the second married wife and his male descendants, and so on.

The ranking of the houses depended on the time of marriage. The first married wife was the senior wife; the second was subordinate to her, and so on. If any junior house had no heir, it was inherited by the great house. Conversely, if the great house had no heir, it was inherited by eldest son of the next senior house, and so on. Where the man had only two wives, and therefore two houses, the eldest son of each house became heir to that house. Where none of the houses in one section of the homestead had an heir, the most senior heir of the other section inherited all of them. At the end of the period of mourning for the death of a father the personal possessions of the deceased, such as weapons, would on a particular day be brought out. The universal or general heir would choose those that he wanted, after which the other sons in order of succession could select from the remainder. On this day close relatives of the deceased would inform the general heir that he was now the father, and if there were any unmarried sons it would be his duty to assist them to obtain wives.

If the father was wealthy and possessed a large herd of stock they might advise him to give each of the other sons a goat or even a beast, but he was not obliged to do so. However, if he unreasonably refused to hand some stock to them, they could report him to the tribal court. On the same day widows were expected to indicate the men from deceased's relatives with whom they wished to have relations in future, otherwise the family elders would choose for them. If there were no male descendants in a polygamous household, succession would pass to the deceased's father. The order of succession of Batubatse was much the same as with the Pedi, Tswana, Bakone and other black tribes.

The case of *Mthembu v Letsela and Another 1997(2) SA 936(T)* will go down in the history of South Africa as one of the first and greatest judicial pronouncements to vindicate customary law as the appropriate legal system to be applied to millions of black South Africans. It has corrected the error of those who thought that customary law should be abolished. In this case a deceased died without a son or brother and his nearest male relative was his father, who also lived in the house his deceased son had built. The judge maintained that customary law had been accepted by the framers of the constitution themselves on a separate legal and cultural system which could be freely chosen by a person desiring to do so. The judge saw merit in the rule of customary law relating to succession because a corollary to the system of primogeniture was the duty to provide sustenance, maintenance and shelter. If we disagreed with this decision, it would mean that all daughters who inherit, say livestock, upon marriage would be entitled to take all the livestock to her married home, leaving her widowed mother, brothers and sisters with no cow to milk, no oxen to plough the lands, and no goat or sheep to sell or slaughter for consumption.

Traditionally a Mutubatse woman was regarded as a minor under the tutelage and guardianship of her father, husband or brother, incapable of owning or acquiring property. This was due to the recognition of the principle of primogeniture which determines the order of succession: the eldest son succeeding in preference to younger sons. Only males were considered to have the legal power necessary to run the family's affairs and the bloodline was traced through males. However some members of the community believed that last-born sons should inherit the family homestead. This shift to ultimo-geniture was explained by the fact that the eldest son was normally the first to marry, leave home and start a new family.

When the eldest daughter married, her marriage goods would pass on to her eldest brother to pay lobola for his first or additional wife (*mammuwe wa kgomo tša gagwe*). This meant that if the boy was a first-born child in the family, the first-born girl should provide him with marriage goods from lobola delivered to her. If a girl was the first-born child in the family, the eldest boy would retain the marriage goods delivered for his eldest sister as his. He was responsible for the return of the marriage goods in the event of the divorce of his elder sister. Upon their marriage, part of the lobola would be allocated to the youngest boy, while the rest would be retained by the eldest boy as family assets.

An heir was required to perpetuate the deceased's name, sacrifice to his ancestors and look after his widow and children. If there were no heir a levirate* union (*gotsenela*) would be entered into which allowed the widow to pick a consort from male relatives or kinsmen of her husband. If the widow refused to enter into a levirate union but remained with the deceased's family, she was deemed to have repudiated the marriage. The customary law of succession was aimed at preserving the male bloodline. A widow could claim maintenance from the estate since the death of her husband did not end her marriage. Where a woman died with no child, or was proved to be barren, the institution of sororate polygyny (*seantlo*) would apply. The widower would enter into a union with one of his deceased wife's sister in order to raise a child as his legitimate heir. The consent of the woman was not required because young women were brought up knowing that one day they might take the position of their older sisters. The wife's family had to provide a surrogate partner, failing which they had to return part of the lobola. Succession to woman was of significance and there was no need to formulate rules to govern the devolution their estate.

*The custom among some Jews and other nations where, under certain circumstances, the brother or next of kin to a deceased man was bound to marry the widow.

Succession to the position of senior traditional leaders and headmen, among the Batubatse tribes, was hereditary along the male line and was further determined by the traditional law of succession. This provided for a senior traditional leader to be succeeded by his eldest son born by the principal wife or the so-called "candle wife" (*Masetshaba or lebone*). The marriage of a candle wife was rarely the first wife of a chief and was largely ceremonial, unlike the marriage of other wives of the chief. The choice of principal wife was usually made in infancy before a chief or heir contracted any other marriage. Other wives would normally come to stay first in the royal kraal before marriage. When the appropriate time for concluding the "candle wife" marriage had come, the whole tribe would be instructed to collect the necessary marriage goods (*magadi*), to which all members of the tribe were expected to donate something.

All the *magadi* collected in a unit (*kgoro*) would be delivered at the same time. In this way no group in the tribe would be unrepresented in the *magadi* for the candle wife. The rest of the marriage ceremonies was similar to any ordinary marriage except that a councillor would be   chosen to deliver the *magadi*. This was done in a grander scale, coupled with recitation of praise-poems of the previous chiefs in a festive spirit. The transfer of the bride to the groom, accompanied by a woman from her family, would occur as soon as the wedding feast (*monyanya*) was concluded. On the day the candle wife was expected to arrive a big feast would be held in the royal *kgoro* of the groom, usually attended by all tribesmen. Before the bride entered, all *kgoro*-fires in the village would be extinguished. A ceremonial fire would be kindled in her *lapa* after she had entered, and all women would then in their turn fetch an ember from the fire to their units to light the fires in their individual homesteads.

The candle wife was the tribal wife married by the tribe. The first son of this tribal wife, who would be the heir and future chief, was thus a son of the tribe and not only of the royal dynasty. It was the relationship established between the tribe and the tribal wife which made this marriage unique. If an heir to the senior traditional leader position should die before having been initiated he would be succeeded by a younger full brother, or if there was no younger brother and the tribal wife had past the child-bearing age an ancillary wife would be married for her by the chief. The Batubatse candle wives were usually married from the Mmola sub-clan of the tribe. Later other families such as Makgopa, Mampuru, Mashumu and Popela also supplied candle wives. If a senior traditional leader died leaving no male offspring, his wife would be engaged in a levirate union (*gotsenela*) to raise an heir. In such event the inheritance to property and succession to office would be in abeyance for many years – at least until the lineage successor reached adulthood and was formally accepted by the royal council as successor and installed.

Although some of the Batubatse tribes recognised their customary law, it was no longer possible for them to follow its rules. In fact there had been so many changes to the customary law of succession that one could easily argue that the contemporary customary law of succession that we know, was no longer customary law but something totally different. For instance the Constitutional Court had declared the customary rule of primogeniture, which allows only an eldest male descendant or relative to succeed to the estate of a black person, to be unconstitutional and invalid. The declaration and invalidity was on the basis that the rule unfairly discriminates against women and others with regard to the administration and distribution of deceased estates. Women in polygamous marriages and their children have now equal succession rights. Extra-marital children are now brought into the fold of successors. The concept of universal heir (*mojalefa*) is no longer recognised.

In spite of customary law being the law of the original inhabitants of this country, there has never been parity between the transplanted laws and the indigenous law. Initially it was ignored by colonials, then tolerated and eventually recognised and was brought on a par with the common law of South Africa by the enactment of the Constitution of the Republic of South Africa of 1996. The customary law of succession was one area of customary law which has received considerable attention from the legal arena because of its distinctive patriarchal characteristics.

"To exist is to change; to change is to mature; to mature is to create one self endlessly."

– Henry Bergson

10
CULTURAL HERITAGE

Olden way of making fire (tsekga or tshekga)

Olifants River and the beautiful mountains

The Dioke Hills - the centre one being where Lethamago was killed

Moholoholo forest on the slopes of the Drakensberg

If you don't know where you come from, you will not know where you are going. South Africa is a country rich in cultural diversity and this diversity makes it an interesting destination. Heritage comprises the practices and traditions passed down from parents to children, as well as the extended family, the community and the location where one was raised. Culture refers to the way of life of a specific group of people or an entire society. We should be proud of our culture, which includes codes of behaviour, beliefs, values, customs, dress style, personal decorations like make-up and jewellery, relationships with others, language, religion, rituals, law and morality. Culture also encompasses special monuments, sculptures, a cave dwelling or important objects of historic, artistic or scientific value.

Robben Island, the Cradle of Humankind and the ancient city of Mapungubwe in Limpopo are examples of South African cultural heritages. These are worthy of preservation for the benefit of future generations. This is part of the healing that democracy has brought after culture was used to divide South Africans in the past. Culture is not static but changes as each generation contributes its experience and discards thing that are no longer significant.

African people, including the Batubatse, have a rich history and cultural heritage which are at risk of being lost in the tide of contemporary global influences. By reigniting awareness of our proud African heritage and reawakening our awareness of Africa's spiritual origins, we can revive the dignity and true equality of Africans and indeed of all humankind. We learn customs, traditions and memories passed on from one generation to the next.

Karaism is the ancient theology of Africa, dating back to the beginning of recorded history. It was the foundation of ancient African religion and philosophy and influences African tradition and cultural history to this day. Karaism is a word derived from Kara, meaning light or sun. By promoting the cultural heritage and values of Karaism, the Kara Heritage Institute in Pretoria is committed to growing sustainable and empowered communities. Karaism, which is based on the ancient spiritual beliefs that originated in Africa, maintains that Christianity and the festive period surrounding it have its roots deeply entrenched in ancient African philosophy. It holds that the First Fruit Festival was celebrated on 25 December and commemorated our African ancestors and sacred kings of pre-Christian times. In AD 274 Emperor Aurelian of the Roman Imperial Church appropriated this date, which was subsequently used to celebrate the unknown birth-date of Jesus Christ of Nazareth. In our system of counting the years from the birth of Jesus we start on the first day of the first month (January) of the first century (Common Era) and not the twenty-fifth day of the twelfth month of the first century (CE), which should be the case if Jesus had indeed been born on 25 December.

Today this is a time when people in Africa and across the world enjoy the festivities without understanding the meaning and origin of the event they are celebrating. It should be an expression of appreciation for the abundance given to us in this life. If Christmas is not the birth date of Jesus Christ, then Christians celebrate the fact that he was born and not the exact day that he was born.

South Africa has many different cultures and traditions. Many projects have been launched to meet the increasing demand of tourists who are eager to learn more about the cultures and traditions of people from whom they were separated by apartheid. These projects are in the form of cultural villages where the traditional lifestyle of the people is shown to the visitors. Aspects such as traditional dances and rituals, in the rural areas, are some of our defining features.

BATUBATSE CULTURAL VILLAGES

We should not forget or try to obliterate the cultures and traditions of Batubatse or any other black tribe. We should honour those who struggled for justice and set up a dialogue between the past and the present. We should keep the memory of our ancestors alive and preserve the sacred sites where they once lived. The redemption and salvation of South Africa and her people lie in the recovery of the country's heritage and the indigenous knowledge system which were outlawed and suppressed, and replaced by foreign ideologies and religions.

A place where our forebears settled and cultivated the land over a long period of time, like Maakene/Tsubye, should be recognised as a cultural heritage site. Here Batubatse cultural villages or centres should preserve the cultures and traditions of the Batubatse. Batubatse huts and houses from the seventeenth or eighteenth century to the present day should be displayed. People in traditional dress should play different roles to accurately depict the lifestyle of Batubatse tribes. Visitors would have the opportunity to taste traditional sorghum beer and to consult a Motubatse traditional healer in his professional capacity.

At Tsubye and other places that can be identified, the cultural villages should provide demonstrations of traditional beadwork, weaving and the famous Batubatse arts and crafts. They should display indigenous food, dance, music, instruments and other cultural objects. During Heritage Month diverse communities in South Africa should be encouraged to embrace cultural diversity, human rights, nation-building and economic development. Visitors to cultural villages could be house guests of a traditional African family.

Marakapula Hill at Tsubye Mountains where some Batubatse chiefs were buried has become a sacred place and a Batubatse place of worship (*badimong* or *dithokoleng*) which should now be respected. The original three sacred drums (*meropa*) or replicas should be displayed here as a tourist attraction. *Boretho* was the largest drum, with a radius of between three and five metres and a height of about one and half metres, and itcould be drummed by not less than five people; *Thannga* was the medium-sized drum and *Phokwi* the smallest one. This place could be declared the Maakene or Tsubye or Marakapula Heritage Site for the Batubatse. Nestling between the small towns of Gravelotte, Mica and Phalaborwa, the picturesque area with its deep valleys, waterfalls and endangered plant species is one of the most breathtaking sights in the Limpopo Province. Its exhibits could include the famous three foot prints that were found imprinted on three separate stones.

At Stoffberg in the Greater Tubatse Municipality the sacred fountain in the bush called *Sediba-Sebore* is regarded as the place of the Batubatse Gods and "The Mother of the Batubatse tribes". It is said that the fountain never dries up. The Batubatse lived there until the Pedi of Sekhukhune came from Bokgatla and occupied the area. Nowadays a large group of the Batubatse of Mmola visits the fountain at least once a year and celebrates their Heritage Day there. Another sacred mountain of importance to the Batubatse was Bolebye Mountain (Kasteelkop) near Gravelotte. This was where a section of Batubatse, led by Masetla Makutuma Maenetja Shai, settled after they separated from the main tribe. A hill forming part of Bolebye Mountain was considered a sacred site by them. Near the hill was a burial place for their ancestors. One of their chiefs used to keep his medicines in a cave on the Bolebye Mountain and would go to the cave regularly to collect herbs. One day he didn't come back and was later found dead in the cave. The royal family closed the mouth of the cave with stones while his body was inside. The exact location of the cave can be observed even today. This list of heritage sites is not exhaustive.

"If you do not have the time to read, you do not have the time to lead."

- Phillip Schlechty

RECOMMENDATIONS

1. Marakapula Hill at Tsubye and other identified sacred sites should be declared heritage sites which have special qualities making them significant within the context of a province, in terms of the heritage assessment criteria within the law of the country.

2. Negotiation to purchase of sites or farms covering the sites, if the places are still being owed by previous individual owners, should take place to provide enough area to accommodate cultural villages.

3. The heritage sites should be resourced through the securing of sponsorship from government departments and the private sector, especially the municipalities and mining industries.

4. Fences or walls should be erected within the identified sites for security reasons and access control. The walls must be shaped like an elephant to symbolise the significance of it to Batubatse.

5. Museums or heritage centres should be erected within the sites housing relevant artifacts. This would include traditional hoes, clay pots, garments and much else.
    Arts and crafts articles must be exhibited and fairly traded at the heritage centres and cultural villages.

6. Submission should be made to the provincial government for tarred roads from major roads to the sites.

7. Erection of big signboards at entrances of the sites and along the major roads to the sites must be done to guide tourists.

8. Creation of websites for the heritage sites to reach international tourists and to promote the sites should form part of the process.

9. Shuttle services between the heritage sites and the nearest town destination should be introduced as a matter of important priority.

10. Arts and craft articles must be exhibited and fairly traded at the heritage centers and cultural villages.

11
BATUBATSE HOUSES/UNITS

Let us take ourselves through each of the identified units with regard to their experiences, life, situations and the conditions which affected them throughout the past generations. Some of the units emanating from the Shayi Royal House are not indicated on the skeleton genealogy of the tribe due to loss or lack of sufficient connecting information to the earlier generations and stem (thito or kutu) of the tribe. These units are, hereunder, haphazardly recorded and discussed, but not according to their ranks. For instance, Mampa and Ntsoane were the two influential sons of Kgoshi Umtubatzi Masie/Masiye. However, the remnants of the house of the younger brother of Kgoshi Mampa, Kgoshi Ntsoane, who remained and had occupied the area covering the present Tjate Heritage Site in the Sekhukhune District are only mentioned in this book, but not discussed in details.

SENIOR HOUSE/UNIT (KGOROKGOLO) SHAYI/SHAI
MAMPA UNIT

The house of Batubatse Ba-Mampa's section, from Makhutswe returned to Ga-Mampa to join the remaining section of the house there with a mission to ensure perpetuation of the tribe as a distinctive community. It is alleged that some of them now refer to themselves as Ba-Moila and had changed their totem of elephant. The reason for doing that is unknown. During tribal conflicts in the Sekhukhune Royal Council, two of Kgoshi Sekhukhune's senior councilors who were half-brothers, Mafefe and Ntwampe, fled to Mmanyaba to save their lives. Mmanyaba helped them to cross the Olifants River and to hide at Mataung, not far from Chief Mampa's territory. They fought among themselves and Mafefe triumphed. Oral-historical accounts reveal that Kgoshi Mafefe and his people found the Mampa community already living there and subdued them. Their independence ought to have been recognised by the present government.

The Ga-Mampa valley is a rural area now in the Mafefe territory, which was previously under the Lepelle-Nkumbi Local Municipality. It covers a large area and gets water from Mohlapitsi River, a tributary of the Olifants River. The valley is surrounded by nature reserves which the local population exploits for fire wood, grazing land, as a hunting area and for wild plant collection for their livelihood. The two main villages in the valley, Ga-Mampa and Mantlhane, each had a chief, now regarded as headman (traditional head of the people), who is responsible for the allocation of communal land among the community and authorizing the harvesting of natural resources within the wetland. Nearby to the area where the Mampa people settled is a village known as Seokodibeng.

In 1940 families from Ga-Phasha, a nearby village, moved there to be closer to the Motse River and to acquire more land for agriculture and grazing. Seokodibeng could be thus considered an extension of Ga-Phasha under Chief Phasha's authority. In time tribal conflicts arose in the Mafefe region resulting in Chief Ntwampe and his tribe being compelled to leave the Mafefe area and return to Sekhukhune with the assistance of Mmanyaba. As a relative of Chief Phasha, Chief Ntwampe obtained land in Moroke, a nearby village, and settled there with his tribe.

A related section of Chief Mampa's tribe also arrived from Mafefe and settled in the area. Later, people from both Ntwampe and Mampa's tribes moved to Sekodibeng. In 1984, a fight broke out between two clans of Chief Phasha, one following him and one rebelling against him. Chief Mampa supported the rebels. The outcome of this conflict was not clearly resolved and Chief Ntwampe's people took no part. Seokodibeng now falls under the Fetakgomo Local Municipality.

The followers of Ga-Mampa at Mafefe have now formed a forum with the aim to develop the area.

MAPITI/MOHLABE UNIT

Batubatse Ba-Mohlabe is a breakaway section of the original Batubatse Tribe. Previously they stayed with other sections of Batubatse at various places. Part of this group initially settled at Mphanama and thereafter at Ntsoaneng. When they couldn't tolerate the irksome rule of the Pedi, they joined a larger group led by Mashishimale Tefo en route to Makhutšwe. Thereafter they were on their own under an independent senior traditional leader (induna). The house of Batubatse Ba-Mohlabe's section settled at the foothills of Mogokoloni Mountain. There they erected a permanent settlement at Sedibeng Sa Lebese, which is now known as Sofaya which is close to Trichardsdal where Kgoshi Sekororo has now established himself.

The intention of the Mohlabe house when they settled there was to establish themselves as an independent tribe with their own chief. This section, originally known as Ba-Mohlaba, was led by a powerful senior councillor from Shayi Royal House. One source asserts this councillor was Mapiti who, with a small group of his supporters, later decided to join his brother, Dipholo, at Modubeng. Another source claims that Mapiti disappeared mysteriously leaving the community under the leadership of his two sons. Until today nothing has been heard about him and his name is lost to memory. One of his two sons, whose name is unknown, moved to Tsubye and nothing further has been heard of him. The Mohlabe group did not move to Tsubye.

The other son known as Segopane remained with the tribe ploughing the land and was recognized by the community as their leader after the disappearance of his father. Because they toiled the soil (mohlaba) and their chief was a seed-planter (mohlaba peu), they became known as the Ba-Mohlaba tribe, meaning people of the soil and people who plant seeds in the soil. They had control of a large piece of land.

The Malepe community was the first to be offered land by Kgoshi Mohlabe when they arrived in the area. At the time Kgoshi Mohlabe's tribe was independent. The Malepe group was followed by the tribes of Mametja, Letsoalo, Lewele and a few other smaller groups. Since the Mohlabe community was already established there, their leaders paid tribute to Kgoshi Mohlabe in return for being offered a place to settle. A good relationship existed between Kgoshi Mohlabe and these tribes, particularly the Mametja people. To confirm this Kgoshi Mabine Mametja's first wife, Mmalokweng of the Mashumu's family, came from the Mohlabe tribe. Mmathobele, the daughter of Kgoshi Mabine Mametja and Mmalokweng, was married to Serite, the younger paternal uncle of Kgoshi Mohlabe.

After the death of Kgoshi Mabine Mametja his younger brother, Seopa, became regent as the deceased's heir Madie was still a minor. Fearing that their uncle Makwala might make an attempt on Madie's life in order to seize the chieftainship of the Mametja tribe, Seopa took his brother's children to their maternal uncle, Kgoshi Mohlabe. The heir apparent Madie was killed in a shooting incident with the Swazis before he could assume the Mametja chieftainship. His younger brother, Sekoko, after coming of age, became Kgoshi Sekoko Mametja by virtue of his brother's marriage to Mmapholo from the Mashumu family of the Mohlabe tribe.

Kgoshi Segopane, regarded as the first recognised chief of this tribe, later assumed the Royal title name of Kgoshi Mohlabe 1. It was during his reign that the Malepe tribe arrived in the area and their leader paid tribute to him before his people were allowed to settle. It is not known where he married his candle wife with whom he fathered a son called Matome. Kgoshi Segopane ruled his tribe from his head kraal at Sedibeng Sa Lebese. When he died he was buried at Serobeng. During his reign the extensive area surrounding his head kraal was unoccupied for a radius of about thirty to forty kilometres. Due to the fact that another Tsonga tribe was known as Mohlaba, the tribal name was altered to Mohlabe. It is not known when this was done. Despite this change of name, some members of the tribe still use Mohlaba as their surname.

According to oral sources, after the death of Kgoshi Segopane Mohlabe, his son Matome assumed the title of Kgoshi Mohlabe ll. He also ruled his tribe from Sedibeng Sa Lebese. Kgoshi Matome Mohlabe married his candle wife (Masetshaba) from the Popela family. Her name was Marebole. They did not bear an heir to the throne. It was during the reign of Kgoshi Matome Mohlabe that Kgoshi Timamogolo Sekororo Mahlo and his followers arrived in the area and paid tribute to him. They were more numerous than the Mohlabe group but the Mohlabe people continued to follow their independent life. Both chiefs agreed that the Sekororo tribe should settle in the area surrounding Lephatse Mountain near Makhutšwe River. After a while Kgoshi Matome Mohlabe suspected that a relationship had been formed between Timamogolo Mahlo and his wife, Marebole. He departed from the area in fury, never to return. When he left his wife Marebole became the ruler. After many years of searching, his grandson, Mashele Benny Mohlabe of Sofaya village, discovered Kgoshi Matome's grave on the Moletlane Mountain at Ga-Mogotlane, Zebediela in 1958.

Marebole led the tribe as a regent during the absence of Kgoshi Matome Mohlabe. She didn't assume the royal's title name since she was just a caretaker leader. Since Marebole could not bear a child and an heir to the throne, the Royal House realised that the tribe would be leaderless after the death of Kgoshigadi Marebole. By agreement between her and senior councillors a candle wife, Mokgadi, was appointed from the Mashumu family, and she was allowed bear children from one of the male members of the Royal House. She gave birth to two sons, Maabyale, the elder and Sekwai, the younger. Unfortunately Maabyale died at an early age leaving the tribe without an issue to ascend the throne.

During the rule of Kgoshigadi Marebole, Kgoshi Timamogolo began to work with her under the pretence of helping to run the affairs of the Mohlabe community. He exerted more influence on her than her councillors and she trusted him too much. He interfered in all Mohlabe matters and betrayed her by approaching the Native Commissioner at Haenertsburg who had requested all senior traditional leaders to register their chieftaincy with him. Timamogolo did not inform Marebole when he registered himself as the chief of the whole area of Mohlabe's territory.

Another account of the event is that in 1882, during Kgoshi Sekoko Mametja's reign, the first Republican Native Commissioner, nicknamed Segwatagwatane, did not wish to recognise all the chiefs as independent and required some of them to consider themselves the subjects of others. Thus Kgoshi Mohlabe and Malepe were ordered to put themselves under Kgoshi Sekororo. But Kgoshi Sekoko Mametja refused to yield his independence. Even after flogging, he still refused, so they left him alone. As regards Kgoshigadi Marebole and her people, in the long run, they found themselves being under the leadership of Chief Sekororo Mahlo. That is how Batubatse Ba-Mohlabe was robbed of their chieftaincy by Sekororo Mahlo. Realising this treachery, Ba-Mohlabe has tried several times to claim their chieftaincy back without success.

The Sekororo people's claim that Ba-Mohlabe are their subjects cannot be verified because the Ba-Mohlabe are Batubatse while Ba-Mahlo or Sekororo are Banareng. The totem of Batubatse is "Tlou" while theirs is "Nare". The Sekororo subjugated them through the help of the apartheid regime, never having fought and defeated them.

Sekwai, also known as Sekwatapeng, succeeded his grandmother by ascending the throne after her death. He became Kgoshi Mohlabe lll. The campaign by the Mohlabe people to break away from the control of Sekororo continued. Chief Sekororo Mahlo did not want to recognise the headmen appointed by Kgoshi Mohlabe. For instance he ignored the appointment of Hermanus Mohlabe and as a result Hermanus Mohlala was deposed. This infuriated the Mohlabe people and they stopped cooperating with him and disobeyed his instructions.

A letter addressed to the Commissioner in Leydsdorp read thus: "We report to you our complaint in connection with our chairman who was deposed by chief AJ Sekororo and the Native Commissioner, Leydsdorp, without consulting or advised us of his fault. Our chairman is Hermanus Mohlabe and was appointed by us according to old tradition, after which we advised Chief Sekororo and the Native Commissioner on the 14 01 1945."

The chieftainship of Batubatse Ba-Mohlabe was never recognized by the previous regime. For decades, if not generations, the Batubatse Ba-Mohlabe have been fighting for their independence from Sekororo. Till to date, they are still battling to claim their independence. It would seem that their leader has been unfairly reduced to a mere headman under Sekororo by the previous government prior to 1994.

After the death of Kgoshi Sekwai the absence of an heir to the throne caused confusion within the royal council. While the discussions were still taking place within the Royal House to determine who was to ascend the throne, Morabudi became the acting chief with the title of Chief Mohlabe IV. Together with the tribe he continued to fight for the recognition of a senior traditional leadership out of Chief Sekororo Mahlo's control. Unfortunately he died before the leadership dispute could be resolved. However a young male, Maitjeng, had been identified as an heir to the throne and was being groomed take over the reign from him.

While Chief Morabudi was still seriously ill and could not run the affairs of the tribe, the inner circle decided to appoint Ms Maatsebe, the daughter of one of the previous chiefs, to act as regent for Maitjeng. She and Maitjeng's father were brother and sister. She continued to lead the tribe as a regent from Sofaya. However Maitjeng predeceased Maatsebe before he could become a chief. Ms Maatsebe then ruled the tribe on behalf of the young Soo Samuel Mohlabe who was in line to the throne of Mohlabe chiefs. As a caretaker chieftainess she could not use the title name of Mohlabe. Together with members of the Royal House she continued to fight for recognition of Mohlabe's independency from Sekororo. During her reign there was some dissatisfaction within the inner circle or the Royal House. As a result she moved from Sofaya to Mahlomoleng but while she was still living there she became passive due to old age and illness. She died while Morabudi was still alive and it is unclear who assumed the throne after her death.

Soo Samuel is the present reigning chief of the Mohlabe Tribe after assuming the leadership in about 1995. Prince Soo Mohlabe was born at a time when the chieftainship of Ba-Mohlabe was in a precarious state. From the time of Kgoshigadi Marebole until to date members of the Ba-Mohlabe are still being forced to submit to the jurisdiction of Kgoshi Sekororo Mahlo. As a result Soo cannot be called chief or headman and lives the life of an ordinary person without any leadership status. This is something that needs to be addressed and brought to finality by the Disputes and Claims committee of the Commission on

Traditional Leadership. The Mohlabe Community and the Batubatse people in general, however, still recognize him as chief.

After the breakaway of the house of the Batubatse Ba-Mohlabe from the entire tribe of Batubatse Ba-Shai, they continued to lead an independent existence from the other group. Although they were on their own, they still remained in contact with other Batubatse Ba-Shai tribes with whom they consulted on matters of mutual concern, in keeping with their strong ancestral relationship. It is understood that Chief Segopane Mohlabe I had a biological brother, whose name cannot be recalled, who visited the other group of Batubatse at Tsubye as another sign of their strong ancestral ties.

A sign of their independence was that, of all the neighbouring tribes, they refused to pay tribute to Sekororo Mahlo. In all their dealings, the Mohlabe community never asked permission from Chief Sekororo and continued to defy his orders. But because of hardship Mohlabe's subjects had no choice but to look at Sekororo for assistance as he was recognised by the government, particularly on matters that require the Chief's rubber stamp. By doing so the Mohlabe community was not endorsing the control of Chief Sekororo over them. Sekororo, of course, knew very well that his authority was due to the cheating by Chief Timamogolo and apartheid government.

The only people who threatened the independence and peace of Batubatse Ba-Mohlabe in the early days were the burgers of the Zuid Afrikaanse Republiek (ZAR) who established a Boer Republiek in the Transvaal headed by Paul Kruger. The ZAR appointed a Location Commission on 20 June 1892 to define boundaries between whites and black tribes in the Lowveld. In 1886 the ZAR laid down new boundaries in the areas occupied by Mohlabe community. This was in terms of Act 8 of 1886 which demarcated the land into farms and allocated these to burgers in an effort to expand white settlement in the Lowveld. This was in spite of the fact that the Mohlabe community and other black tribes were occupying this land. They were instructed to move to their new location. Although some of Mohlabe's subjects complied with the instruction, most of them remained where they are till to date. Consequently, Batubatse Ba-Mohlabe have laid claim to some of the farms in a land claim lodged with the Regional Land Claim Commission (RLCC).

DIPHOLO/MMANYABA UNIT

Having arrived at Maakene the remaining tribe of Batubatse broke into two groups; one led by Tefo and Mabine and the other group by Dipholo Shayi. The group led by Dipholo (senior) decided to return to the vicinity of Tubatse. Dipholo (senior) had three wives and had become of age at the time and it was going to be difficult for him to lead the tribe back to Tubatse. His son Mashabane or Mashabake Mmanyaba took the leadership of the group, crossed Olifants River and the high mountains back to Tubatse. He was with his younger brother Mapiti. Khashane, a half-brother of Mashabane from the senior house remained at Tsubye.

Before they reach Modubeng, they first settled at Leboeng, then at Maabotja, a place between the present Penge and Praktiseer. Some of their siblings settled at the present Bothashoek between Burgersfort and Praktiseer. From here they trekked to Sekopung near the present Makhofane village. It is here where they began to scatter. This time Mashabane Mmanyaba had come of age. His brother-in-law, Lesetja Sebetlakoma Mahlakwana, invited Mmanyaba through his son Dipholo (junior) to come and stay with them at Tlading, not far from a place which today is known as Modubeng.

According to the informant Lekola Simon Makgopa, supported by Ngoato Movad Shayi and Chichila Morebudi Shai, Mashabane or Mashabake found this small section of Mahlakwana people as a family, led by the same Lesetja Sebetlakoma Mahlakwana, a traditional healer, residing in the area. The section recognised him as their chief since they knew that he was from the Batubatse Royal House and had married a lady of a high quality and standard as candle wife from them. He was their brother-in-law. Mashabane fought bravely to secure control of the area. His tribe lived there in the absence of Khashane. Sebetlakoma Mahlakwana is the one who introduced an aged Dipholo (senior) as chief to Kgoshi Sekhukhune. The Batubatse named the place Tsubye in honour and remembrance to their Tsubye near Phalaborwa where they came from. Dipholo (senior), the father to Mashabane Mmanyaba and Mapiti, probably died there.

The whole place had a lot of water everywhere and when one was walking on feet one would feel as if his legs were making (dubaduba) mud. As the time went on they talked amongst themselves that they are at Modubadubeng, meaning that they were at a place where the process of making mud takes place. Another account states that the area was covered by many trees known in Northern Sotho as meduba, single moduba. Each of them used to sit under the shadow of this moduba tree, hence modubeng. Ultimately they gave their new place another name of Modubeng, meaning a place of making mud or a place of the moduba tree, in addition to that of Tsubye. According to my informant, Lekola Simon Makgopa born in 1936, because this section of Batubatse had plenty water there they were able to plant and reap enough peanuts, sweet potatoes and malt for a living.

His son, Mashabane was installed as Kgoshi Mmanyaba l (one). During the reign of Kgoshi Mmanyaba l Khashane came from Tsubye and made an attempt to wrestle the chieftainship, claiming that, as the eldest son of Dipholo (senior), he was the first in line to take the leadership of the tribe. His attempt, however, didn't yield any dividend because Kgoshi Sekhukhune recognized Mashabane as the leader of Batubatse in that area. When Mashabane Mmanyaba intent to open an initiation school, he would get a muti-permit (sesa/pheko) from Mapiti at Tsubye, Maakene. His first initiation (koma) school was called "bogwera". Later he got his own muti-permit sesa/pheko with the help of one Malepe.

During tribal conflicts in the Sekhukhune Royal Council, two of Kgoshi Sekhukhune's senior councilors, Mafefe and Ntwampe, ran to Mmanyaba to save their lives. Mmanyaba helped them to cross Olifants River and hide them at Mataung, not far from Chief Mampa territory. Mafefe and Ntwampe were half-brothers. They fought among themselves. When it became tough for Ntwampe, he returned to Sekhukhune with the assistance of Mmanyaba where after he settled at Moroke area. Kgoshi Mmanyaba l ruled the tribe for a considerable period of time and died, leaving his heir apparent son, Dipholo (junior), to succeed him on the throne. Dipholo married his candle wife from Mahlakwana family as well. Upon his father's death he ascended the throne as Kgoshi Mmanyaba ll (two).

It would appear that, for some time the Mmanyaba Shayi group was never involved in any leadership squabbles. Even if there was such a dispute, it never reared its head up before calling for investigation. The leadership dispute appears to be a guarded secret in the community. Upon his death after ruling the tribe for a long time, Kgoshi Mmanyaba ll was succeeded on the throne by his son Malapane with the title of Mmanyaba lll (three). His candle wife from Mmola family gave birth to a son and the heir to the throne. After his death, the son ascended the throne under the title of Mapalakanye l. He too got his candle wife from Mmola sub clan. When he died, his son and heir to the throne took the reign and assumed the title of Mmanyaba IV. His candle wife, Makalela Mida, came from Mampuru kraal and, for reasons unknown, she presently rule the tribe as a regent in the absence of the chief who reside a distance away from his royal palace with no interest in the running of the affairs of his tribe.

What is interesting about Mmanyaba Shayi Royal House is that all conflicts affecting traditional leadership or chieftainship were resolved without bloodshed, as compared with other tribes. Until to date this tribe exist while fully entrenched at Modubeng, a mountainous place, about sixty (60) kilometers from either Lebowakgomo or Burgersfort. Kgoshi Mmanyaba Shai is, however, not registered as a senior traditional leader and therefore not recognized as a paid Senior Traditional Leader. Probably he is considered as one of the headmen under one of the Sekhukhune chiefs, something that does not go well with the Batubatse community.

Kgoshigadi Makalela Mida Shayi

TEFO/MABINE UNIT

Tefo and his tribe were not deterred by the breakaway groups and had settled at Makhutšwe near the present Sekororo. Before Mashabane or Mashabake led Mmanyaba Shayi group back to Tubatse, Mabine came back to inform Mashishimale Tefo (sometimes referred to as Mashishimale I) and others that he had found a good and fertile land along the Mountains at Maakene. Tefo was given the name of Mashishimale in honour of his great-grandfather Masie. Tefo moved on with the tribe to follow Mabine until they reaches Maakene, a rich place near a place known as Mica today, not far from Phalaborwa. He settled or established himself along the hills which were later named Tsubye and started agriculture on the land for survival. The principle or yard stick to determine the size of their land or area was "As far as the eyes could see when standing on a mountain".

With him from the senior house, there were his key sons, among them was Matome, Tlhogotlou Masetle Maenetja, Seanego and many others who later became famous traditional healers and leaders with great influence on any key decisions to be taken affecting the tribe. After a while, Mashabane Mmanyaba's father, Dipholo left with his son to Modubeng. The land was indeed good, beautiful and fertile. They stayed there together as brothers and they established their capital and dwelt for generations. That was when Tefo was given the praise-name of Selota, meaning a "follower", as he had followed his younger brother. The tribe established its independent chieftainship at Maakene having three sacred dikomana drums: boretho - the largest one, thannga - the medium size one and phokwi - the smallest one, like its neighbours of Phalaborwa. When they arrive there they found a small portion of Batubatse community led by Sekhula living alongside a certain old man known as Modiamofe, who had been there with his people long before all of them. It is said that Sekhula was one of the Batubatse families that left the tribe earlier before.

Sekhula knew that Tefo Selota, Mabine, Dipholo and others were solidly united and had formed a larger tribe than that of Modiamofe. Tefo and Mabine conspired and hatched a plan in order to rob Modiamofe the leadership and chieftainship of the whole the community in that area. They suggested to him, with the support of Sekhula, a contest which would determine who would be the chief of the two groups combined. The challenge was that each of the two communities should get enough people to hold each other with hands to embrace the mountain in the form of a ring surrounding it. Further that, he who succeeds to completely embrace the mountain as such or his people completely surround the mountain holding each other with arms shall become the leader or chief of the two communities combined. This was a test to determine who was having more subjects than the other between Tefo Selota and Modiamofe. Modiamofe initially agreed to the suggestion, unaware that Tefo had too many subjects than him and was stepping into a big trap.

Modiamofe was confident as he was the first to surround the Mountain with his people. He failed to get enough subjects to accomplish the agreed mission. When Tefo and Mabine gather their own people Modiamofe realized that Tefo had many people who could surround the mountain many times as agreed. He then raised his hands up together with his people as a sign of defeat. Further than this, the brothers had conspired to outsmart him and during the night, after Modiamofe had failed to secure the leadership position, Selota and Mabine set a small bush surrounding the mountain on fire. A bushfire covered the whole mountain. Apparently, at the time, Modiamofe and his people were unaware of fire and were frightened by the flames of the bushfire.

They did not disclose to Modiamofe the knowledge that there was a fire which can burn the bush or forest. Modiamofe accepted defeat and lost the leadership position. Tefo Shai assumed the leadership of the whole tribe and became the first kgoshi at Maakene under the title of Kgoshi Selota

In realizing that his position as a leader of a small section of the community of Batubatse in the area was under a threat, Sekhula moved away with some of his followers to Ga-Maupa and Bolobedu.

Another verbal source states that the Batubatse Ba-Shai, including the Sekhula family, upon arrival at Maakene, they found a weak and small Modiamofe community with no knowledge of fire, living like wild animals, eating raw meat; their huts were badly constructed and dirty; they tilled the soil with sharpened sticks in comparison to the hoes used by the group who found them; and the uncivilized impression which they imparted was further bolstered by the fact that they had no chief or any visible form of government. The cultured Shai people took upon themselves the task of educating and teaching these savage people the uses of fire.

The Batubatse mode of making fire was known as tsekga, whereby two special dry sticks were rubbed together until the friction produced fire. This community was reportedly enthralled by the taste of cooked food and the warmth of the hearth fire. In exchange for the knowledge and skills imparted on them by the Batubatse people, they were expected to adopt Shayi/Shai as their only surname and in clear terms they were told never again to refer to their old surname and names. As a result the identity of Modiamofe community was forever changed and never heard of again. However, some of his remnants later became known as Motodi people, now living in Sekhukhuneland under a senior traditional leader.

When the Malatji people arrive at the present Phalaborwa, they found the Batubatse already settled there. One of Chief Malatji's wives was given to him by Batubatse upon their arrival. According to information the Malatjis are the son-in-laws of Batubatse Ba-Shai of Mashishimale. On a certain night the Batubatse set the mountain hills nearby on fire. Malatji and his people saw a big flame of fire for the first time in their lives and were frightened. The following morning they went to Batubatse to inquire about a big flame they saw at night around the hills near them. The hills or the mountain was covered with black ash (letsubye). After they got the explanation from the Batubatse of what had happened the previous night, the Malatji people began to call the burned hills which were covered by the black ash as "Tsubye". Since then till to date those hills at Maakene are referred to or called Tsubye or Tsuubye. The words 'tsubye or tsuubye' is derived from the Sotho words tsube or tshuba or tshuma, meaning to cause wild fire.

Members of the Batubatse who once stayed there before they break away to other places are sometimes referred to as the Batsubye, meaning people from Tsubye. At that time the Batubatse were under the leadership of Selota. One may, correctly, say that Kgoshi Mashishimale Selota 1 was an icon, the originator and pillar of strength of Batubatse at Maakene. He was someone too important, or too highly thought of. Kgoshi Selota 1 stood for something greater than his family's peace of mind. As a true leader, he was inspired by love for his people and not by hatred for his enemies. He wanted a total emancipation of his community and was willing to lay his life down for that. His reign stands out boldly because of his subjugation of the Modiamofe community, primitive denizens of the forest of Tsubye.

He, together with his brothers, Mabine, Dipholo and many others ventured in the wilderness, forests and thorny bushes to bring the tribe in the land flowing with milk and honey, just like Moses in the Bible who led the Israelites to a similar land of milk and honey, Canaan. This great man lived to ensure that there was progress of the Batubatse in general. He was a man the Batubatse entered the land with him before something terribly went wrong.

In desperate need of brave leaders there couldn't be a better story to tell the future generations than the true story of Kgoshi Mashishimale Tefo Shai, who the name of the present town of Mashishing came because of his braveness. As one could understand talks about him, he was a leader who stepped into the hearts of his people with charm, courtesy, a self-deprecating sense of humour and a smile that could smelt a heart of ice. Mashishimale Tefo Shai could zoom in on the essence of what the tribe needs and connect with them. He has the capacity to understand the bigger picture of Batubatse complex and dynamic political landscape. He was astute enough, they say, to garner huge support at the conscious risk of alienating important minority groups and then, at the right time, tone down his message or package it so that it slowly draws in many of the alienated groups.

The Batubatse called Kgoshi Mashishimale Tefo Shai "Molomo wa go sebolele phosho (The Mouth that speaks no wrong)". We believe that his charisma not only won the admiration of the Batubatse, it also conquered the hearts of the majority of his opponents. The Batubatse Royal Houses and families could have been easily wrestled out by other tribes or completely disappeared had he not played his cards very cleverly. For that he became not only the most beloved chief of Batubatse communities ever known, but also one of the most revered fathers of Batubatse. This man left an indelible mark in South Africa of today. He was a gift of hope to us, Batubatse. None have ever been able to find words to describe exactly what happened in his or her heart the day he or she heard about him. He is an historic figure, as well as the legendary hero of both ancient and modern Batubatse communities. Kgoshi Mashishimale Tefo Shai died at Maakene and was considered by us, Batubatse, as being among the greatest leaders in human history and was buried there.

Mabine, of course, cannot be ignored. He, leading members of his circumcision regiment, discovered Maakene as a fine area for the Batubatse to settle. His view was that the question of their final settlement could not be decided by talking and resolutions, but by venturing through the thorny bushes with his armed warriors in order to find a settlement. Mabine was not only the master at war, but was also able to read the minds of the members of his regiment and the people they were serving. He guided his men under extreme and dangerous circumstances to the brink of fulfilling the wish of Batubtse of finding a good permanent home.

His constant dedication to help his brother, Kgoshi Tefo, build a strong Batubatse tribe affected his health yet after several months of illness he insisted on returning to his many tribal duties. He maintained that nothing beats dedication, passion and being prepared to work long hours. Unlike some of his half-brothers, he never attempted to wrest power from his elder brother. Indeed he paid him the utmost respect that a chief deserves. He was conscious of the attempts of those who were secretly planning to seize power from Kgoshi Mashishimale Tefo. He was quick to confront them and put an end to their efforts. He was well respected and got on well with most people within the community.

His presence, charisma and gravitas attracted the attention of anyone with whom he came in contact. Yet he didn't look uncomfortable because of it. This was a space into which he naturally fitted. He had strong views and was not afraid to voice them. He promoted a cause with passion and vigour. They say while he was leading his regiment, he consulted with his team and allowed them to lead him. Those who were close to him described him as a simple man, an open book. He was a hero to those who believed in peace against troublemakers. He was regarded as one of the Batubatse's great men. In their darkest hour he gave them inspired leadership and a place to stay.

Kgoshi Mashishimale Tefo Selota 1 had a number of powerful sons; among them was Matome, Makutuma Maasetla (Tlhogotlou), Seanego and many others. It is said that Matome was the first and heir apparent but did not ascend the throne after the death of his father for fear of being killed. Neither of his two younger brothers dared to accept the throne for the same reason. Instead, his younger paternal uncle, Mabine, took over and became Kgoshi of Batubatse Ba-Shai under the title of Kgoshi Mabine l.

Mabine l played an important role in the search for green pastures and opened the way for the unification of the scattered Batubatse communities. He enabled his elder brother Selota l to reach Maakeneand respected his position as Kgoshi until his death. Kgoshi Mabine passed away at Tsubye and was buried there. After his death his son, Dipholo, who assumed the title of Kgoshi Selota II, ascended the Batubatse Ba-Shai throne at Maakene, but went on to settle at Mabye-A-Shosho (Enable) before moving to Dioke, which was part of Maakene. Kgoshi Selota II passed on at Dioke and was, probably, buried there. From his candle wife he fathered three children, Mokgadi Makoma, Taola and Khashane Mashishimale and from his second wife he beget Nkurwane, Modume and Leshwene as his children.

TAOLA/MASHISHIMALE UNIT

Upon the death of Kgoshi Dipholo Selota II, Taola ruled the tribe for a short period and died unexpectedly. He left his two wives, the candle wife from Mmola and the other one from Malepe with three young children each. A leadership squabble ensued amongst those who were gunning for the vacuum left by the death of Kgoshi Taola. It was then suggested that, his elder sister Mokgadi, should act as regent for Kgoshi Taola's son as he was still very young. She ruled the tribe for a short period when a leadership squabble ensued again. There was a period of tension within the Royal House, exacerbated by those opposed to her leadership.

The majority of the members of the Royal House were not in favour of being ruled by a woman. They also feared that Mokgadi's son, Thakadu, may wrest the throne from his mother, and if that happened, it might be difficult to remove him or prevent his son to take over the reins from him. Apart from that, Mokgadi could not give birth to an heir to the throne since she was not a candle wife, but a kgoshi's daughter. Ultimately, by agreement, Kgoshi Taola's younger brother, Khashane Mashishimale, succeeded him and ruled the community, also as a regent.

Kgoshi Khashane Mashishimale was one of the sons of Kgoshi Selota ll and although ruling as regent, he was given the title of Mashishimale ll and was a good leader. It was, therefore, traditionally not out of order that he should step into the shoes of his elder brother to preserve the Batubatse Royal House since Taola's son and heir to the throne was still too young to take over the chieftainship. Initially, the understanding was that Mashishimale would make way for Kgoshi Taola's son as the heir to the throne when he had grown up and was ready to take over. But it transpired that that was not the case and the chieftainship was not immediately handed over to him.

According to observation and assessment of the situation at the time, Kgoshi Mashishimale was loyal to the house of his brother, Taola, and carefully looked after it. It is understood that he kept on saying openly and publicly that "The chieftainship is not mine; it belong to the main house." It would seem that Kgoshi Taola's children did not worry much about the chieftainship but looked at the progress of the tribe, hoping that it would one day revert back to them when the opportunity arise. Kgoshi Mashishimale's candle wife, Mmammola or Mmalefaru, came from the Mmola family. During my research information was obtained that she gave birth to Lethamaga Molotolo and another Mabine. Another version of the story, however, holds that Mabine was not Lethamaga's brother, but his son.

It is also said that Mmalefaru was in fact Lethamaga's wife from Mmola sub-clan of the tribe. Lethamaga and that Mmalefaru gave birth to Kharitje Majatjebotse (son), Mabine (son) and Shabeshabe (daughter). Shabeshabe married a man from the Mutswi sub-clan of the tribe. She was killed in a raid by Gungunyana's people. From his second and chief wife of the Makgopa sub-clan he fathered one son, also known as Mabine. Kgoshi Mashishimale ruled for an extremely long period; some say for 20 to 30 years. It is not known which year he became a chief, probably around 1860 to 1870. It is thought that he was still a chief at the time of the attack on the Mapulana stronghold of Maholoholo on Mariep Mountain. Furthermore, it is alleged that he lived for more than 100 years.

LETHAMAGA UNIT

When Kgoshi Kgashane Mashishimale II became of age, matters in the Royal House took a different turn. A struggle for leadership ensued. On the one hand Taola's children from the candle wife campaigned to take the throne back to the first and principal house, where it belonged, while on the other hand there was a conspiracy by Lethamaga and others to usurp the throne for themselves or to share it with Taola's children. This conspiracy was supported by the Mmola sub-clan and other members of the Royal House. When Lethamaga requested his father, Mashishimale, to hand the chieftainship to him, he was told that the throne did not belong to him but to Taola's main house. When Lethamaga insisted that he hand the throne over to him, Mashishimale told him that the only way to get the chieftainship was to 'eliminate' all the children of the main house. Accordingly some of these children were secretly attacked and strangled to death at night. All Taola's children from the main house who were in line to the throne, Leshwene, Modume and Nkurwane, were eliminated. Nkurwane's son, Matidimane, was spared. The wife of Kgoshi Taola's second and lower house came from Malepe family at Makhutšwi. She gave birth to three sons Mapiti, Sekgasane and Mariti Lethabanaga. When they realised that the siblings of Taola's houses were being murdered, they fled to their uncle Malepe at Makhutšwi. Some of Taola's family members, his other children and supporters secretly left the area to Ga-Maupa, Bolobedu and Mapulaneng. Others returned to Modubeng to join another section of Batubatse.

According to Masegare I Shai, after Lethamaga had eliminated all suspected potential opponents, he asked his father once again to hand over the chieftainship to him or give part of the land and the tribe to rule. Kgoši Mashishimale told him that he could not do that while still alive. He further indicated that his request could be acceded to after consultation with the elders of the other house at Modubeng. From the look of things it would appear that by then Mashishimale had already discussed Lethamaga's request with his half-brothers at Modubeng. Kgoshi Mashishimale and his councillors were not in support of the request or proposal by Lethamaga.

After hearing what his father told him, Lethamaga and his cousin, Thabalešoke, travelled to Modubeng to seek approval to his request. In the meantime, Kgoshi Mashishimale and his counsellors had already dispatched people to Modubeng to brief them about the purpose of Lethamaga's visit. He also sent a message that Lethamaga should be killed at the place where he intended to settle as chief. Upon arrival Lethamaga presented his case to Kgoshi Mmanyaba Shai of Modubeng. They agreed with him and thereafter selected a few warriors to accompany him up to the spot where he intended to settle and rule. They crossed the Olifants River and when they arrive at Dioke Hills, about ten to fifteen kilometers from The Oaks, Lethamaga pointed out to them a beautiful place lying under those hills where he intended to erect his own kraal (moshate) and he indicated the proposed boundaries of his territory. One of the warriors called Thabalešoke aside and secretly advised him to escape. At that point the warriors took a head-cloth, covered Lethamaga's head down to the neck and throttled him with it until he expired. He died the death of a martyr, killed as a result of his political and religious beliefs. Had he not being killed, today that beautiful land would have been the immovable asset of the Batubatse community.

If we put aside the line of succession on the side of Taola, Lethamaga, born by the principal wife, was supposed to step in the shoes of his father, Mashishimale, upon his death. Lethamaga had two wives. The 1st wife came from Mmola family and was considered as his principal and candle wife. She gave birth to Kharitji Majatjebotse who was to become chief after the death of his grandfather, Kgashane Mashishimale II or his father Lethamaga. The candle wives of all previous Batubatse chiefs had always came from Mmola family unit. Lethamaga's second wife came from Makgopa family and thier eldest son was Mabine. Mabine could only assume the throne of Batubatse Ba-Shayi-Ditlou as regent because his mother was not a candle wife, and also if Kharitji Majatjebotse, for any good reason, cannot assume the chieftainship.

When Kharitje Majatjebotse, son of Lethamaga, heard of the gruesome murder of his father he was enraged and vowed to revenge the death of his father. Taking his firearm he went on an angry rampage in the company of his supporters and shot to death senior councillors Marabe, Podume, Mokgashane and Mokgale. Surprisingly, he spared the life of Kgoshi Mashishimale but showed him the firearm he used to kill the others. The other children of Lethamaga joined the crusade and killed everyone they met. After crossing Letsitele River they destroyed anything they came across on their way to their maternal uncle, Letsie Phohlo Mmola at Mogonyeng. They were welcomed with loud applause, praise poems and victory war songs. Kgoshi Mashishimale was shocked and affected by the events. He passed away, leaving the head kraal at Maakene in great misery, sadness, grief and mourning. When he died at Maakene, his heir Lethamaga had already predeceased him and his grandson, Kharitji Majatjebotse, was nowhere to be found to come out and assume the throne. Some say his wife was, at the time, very sick and this prevented him to take over the throne and had left his half brother, Mabine, to warm the seat in his absence.

By agreement of the community, Lethamaha's son from the second and senior wife, Mabine ll, succeeded to his grandfather's throne at Maakene as Acting Chief and Mabine ll,. Kgoshi Mabine ll's wife was Pulane Maketjemane from the Makgopa sub-clan of the tribe. She gave birth to Leshwene (m), Mosebutjane (f), Mokgadi (f), Manko (f) and Kabelo (f). There is a difference of opinions as to whether Mokgadi was his daughter or his second wife or was just brought to him. Nor is it known from which family she came.

Kgoshi Mabine ll ruled for some time at Maakene, through three circumcisions and eventually died there, probably in 1899 or 1900, during the bogwera initiation of the Melau/Malau regiment, at the time of the war between Sekororo and Maake. The tribe was scattered in those days owing to drought. It is understood that during Mabine II's rule, Kharitji made several attempts and demand for the return of his position as chief from Mabine, but Mabine refused. That is when the issue of candle wife from Mmola Unit was lost. Mabine ll was succeeded by his son Maphokwane Leshwene who had about ten wives as follows:

1. Mosebutšane, daughter of Sekhwela from the Makgopa family of the tribe, who gave birth to Mokgadi (f), Lebeko (f), Mpopane (f) and Mabine Johannes (m) who later assumed the title of Mabine lll.

2. Mapeu, daughter of Manaba from the Malatji family of Phalaborwa. She gave birth to two daughters, Manko and Makoma.

3. Mokgadi, daughter of Serupu from the Makgoba family. She begot two sons, Khashane and Nkurwane.

4. Mmashai, daughter of Mokhashe of Marobela sub-clan of the royal house. She begot two daughters, Nkhaka and Mosebudi.

5. Manku, daughter of Meriri from the Monyela family. She subsequently absconded to Modjadji area and had one daughter named Mokgadi.

6. Mmakgoshi, daughter of Rakhuma from the Malatji family of Phalaborwa. She subsequently left to stay at Makhushane village with one son, Matome.

7. Mmaletshira, daughter of Madiele from the Malatji family of Phalaborwa. She ran away and remarried to Nkwana of this tribe. She had one male child, Morakene or Morakane. The lobola cattle were returned to Kgoshi Mabine ll.

8. Ditshwantsho, daughter of Marakene from the Malatji family of Phalaborwa. She also ran away with her three children, Shai (m), Molewane (f) and Maropene (f), to live with her brother at Mohlaba village.

9. Nkatla, daughter of Matema from the Malatji family. She had no children.

10. Morongwa, daughter of Fereki from the Pilusa family, Kgoshi Malatji's councillor. She had two children Matjepe (f) and Mothoka (m).

Under the leadership of Kgoshi Leshwene the tribe moved away from Maakene to the Mohote River, on the western boundary of the farm now called Lekkersmaak 209. Around

1902 or 1903 the tribe experienced a famine known as "Tlala Ya Ditlouma".

In about 1922 the tribe settled at its present reserve at Ga-Mashishimale. Leshwene died there on 28 July 1936 and was succeeded on 25 October 1936 by his son Mabine Johannes, who was married to Mmapatene Makgopa. When he paased on in 1962 his son, Daniel Modume, was still very young to rule. His paternal uncle, Mackson Morakeng Shayi, became Acting Chief on his behalf from 1962 till 1977. Modume Daniel, after he passed on his son, Modume Shayi, became Kgoshi of the Mashishimale tribe in 1978. He married Mokgadi Catherine, the daughter of the late Matome Daniel and Seletja Makgopa. His life was short- lived when he was laid to rest in 1991.

His wife, Mokgadi Catherine, took over from her late husband as regent and was inaugurated as Kgoshigadi of the Mashishimale Ba-Shayi-Ditlou tribe in 1992. She met her death on 2 July 2015, after she sustained a stroke, and was laid to rest next to her husband's grave on 11 July 2015 at Mashishimale Royal Cemetery. She is survived by five children. From the above discussion, it is clear that, if we go back to Kgoshi Taola, the traditional custom line of succession of chieftainship of Batubatse Ba-Shayi-Ditlou in regard to candle wife, was lost from Mmola family to Makgopa family when Mabine II became chief.

Kgoshigadi Mokgadi Catherine Shayi

NKURWANE UNIT

In the words of Masegare Isaac Shai, Nkurwane was the youngest son of Kgoshi Taola and was in line to occupy a senior position in the Royal Kraal. He was eliminated before he could challenge anyone who aspired to become chief of the tribe. His wife came from the Malepe family and was blessed with three children, Matidimane, Choma Mokeketi and Pebane. Matidimane, like his father married his second wife, Maabale, from the Malepe family. They had five children; Mokgano, Magofane, Mangwato, Mapule and Makhoo. Makgano acquired his third wife from the Malepe family as well. He had more than ten children from his wives. When he realized that there was no paid job at home he travelled to Johannesburg to seek paid employment. He left while most of his children were still small.

Since then his whereabouts were never known. His younger brother, Mkhoo, remained taking care of his children and their mother in addition to his wife and own children.

Makhoo was married to Motjatji Mpholwane who gave birth to Masegare Andries, Mmerika Freddy and Kgabashai Wilson (Mosapalome). At the time his household was at Sedawa, close to his uncle, Malepe. While going around the area he was attracted to an area with good grazing land and sufficient water near Olifants River and decided to move there. The new locality was well-suited for agriculture, unlike Sedawa which was mountainous and dry. It took him two years to convince his mother to relocate away from Sedawa. He settled with his whole family at the new place in bush populated with various species of wild animals which he named Dingapong. Makhoo was the only brave man who maintained and urged Nkurwane's unit to remain together until he was no more.

MASETLA/TLHOGOTLOU UNIT

Masetla (Maasetla) Makutuma Shai, the younger brother of Matome Shai and a traditional healer as well, left Maakene with a separate group of about ten families after Matome Shai had left, and proceeded to settle at Bolebye Mountain after being advised to do so. At the same time other families, such as that of Mmola, Moshole, Phaladi, Makwala, Mapaila, Matlou and others moved to other areas, all from Tsubye. Masetla Makutuma's group later became known as Maenetje or Maenetja people. His house and followers stayed close to Bakgaga Ba-Maake under their King. Masetla Makutuma, a traditional healer and herbalist, was also known by the name of Tlhogotlou after he skillfully removed the brain of an elephant out of its skull through its ear-hole in a surprising way. Together with him when he left Maakene/Tsubye, were his younger brothers Seanego (senior) who was fond of narrating stories, Marobela who managed to kill a giraffe single handed, Mokgomola who was always sent to be on the lookout for enemies and Mogonone who was always in doubt to everything.

According to the late Phetole William Maenetja, the informant, Masetla Makutuma Shai became chief after his group, later known as the Maenetja group, separated from the senior section, Shai, at Tsubye. His house included people who later became known as Maenetja, Masetla, Seanego, Marobela, Mokgomola, Mogonone, Ratlabala, Ramonyathi, Selaelo, Kgoahla, Moloise, Mamanyoga, Mafedi, Magodiele, Rathete, Thema and few others. One oral source of information state that Ba- Maenetje, also known as Balebye, had their own chief while another source says that Masetla Makutuma Shai was a headman under Bakgaga Ba- Maake, using Maenetja as his surname. From Tsubye, Masetla and his people settled where the present farm of Kasteel is found. They occupied the highest peak of the nearby mountain known as Kasteelkop and the immediate area at the bottom of it.

As indicated above the group comprised about ten families, probably less than two hundred people, and could only have occupied a mall part of the area. According to Phetole William there is an archaeological site at Kasteelkop that confirms the exact location of their stay. The mountain as well as the area surrounding it, "as far as the eyes could see when standing on a mountain", was known as Bolebye. The peak of the mountain called Bolebye (Kasteelkop) together with other small peaks such as Moreofetše, Ntopele, Tshwenyane and Mafologela, formed the Murchison Range. Spitskop, 874 metres high, is the highest point in the Murchison Range. The name bolebye refers to a sticky fluid used to catch birds, emanating from a fruit bearing trees which covered most part of Kasteelkop. Families frequently quarrel amongst themselves and eventually break away from each other. The Maenetja families were no exception.

The first one to break away from the senior household of Masetla was Kgoahla, the son of Mogonone. At the time of his departure, Kgoahla told the senior house that they would have to follow his track (kgoatla) to find his family, hence the origin of the surname of Kgoahla. The remnants of his people are to be found in the vicinity of Polokwane (Pietersburg). The remainder of Mogonone's family members stayed with Masetla at Bolebye (Kasteelkop). Masetla Makutuma Maenetja had two official wives. His first wife passed away after she gave birth to her son, Mafedi. Mafedi grew up under the care of Masetla's second wife from Malatji Makhushane clan. Masetla Makhutuma Maenetja died at Bolebye. Before his death he said to his people that he was going to look for medicines and herbs in the bush and never returned. A search for him or his body was unsuccessful.

Upon his disappearance or death, Mafedi Maenetje, his son from his first and senior wife stepped into his shoes to lead the tribe. Kheselo (Seselo), the son of Masetla's second wife, became unhappy with this arrangement. He broke away and moved to an unoccupied area at Mulati farm. After a short stay at Mulati, he trekked to Modjadji, where after he moved with his people to Mogoboya to join the remainder of Matome Shai's family members. His great grandson, Simon Masie, named after one of Batubatse earlier chiefs, is a headman at Mogoboya at present. Mafedi, like his father Masetla, was an herbalist. He used to keep his medicines in a cave on the Bolebye Mountain (Kasteelkop) and would go to the cave regularly when he needs some herbs and come back. One day he also didn't come back and was later found dead in the cave.

The royal family closed the mouth of the cave with stones while his body was inside. The exact location of the cave could still be observed even today. Mafedi had eight known wives and forty two children. His eldest son from the candle wife, also known as Seanego (junior), led the tribe from 1913 till 1920 while resident at Lesholo (Prieska), but was expelled by the apartheid regime as the land was earmarked for Hans Merensky Nature Reserve. He crossed the Letaba River and went to live at Maleele where he became headman in 1925 under Kgošigadi Modjadji. From Bolebye some of them moved further to Rita and other areas, using Shai and other nicknames as their surnames.

When the mining activities commenced in 1920, the Batubatse of Masetla Maenetja's people or Balebye tribe scattered over a large area not far from Gravelotte. Seanego (senior) and Mokhomola families were allocated the land along Tshapare Mountain (Granville and Begin); Marobela and Masetla families moved to Thabanapedi (Black Hills); Mafedi, Ratlabala, Ramonyathi and Mamanyoha families moved to Mamotswapi (Eiland); Magodiele family moved to Sekgotopitsi (Gondweni) between Magwena and Sekgotopitsi streams; Seanego (junior) family went to settle at Maleele near Dzumeri and Mohaleamalle and/or Rathete families went to Modjadji. In fact members of Mokgomola family formed part of Seanego senior's group. It is not known where he died but it is believed that he was laid to rest at Tshapare.

MATOME UNIT

Matome Shai was the eldest son of Kgoshi Tefo Selota 1 from his principal wife and was, probably, the heir apparent of Batubatse Ba-Shai Royal House. Leadership conflicts in the Royal House, however, discouraged him from assuming the chieftainship. He feared that he might be eliminated by those who desired the throne. He was a famous traditional healer, and was assisted in his healing practices by his three official wives and a number of his mistresses sometimes referred to as secondary wives or concubines, all of whom bore him children. His first and principal wife was known as Malephata, from Mmola unit. The names of the other two wives are unknown. According to one of my informant, Moile David Shai (born in 1939) presently residing at Mojetene village near Lenyenye, due to leadership squabbles within the Shai Royal Council and members of the inner circle, Matome Shai's house together with his three (3) wives, a number of concubines and a sizable number of community members who supported him broke off and left Maakene/Tsubye.

He settled for a short period near Bolebye and proceeded to a place known today as Ga-Mogoboya, Thabine, leaving part of his family members and supporters along the way. According to Mokanthiane Moses Shai Ragoboya, supported by the author, some of Matome's siblings scattered all over in areas such as Bolobedu, Sekgopo, Dikgale, Mamabolo, Moletji, Seshego, Ramalapa, Matlala, Thabazimbi, Ga-Maupa, Relela, Ga-Moleketla, Rita, Thabine, Motlatlareng, Mokgoloboto, Shilubane, Parare, Lenyenye, Lephepane, Phepene, Ga-Kgapane, Dan, Sekgosese, Ga-Malematja, Mthommene, Ga-Ramaroka, Ga-Phapadi, Ga-Ramohlola, Ramokaku, Sasekane, Mohlabaneng, Ga- Koranta, Ga-Ramotshinyadi, and many other areas.

MATOME AND MASETLA SHAYI/SHAI FAMILY TREE

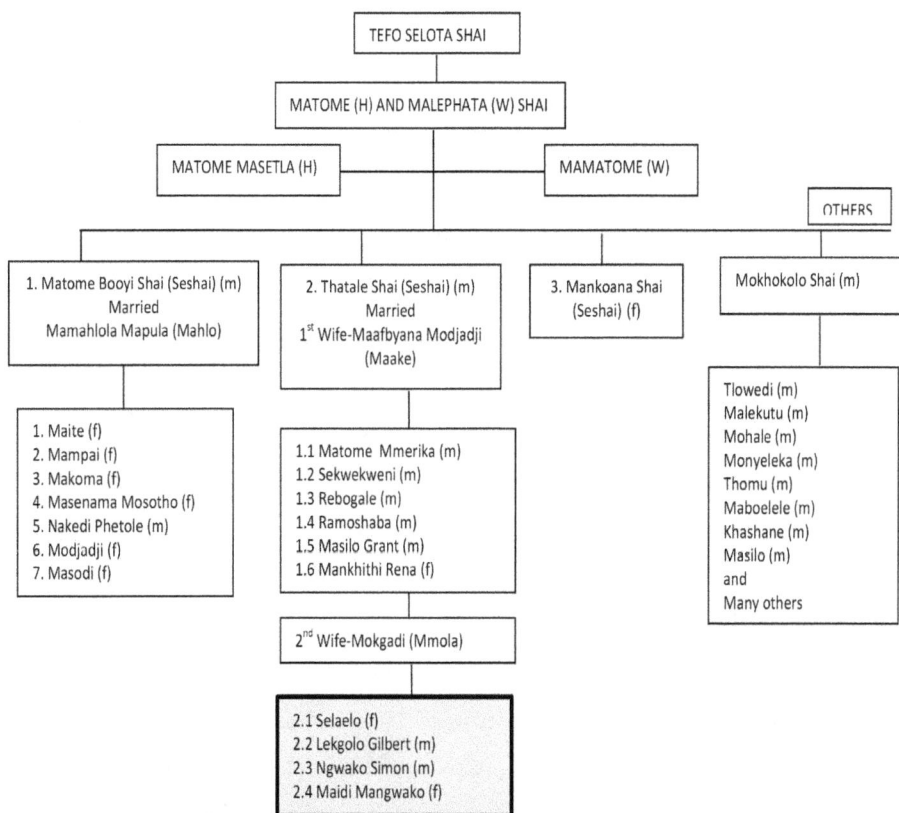

Two of those children who are still remembered are Masetla or Masetle Matome Shai (junior), born around 1820, probably, named after his paternal uncle Maasetla/ Masetla Maenetje (senior) who led the other group of people to Bolebye and Malope, born around 1826, both from his first wife, Malephata. Both Masetle Matome Shai (junior) and Malope were revered traditional healers in their own right with many wives and concubines under their control. Some of Matome's children, including Masetle, remained at Rita and Motlatlareng near Lenyenye when Matome trekked to Thabine. To the author, Masetle Matome Shai (junior) was his great-grandfather, and was one of those children who remained at Rita and was later joined by Mokgomola who trekked away from Bolebye. But because of his good relationship with his paternal uncle, Masetle Shai (senior), he left Rita for some time to live at Bolebye and returned to Rita few years later. Rita is a mountain forming part of chains of mountains leading to the ancestral secret place of Baroka/ Bakgaga nationality at Seribane/Theribane. When the Shai group increased in number they scattered all over Bokgaga territory and other neighbouring chiefs. Some became headmen under Kgoshi Maake.

In 1840 many of Batubatse communities settled at Tsaneni and Bolobedu territories. At that time Kgoshi (Chief) Makgotlo Maake, one of the sons of Kgoshikgolo Monyewede, was already an independent Chief of Bakgaga Ba-Maupa beyond the Great Letaba River living in Tsaneni territory, commonly known as Tzaneen. No information could be found as to whether Masetle left Rita with other Shai people who were part of Bakgaga Ba-Maupa or he remained there until his death. Some of Masetle Shai (junior)'s sons from his first wife Mamatome, were Matome Booyi and Thatale. They had one elder or younger sister, Mankoana.

The two sons spent most of their life as members of the Bakgaga Ba-Maupa tribe. They played an important role in the administration of the Bakgaga Ba-Maupa. Thatale, in particular, acted as one of the senior headmen and was close to the Royal Council and specifically Chief Maupa Maake. Masetla's sons changed their surname from Shai to Seshayi/Seshai. Other known sons of Masetle Shai (junior) from his other wives include Matome Mokhokolo, Pheagane and Tsetsetse. Some of Pheagane's grandchildren use Shai Ragoboya and Nakampe as their surnames. Tsetsetse sired Maesemane, who in turn fathered Butane Shai, residing at House 602, Kgapamadi/Mountainview- Gakgapane.

There are various versions of the deaths of Masetla, sometimes pronounced Masetle, and Malope Shai and their place of burial. One source states that Masetle became ill and was taken to Bolebye for medical treatment. Upon his death, he was buried there, not far from his paternal uncle, Masetle (senior) who was already deceased, honouring his wish. It is also rumoured that an unnamed Shai man died while staying at Rita, but was buried near Shilubane, about 10 kilometers away, where some of his children lived. A century-old grave is still visible near Shilubane and is believed to house a Shai Royal member. This is a likely final resting place for Masetla or Malope Shai or another member of the Batubatse Royal House, but information about the grave has sadly been lost.

It is understood that while at Thabine, Matome experienced some problems with his first wife. He became so angry that he decided to leave his three wives and other children for Johannesburg. He continued with his traditional healing practice there. Besides being a traditional healer, Matome was described as a leader of note, with acumen, insightfulness and an eagle eye for leadership opportunity. He made prudent leadership decisions even if some choices were unpopular or a potential for disagreements with other members of the Batubatse of Shai inner circle. Memories may fade and adulation fray as history marches on. But what the wind of time could not erase was the responsibility that Matome and his peers left us- to pick up the baton and continue the long walk to freedom. His fame as a great traditional healer was respected as far as Lesotho. He was known for his skill to perform magic, medication and spells. Above that he was able to deal severely with witches and sorcerers who caused trouble within the community.

While resident in Johannesburg, a Lesotho Chief heard about his fame and invited him to visit his Chiefdom to help him to solve the problem he was encountering at his village. After Matome had successfully, through his knowledge of spells, medication and healing process, did what he was requested to do, he was honoured with a girl to be his wife, as well as cattle and a place to establish himself as headman. The place where he lived in Lesotho was named Mashai, meaning Shai's mother or wife, in recognition to his wife. As culture allowed, he had other additional women as his wives. Matome, died in Lesotho using Shai as his surname, which surname still rule supreme there to this day.

This unit, like other units, boasts of a number of businessmen and women, medical doctors, graduates, advocates, politicians, authors, and many other important people. For instance the late Matome Shai Ragoboya was a school principal and had written seven books; his son, Mokantiana Moses Shai Ragoboya was also a school principal and lecturer at the University of Limpopo; Nakampe Lincoln Shai was a principal and Mayor of Thabazimbi; Matome Mikiele Shai was a businessman; Masilo Koranta Shai Seshai and his son, Ngwako Gabriel were businessmen; Booyi Phillip Makeke Seshai Shai was an administrator; Advocate Isaac Shai; M. V. Shai, the author of Diphororo Tsa Bophelo and many more books. The name 'Matome' dominates nearly all households from this unit and beyond.

MMOLA UNIT

Mmola clans are the offspring of candle wives of most chiefs of Batubatse communities. The surname, Mmola, originated through one princess, Letlaka, the daughter of one the earliest Batubatse chiefs. Princess Letlaka was unmarried but she gave birth to an illegitimate son, known as Mohleng, with Prince Skosana, the son of another Ndebele tribal chief. Princess LetIaka and Prince Skosana never stayed together as husband and wife. She remained part of the Batubatse tribe, while she met Skosana at their secret place. For this reason Mohleng didn't use Skosana as his surname, but Shai. Mohleng enjoyed hunting and once told his mother that he dreamed of a large animal. She did not understand what the boy was telling her and took no notice. One day the boy, while hunting, came across a dead giraffe in the bush. It was too heavy to carry and when he returned home to tell his mother, she informed the elders of the Royal House. They immediately organized a search party to accompany Mohleng on his long journey to the site where he supposedly came across the dead animal. When they arrived at the scene several days later, they indeed found a dead giraffe, which was already decomposing (mmola). Since then the boy and his mother's family have been known as the Mmola family. Because of the bravery shown by Mohleng, the Royal House decided to look at Mmola's family when selecting candle wives.

When the Batubatse tribe lefts theTubatse area (Burgersfort and Steelpoort) the Mmola section also joined them and they settled for generations at the present Makalali farm near the present Sekororo. Part of Mmola section left Sekororo and stayed at Bokgaga under Kgoshi Maake and Sejabeng under Kgoshi Maupa Maake who subsequently made their leader one of his headmen. Those who remained at Makalali later returned to Burgersfort and Steelpoort area and got scattered all over neighbouring places.

The only known traditional leader of this section of Batubatse tribe at Ga-Maupa was Mabopa Diale Lucas Mmola. Upon his death the leadership went to his son Matome Johannes Mmola. After Matome's death everything concerning succession came to a stop.

No one came forward to take the leadership and the Mmola group did not want to talk much about them. Some of this group of people can still be traced in large numbers from various places such as Sekororo, Mametja, Bolobedu at Ga-Matswi, Mohlakone and Polasene, Ga-Sekgopo, Bellevue, Ga-Mamabolo, Bodupe- their secret ancestral place of worship (dithokoleng) near Duiwelskloof (Modjadjiskloof), Malokele, Modubeng, Burgersfort, Steelpoort, Moroke and many other places.

MATLOU UNIT

From Ga-Mampa the Batubatse arrived at a place suitable for agriculture called Lekgwareng-La- Malatji. Tefo remained there ploughing the land while Mabine proceeded on with a group of hunters of his circumcision regiment. A rumour that Kgoshi Sekhukhune was still after him again, reached Tefo, who then decided to leave the place. By then they had enough mealies to live on during their journey. A certain man from Shai family was having much more mealies than all of them and had manufactured a unique number of special granaries (storehouses for threshed grain) called "Matlou" (singular is Letlou-granary) in which to store his mealies. He did not wish to continue with a journey and had decided to remain behind. With his decision to stay behind he effectively removed himself temporarily from Batubatse of Shai group and was then on referred to by a different name, Matlou. People stopped calling him Shai. Among the Batubatse, the Matlou sub-clan came into being because of this very same man who did not move with the tribe, but followed them later.

MPHAGE UNIT

The Batubatse people have dispersed over a vast area of Southern Africa largely as a result of certain historical factors. Succession to the chieftainship lies within a royal descent group. Membership of the dynasty was transmitted only through the male sex. This system coupled with the system of polygyny, resulted in the chief having a number of sons who might make strong claim to the chieftainship. To overcome this difficulty one son was designated as the heir to the throne and eliminated all other sons of the chief as ineligible. The ineligibles thought that they were just being overlooked or sidelined. Ultimately they were able to express their natural desire for political office by seceding from the dynastic royal unit and attempted to establish their own royal units (kgoros), which gave them a measure of independence and new status without disrupting and splitting the well-oiled original tribe.

When there was dissatisfaction regarding the restructured Shayi or Shai Royal House at Tsubye/Maakene, a number of mature sons of the chief decided to leave the place without bloodshed. One such son of Chief Shayi was Mphage Shayi, who left at night with his family. He journeyed along the Drakensberg Mountains after crossing the Lepelle (Olifants) River and ended up settling along Lewalemagodi, Rotseng and Matlabong Mountains, covering the area known today as Leboeng, not far from Ohrigstad. There he was found by another section of Batubatse that left Maakene after him, however this other section left him and proceeded to the present Mapulaneng district. Another account state that Mphage's family was part of Mmanyaba section that left him at Leboeng on their way to Mudubeng. The whole area of Leboeng was still unoccupied by then.

After a few years the children of Mateu Motubatse, a member of Batubatse community from Gautswane, joined him. The wife of one of Mateu Motubatse's siblings, at a later stage, was Mayor of the Greater Tubatse Municipality and her son, Mosinki Justice Motubatse, is a magistrate at Lulekane Court near Phalaborwa. Presently Nkwana, Moraba and Molapo, traditional leaders, live together with some of Batubatse people there and are, separately, in control of certain areas. How this came to be is not clear.

He was known to have had more than one wife but it is unknown now how many. His only known son, Mosomedi (senior), was married and fathered Morebudi (d), Sodi (s), Kgopamoshodi (s), Motlanalo (d), Mantsana (d) and Magopalo (d). Sodi had three wives, Monawane Monashane from Segorong, Tigane Mathulatjatjing from Gautswane and Mamokwale Malepe from Maatshokgeng at Leboeng. From his first wife Sodi fathered Tshabakwane which meant "we ran away from a certain place", Morakeng which meant that "we arrived at a new place", Seyalenaga which meant "we wandered with the country" and Molata which meant that "I followed all of them". He also had four daughters from his second wife and five children, three daughters and two sons, from his third wife. Mosomedi passed on at Leboeng.

At some stage Kgopamoshodi left Leboeng to settle at Makouke, Seraganeng, and died there. His wife came from the Malepe clan and their children were Mongene, Machubeng, Motjatji, Mokibela, Mashishimale, Nnoi, Moholoholo and Papa. Mokibela was born at Makouke village near the confluence of Olifants (Lepelle) and Steelpoort (Tubatse) rivers and passed on at Shakung, near Moroke. Mashishimale passed on at Mabotja village towards Penge near Burgersfort. Sodi, Kgopamoshodi, their siblings and their children gave birth to a number of siblings which increased Mphage's unit. These siblings scattered to different areas though keeping a close to each other. Two sons of Mokibela, Mosomedi (junior) and Matome, are some of those siblings and had provided valuable information concerning Mphage's unit. Sodi was one of Mosomedi (senior's) children who became a famous rich stock farmer at Leboeng.

While travelling around the area, before becoming wealthy, Sodi came across some good grazing land with sufficient water, well-suited to livestock and agricultural production, as well as being the habitat of many wild animals. He settled with his whole family here, some distance from his father and other siblings. It took him two years to establish Lekaung farm. He also opened a shop there which gave him income which he gave to his brother, Kgopamoshodi, to purchase cattle. He also slaughtered wild game to provide biltong. Ultimately his herd of cattle increased considerably. Kgopamoshodi's son Mokibela and Sodi's son Seyalenaga together looked after those cattle. Sodi died at Leboeng and was buried there. Both Sodi and Kgopamoshodi were brave men who maintained and made Mphage's unit to remain united and be together until he was no more and thereafter. His idea of becoming an independent traditional leader did not materialize. Mphage Shia passed on at Leboeng and his mortal remains were buried there.

MUTSWI/MOTSWI UNIT

Very little is known of the history of Motswi section of the Batubatse tribe from the earlier generation before they seceded from the parent group, Shai/Shayi. It is not known who led this section during their secession; however, what is clear is that their earlier ancestor was Mutswi or Motswi Shayi, who appeared to have been one of the senior members of the royal family. This might be confirmed by the fact that his name is mentioned in the Shai praise poem. Probably this section seceded from Shai very early after arrival at Maakene, hence only few of them remember having settled at the vicinity of this place. It is understood that when they left Maakene/Tsubye they were less than five families, which implies that they comprised barely fifty (50) people and could only have occupied a small part of the area where they settled. This group eventually gave rise to the now increased Motswi sub-clan.

From 1908 to 2006 death notices of some 90 members of the Motswi unit were recorded in the South African Death Records, indicating the increase membership of this sub-clan. Among them with their birth year opposite each name, we have Mankwana and Matapa in 1908, Lobela Gilbert in 1924, Šai John in 1928, and many others. By 2014, 310 people had Motswi as their surname in South Africa.

SEANEGO UNIT

Seanego Shai was the younger brother of Masetla (Maasetla) Makutuma Shai. The origin of his sub-clan could be traced back from Bolebye near the present town of Gravelotte. Seanego's family was one of the ten families that left Tsubye under the leadership of Masetla Makutuma Shai, the younger brother of Matome Shai. He was also a well-known traditional healer. With the passing of time his family grew up into a larger group. When mining activities commenced in 1920, the Batubatse of Masetla Maenetja's people, known also as the Balebye tribe, scattered over a large area around from Gravelotte. Seanego Senior, though very old by then, and the Mokgomola families were allocated the land along Tshapare Mountain (Granville and Begin). In fact members of the Mokgomola family formed part of the Seanego Senior group. One of his grandsons was named Seanego Junior after him.

Seanego Junior's family later left Tshapare and settled at Maleele near Dzumeri. Other members of the Seanego unit broke away from the senior household of Masetla and went in different directions. At the time of their departure they used Seanego as their surname, hence the origin of the surname of Seanego. Why the unit took on this surname is not clear. It might have been because they lived at Bolebye or from a distinguishing physical trait. It was not unusual for a last name to be altered when an ancestor entered a new territory. Understanding where your ancestors lived, how they worked, and what they did in their leisure time may give one a better appreciation of one's heritage.

Ancestry research revealed that the first known Shai member to use Seanego as a surname was Monametji Matheka Frans in 1901, Matome Piet in 1906, Mothepa Emma in 1007, Setaki in 1908, Ngoako Alfred in 1910, Ngako Jacob in 1910, Kgabu in 1914 and many others. From 1880 to 2007 death notices of more than 600 members of the Seanego unit were recorded in the South African Death Records, indicating the increase membership of this sub-clan. Some of Seanego people can be located in other parts of the country through research into the records of passenger arrivals, naturalization, border crossings, and emigration and passport applications and even convict transportation.

The remnants of his people are to be found in all part of the country. It is presumed that Seanego Senior passed away and was laid to rest at Tshapare. There are no two authorities that give similar accounts of the successors of Seanego Senior for the previous generation. Only the most likely account will be given, as far as this could be deducted from oral information, without discussing at any length the various points of view. It seems that, at some stage Seanego (senior) was succeeded by his son, whose name is unknown, to lead the unit, followed by Monametji, born in 1880. After him Seanego (Junior) took over the leadership before he went to settle at Maleele.

Among the Batubatse of Seanego unit there were several legendary figures. One was Charles Seanego, a lawyer who spent fifteen years practising in North West Province before his father passed on. He was the only child at home, and although he was reluctant to go into business, the dread of watching his father's legacy, accumulated from the early sixties, slip down the drain worried him. So he forthwith took charge of his father's chain of general dealerships and service stations. Together with his teacher wife, he successfully managed the family enterprise and in two years he added two more service stations to his steadily-growing portfolio as well as establishing Seanego Arms and Securities.

In 1996 Molatelo Christina Seanego, a graduate of the University of Venda, wrote an 86-page book titled Problems Encountered by Foster Parents in Bochum (Northern Province). Malapile Aaron Seanego, a graduate from the same institution in the School of Health Services, Department of Nutrition, had written a 234-page book in 2008 titled An Assessment of the Dietary Patterns of Adult Women of the Greater Letaba Municipality in Limpopo Province. Another prominent figure from the family was Noko Seanego, Municipal Manager of Mbombela. He was accused of misconduct after appointing specialized security officers for the municipality but was cleared of the charge. The individuals who had attempted to manipulate the process failed to benefit.

MOHOLOHOLO UNIT

As indicated above, succession to the traditional leadership among the Batubatse tribe was from the male descendant of the royal house. Through the system of polygyny, the chief would have a number of sons who might have strong claims to the chieftainship. Those who were overlooked or sidelined often seceded from the dynastic royal unit and established their own royal units (kgoros), which gave them a measure of independence and new status without disrupting or splitting the original tribe. They would go out and bravely fight to overcome some weaker communities in order to attain their new status.

Moholoholo Shayi/Shai, also known as Poi or Booyi, was the son of Mashabakgole one of the senior councilors (magota/makota) of Shayi's Royal House. Mashabakgole passed away at Maakene/Tsubye and was buried there. His wife is unknown. Moholoholo, whose praise name was Mamaseka, was their eldest son who wished for independence and new status. As a young boy he was known for his bravery and being an impudent person among the graduates of his circumcision regiment. He enjoyed fighting to the bitter end and would start a fight with any of his peers for no apparent reason. Accordingly few boys of his age wanted to associate with him. His fighting behaviour caused his to be loggerhead with other members of the community. Nevertheless he had many friends.

As an adult, Moholoholo left Maakene/Tsubye unceremoniously at night with his family and several supporters. He went in the direction of the present Mapulaneng district. After crossing the Lepelle (Olifants) River he settled in a verdant rain forest on the slopes of the majestic North Eastern Drakensberg along the Blyde River Canyon (largest green canyon in the world), with a number waterfalls nearby. The area was still unoccupied though there is evidence that early stone-age San once lived in the canyon. Being mountainous the place provided him with good security consisting of dense bush, forbidding caves and overhanging rocks. He knew the area like the palm of his hand. When attacked he would hide himself and his people inside one of those fearsome caves or he would ascend the mountain and roll rocks against his enemies. The land was large enough for habitation with plenty of water. He never lost contact with other sections of Batubatse staying in Mapulaneng, Leboeng and nearby areas.

During their first battle against the Swazis, the Mapulana people came across Moholoholo while seeking refuge there. He guided them to safety along the mountains and showed them how to roll rocks down against their enemies. Following his advice, the Mapulana crushed the Swazis to their first defeat. In the next encounter with the Swazis, Moholoholo and the Malepe people again sided with the Mapulana and once again by applying his war methods the Mapulana warriors inflicted a second defeat to the Swazis. The final and decisive battle, known as the Battle of Moholoholo, was fought in 1864 at

Mariepskop, a mountain named after the Mapulana chief, Maripi Mashile, who led his men to victory against the Swazis in the Blyde River Canyon. Moholoholo and his people played an important role during these fierce battles and to commemorate his name, the forest between the mountains was named Moholoholo.

This forest is now a private game reserve with a bush camp overlooking the magnificent Marepe (Malepe) Mountain which forms part of the Drakensberg. Within this wooded area many wild animals come to quench their thirst at the waterholes shaded by the canopy of large tree, under the watchful eyes of monkeys and birds. Today Moholoholo Forest Camp is known for its beautiful waterfalls (diphororo) and is ideally situated for day excursions to Kruger Park and Blyde River Canyon. It offers visitors a chance to meet anything from rhino to aardvark and to experience the lore of the African bush.

Moholoholo Shayi was a traditional healer and had two official wives; Nateng, from the Mmola sub-clan of the Batubatse tribe, and Madithepa from the Maile family. He also had a number of secondary wives or concubines. From his first wife, Nateng, he fathered three daughters, Maathabana, Mosibudi Mmamokgadi and Mmashai, and two sons, Mashabakgole and Legaro Pasopa. For reasons unknown his second wife returned to her parents leaving him with two children whose names cannot now be remembered. After the war many people were familiar with the area and Moholoholo, now an old man, realized that his presence in the forest was no longer secure. So he departed and settled with his family at Sedawa, Ga-Mametja, where his grand- and great-grandchildren could still be traced. His ambition of becoming an independent traditional leader and of acquiring a new status did not materialize, but within the Batubatse communities his legacy is recorded in the Battle of Moholoholo and the Moholoholo Forest. He died at Sedawa village where he had a big family and was buried at the nearby dense forest on the Sedakwe Hill.

His first daughter, Maathabana, married a member of the Malepe family while Mmashai married into the Mahlako family and gave birth to Pitsane. Mosibudi was apparently unmarried. Mashabakgole, named after his grandfather, was a traditional healer like his father Moholoholo. He was married to Mahlona from the Moloto family at Bokgaga and was given a necklace (pheta ya thaga) to symbolize that his wife came from a dignified family house. His ancestors blessed him with five children from his principal wife, Podudu, Sereko Sheleng, Maatloo, Motsakwe and Sello. He also had other children from his concubines or secret wives. Moholoholo's youngest son, Legaro Pasopa, was married to Dingwati from the Malepe family and fathered seven children, Ledwaba, Legashe, Taile, Shoroane, Maphaba and Maalabi. Moholoholo's great-grandchildren such as Makhoo, Boshego, Ledwaba and Sello are intrepid men who are presently striving to keep the Moholoholo unit together. Both Mashabakgole and Legaro died at Sedawa and their mortal remains were also buried in the forest of Sedakwe Hill.

*   *   *

12
MY VIEWS OF RELIGION

What was the origin of life was a question that bothered the ancients as much as it bothers moderns today. Our ancestors had no science or written history – just their imagination. It is exciting to stand on the threshold of a concept but not to know where it originated except to guess and make predictions. How will these differ from one's preconceived notion and which of these predictions will stand up to one's own experiences and observations? You look up to the sky and see clouds, darkness, the moon, stars, other planets, unidentified objects, without reaching the end of it. You look down at the earth and see mountains, trees, rocks, water, animals and many other things. You dig down and go beneath the surface of land and sea find many things without reaching the end. Some speak of the existence of the so-called heaven which none of the living beings ever reached.

What will be discussed in this chapter may bring robust criticism, condemnation, censure, vigorous reactions and the like. This will be so because we understand things differently, but everyone has the right to freedom of speech and his or her views about life. Equally anyone can oppose these observations but any criticism will not dampen our determination to reveal the truth that can be proved with evidence. What can be asserted without evidence may be dismissed without evidence.

Earth is the only planet known to support life, and its natural features are the subjects of many fields of science. Earth, through Nature, has evolved through geological and biological processes that have left traces of original conditions. According to the scientists, the planet Earth is estimated to have been formed 4.54 billion years ago from the solar nebula (the evolution of the solar system) along with the sun and other planets. The moon was formed roughly twenty million years later. The origin of life on Earth is not well understood but research indicates that the first life on earth in the form of bacteria dates back about 3.2 or 3.5 billion years ago. Only several million years ago a species of small ape gained the ability to stand upright. Anatomically modern humans first arose about two hundred thousand years ago in Africa and developed more rapidly than any previous life form. Species that were unable to adapt to the changing environment and competition from other forms became extinct. However, the fossil record retains evidence of many of these older species. Through Nature the current fossil and DNA evidence shows that all existing species can trace a continual ancestry back to the first primitive life forms. Fossils are the preserved remains or traces of animals, plants, and other organisms from the remote past.

When and how our lineage then dispersed out of Africa has long proven controversial but evidence had suggested that an exodus took place some 60 000 years ago. All the population groups outside Africa are descended from a small band of human that left Africa, probably 50 000 to 80 000 years ago. In a sense, we are all Africans. If modern man is two hundred thousand years old and Christian religion only about six thousand years ago because it was not until man garnered the communication skill, and the intellect to ask the proverbial question of all time, *"Why are we here?"* Without the science and knowledge of the cosmos we have today, people only understood one answer…. creation. They then deemed there must be a creator, and proof….god was born. If a creator existed, who created the creator? Nature.

This belief system was uncontested for thousands of years -- thousands of years of parents indoctrinating children into this belief of a god. Four hundred years from now humanity will look back and laugh at a belief that an invisible magician who lived in the sky made everything from nothing with a nod of his head. Perhaps we should find interesting that there is one religion which believes that matter is eternal and had always existed. And, yes, the laws of Nature are also eternal, and the Biblical God has always been subjected to those laws, thus He cannot do good things for others and fail to prevent bad things to happen to others. Hence one may correctly say humanity would be better off without belief in Biblical God but to Unknown Creator God, Nature or Ptah.

The celestial maps show that the universe is a living organism consisting of parts that are inter- related, inter-connected and inter-dependent. The earth and humanity are parts of this organism. If this assertion could be true, then this organism is Nature since no one knew who created humanity. Most scientists believed and believe that our universe never had a beginning. They believed and believe that mass, space and energy had always existed. Science is unable to tell us what or who caused the universe to begin. To be correct physicists calculated that for life to exist, gravity and other forces of "Nature" needed to be just right or our universe could not exist.

According to Wikipedia, the free encyclopedia, a miracle is an event not explicable by natural or scientific law. Theologians say that Biblical God and Ancestors regularly work through created nature yet are free to work without or against it as well. This assumption is incorrect because no one can work against Nature. The word "miracle" is often used to characterise any beneficial event that is statistically unlikely but not contrary to law of Nature, such as surviving a natural disaster, or simply a "wonderful" occurrence, regardless of likelihood, such as a birth. Other miracles might be the survival of an illness diagnosed as terminal, escaping a life-threatening situation or beating the odds. Some coincidence may be seen as miracles. Everything done or not done by human beings including miracles is a product of Nature. Anyone who does miracles derives "miraculous power" from Nature. How this "miraculous power" is derived from Nature is debatable.

C.S. Lewis, a 20th-century Christian, said that a miracle is something that comes totally out of the blue, in line with what Batubatse and other African tribes believed. If for millions or thousands of years a woman can become pregnant by sexual intercourse with a man, if she were to become pregnant without a man, it would be a miracle or super-miracle. It has been said that the word "supernatural", first used : 1520 – 30AD, refer to that which is not subject to the law of physics or, more figuratively, that which is said to exist above Nature. This is a wrong and shalow interpretation of the word because there is nothing beyond Nature. We may have super something, but all should be considered to be the creatures of Nature.

A supernatural order through or by human beings is more than a miraculous way of producing natural effect, or a notion of relative superiority within the created world, or the necessary concurrent of our Ancestors, God, Allah, Camagu, Ganesha, Anu, Jah, Jahweh and all the deities that our people believe in in the universe. It is an effect on series of effects substantially and absolutely below Nature, not beyond. We survived and sometimes didn't survive dangerous situations and circumstances because this, naturally, had to happen. A miracle is sometime associated with magic. The two words might appear similar in their connotation, but strictly speaking there is difference between the two. They can both be defined as incidents that somehow make us wonder how something happened.

It is generally believed that magic is the act of human being whereas a miracle is the act of the Biblical God or any divine power like Ancestor's spirit. Magic happens in front of your very eyes much to your delight and astonishment. One would appreciate the skill of the magician, praise and applaud him/her. Miracles do not involve the use of energy, but draw your astonishment and delight. A miracle can be proven otherwise sometimes. For example, think of someone considered dead staring to breathe again. Magic can be used for fun and is not real, whereas miracles were not just for fun and are real. A magic can be used to deceive and is intended to entertain us and show us the magician's talent, whereas miracles are never used to deceive and their purpose was never to entertain an audience or to demonstrate how talented a person was.

It is crucial to stress right from here that until the 20th century people didn't call themselves pagan to discribe the religion they practiced. Paganism is a term that developed among the Christian Community of southern Europe during the late antiquity to describe religions other than their own or Judaism and throughout history the term, as it is understood today, was generally a label used in a derogatory sense. The precise boundaries for the late antiquity period are a matter of debate. The Jewish or Israelites, like any other community, had their own Ancestors such as Abraham, Jacob, Israel, Jesus Christ and many others. The religion of the Jews of Israel, Judaism, was based on the Mosaic Code proclaimed in the first five books of the Bible. Primitive Christianity arose out of the Jewish culture and tradition.

We should remind ourselves that it is a well-known fact that it was Paul of Tarsus, a man who had never himself set eyes on Jesus Christ, who was the founder of Christianity, not Jesus as is widely but wrongly believed. It was Paul who made up a religion for Jesus' followers to follow. Up until the time Jesus died Christianity, as a religion independent from Judaism did not exist, yet people lived badly and happily like today. In its origin, Christianity was a development of the ancient Jewish faith and is founded upon the teaching of Jesus Christ. Its doctrine was immediately appealing and by the end of the 4th century AD it had emerged as the dominant religion. Church leaders then concluded that the organised Christian Church had a unique calling to give leadership to a fallen world, which had not fallen. It could not be subordinate to other interests, and thus expected that this priestly Christian authority should be respected as higher than others. This kind of thinking caused considerable conflict within the church-state relations in the Middle Ages.

Most people today regard Christmas Day as the birthday of Jesus Christ. It is not. History shows that the 25th of December was popularised as the date of Christmas, not because Jesus Christ was born on that day, but because the date was already popular in pagan religious celebration as the birth of the unconquered sun from the rock and was celebrated anciently as the birth of the Persian deity or Pagan Sun God, Mithra. History, further, shows that Christmas celebration predates Jesus Christ by many centuries. Some literatures notes that Christmas has its roots in the Winter Solstice, the day where there is the shortest time between the sun rising and the sun setting. Pagans had a festival on the 25th December to celebrate and worship the sun for winning over the darkness of winter.

Given the difficulties and desire to bring pagans into Chritianity, the fixing of the date of Christmas as the 25th of December was a compromise with paganism. The word 'Christmass', shortened Christmas, comes from the Mass services of Christ, who died for Christians and then came back to life. In AD 274 Emperor Aurelian of Rome declared it to be the "birthday of the Invincible Sun". Many Orthodox and Coptic churches, like in Ethopia, celebrate Christmas on the 6th or 7th of January, which is when December 25th would have been on the Orthodox or Julian calender.

Nowhere in the New Testament do we see Jesus' disciples observing his birthday or Christmas or teach anyone to keep this pagan celebration. Christmas is, in fact an affront of Jesus Christ. The day is a holiday found nowhere in the Bible. No one knew the real birthday of Jesus. His birth probably happened slightly earlier before the year 1 AD, between 2 BC and 7BC. It is difficult to determine the first time anyone celebrated the 25th of December as Christmas, but historians generally agree that it was sometime during the 4th century-some 300 years after Jesus Christ's death. The first recorded date of Christmas being celebrated on this day was 336 AD during the time of the Roman Emperor, Contantine. A few years later, Pope Julius I officially declared that the birth of Jesus would be celebrated on the 25th December. The date was chosen because it was already a popular pagan holiday celebrating the birth of the Sun God.

The 25th of December marked the birth of our primal African ancestors and all sacred kings of pre- Christian times and was the celebration of the yearly First Fruit Festival. Although the exact date is unknown, the new moon in December enjoined the Batubatse community, too, to begin preparations for the yearly First Fruit Celebrations. It is clear that the Roman Imperial Church appropriated this date and used it to celebrate the unknown birth date of Jesus Christos of Nazarene. This is supported by the fact that the counting of a year from the first century of our Common Era (CE), after the birth of Jesus, starts on the 1st day of the 1st month (January) of the 1st century (CE) and not the 25th day of the 12th month (December) of the 1st century (CE) which was supposed to be if Jesus

Christos was born on the 25th of December.

Jesus was probably not born in Bethlehem and he certainly wasn't born to a vigin, both the two fictions were made up explicitly to fulfil Old Testament prophecies. For this reason Jesus was just a prophet for the guidance of Jews or Israelis only and not for the rest of mankind. In this regard see the Book of Mathews, Chapter 15: Verse 24 which Jesus state that: "I was sent only to the lost sheep of the house of Israel". Again read the Book of John, Chapter 4: Verse 22 where Jesus said to the non-Jewish woman from Samaria: "You worship what you do not know; we worship what we know, for salvation is from the Jews".

There is nothing wrong if they talk and show respect to their ancestors in many ways and believe in one God above them, but above their Biblical God there is Nature of all things.

Several religious authors throughout history have advanced the notion that the Biblical God is consistently in character with the Devil. To Christians He is supposed to be all good and all powerful. If that is the case he would not want evil and suffering to exist and would then be able to remove them, yet evil and suffering exist in the world. Religious authors make the case that the Biblical God is a divine force that wreaks sufferings, death and destruction. This is in line with what some of the Batubatse are thinking. They, further, argue that if the Biblical God was good enough, powerful and does righteous things, he could not let male adults molest innocent female kids, he could not let innocent women being raped, he could not let others become more rich and others more poor with nothing to eat, he could not let corruption go on and on while people are suffering, the list is endless. The Biblical God of the believers appear to be less awe-inspiring than Nature itself, and thus not worthy of praising.

The Bible make it clear that the Biblical God is not the only one who works miracles, the Devil too does. The Devil and demons can also perform natural signs, and their miracles are considered to be the major part of the deception, practical joke, mischievous or discreditable acts of the last day. Which last day is the Bible talking about? There will be no such thing as the last day. Billions and millions of years had gone past and billion and millions of people had died with no sign that they will rise up to live again. No one will ever produce facts to guarantee that the last day will ever come. All what people and religious books say or predict about the end of the Earth, resurrection, revival from inactivity or decay and what will happen on the last day are just speculations, which speculations may be true or false.

All what is being said about the Devil is just a distortion of the truth. Whether Biblical God and the Devil actually ever existed or still exist is a matter of endless debate among human beings. Because of fear people will always talk about Biblical God and Devil or Satan. Each person's last day is when he or she dies, whether good or bad. Religion and faith are the basic thing for us to create myths. The word myth has several meanings. It may mean a person or thing having only imaginary or unverifiable existence. The word can be used pejoratively by both religious and non-religious people. People do believe in myths.

Religion is an organised collection of beliefs, cultural systems, and world views that relate humanity to an order of existence. Many religions have narratives, symbols, and sacred histories that aim to explain the meaning of life, the origin of life, or the universe. In all these myths are attached. The origin of religion is uncertain. African traditional religion encompasses the traditional religious beliefs of people in Africa. Religion may include superstition or make use of magical thinking. People look at their faith together with religion as a source of guidance and inspiration.

The English word faith is thought to date from 1200-1250. Faith is confidence or trust in a person or thing or a belief not based on proof. It is a firm belief in something for which there is no evidence. It may also refer to a particular system of religious belief. The term itself has numerous conotations and is used in many different ways, often depending on context. We only speak of faith when we wish to substitute emotions for evidence. Where there is evidence no one speak of faith. For instance we do not speak of faith that three and three are six.

No faith can be defended rationally, and each therefore is defended by propaganda. Evolutionary biologist, Richard Dawkins, had said "Faith is a belief without evidence; a process of non-thinking". He went on to "state that it is a practice that only degrades our understanding of the natural world by allowing anyone to make a claim about nature that is based solely on their personal thoughs, and possibly distorted exception, that does not require testing against nature, has no ability to make reliable and consistant predictions, and is not subject to peer review".

Dawkins, just like ancient and some present Batubatse, contends that "a supernatural creater almost certainly does not exist and that religious faith is a delusion - a fixed false belief held in the face of strong contradictory evidence" . He says the existence of the Biblical God is a scientific hypothesis like any other and that the theory of a universe without this God is preferable to the theory of a universe with this same God. This is so because in the name of this Biblical God, the Bible and other religious books people are being deceived, robbed of their possessions and gruesome bad things does happen daily in His watch and He does nothing. Millions of people pray to this mythical God daily for good things to come their way, but get nothing. Surprisingly those who does not even pray for this mythical God, but work hard, get what they want easy and simple.

Some people are now super-wealthy at the expense of super-poor people at his watch, yet more people keep their faith and hope that a miracle will come out somewhere to save them. Dawkins considers faith as "one of the world's great evil", adding that to be an atheist should be considered praisewothy and that atheists are free-thinkers who should be proud, not apologetic, because atheism is evidence of a healthy and independent mind, and is based in the belief that there is no God. Atheism is the position that affirms the non-existence of God and proposes positive disbelief rather than mere suspention of belief. Dawkins' thinking cannot be disputed. This is so because no simple God who is capable of sending intelligible signals to billion of people simultaneously can at the same time receives messages from all of them simultaneously. It cannot be.

Religion and faith always exist together. On one hand religion comes into being as a result of faith and survives, also, because of it. If everyone lost faith in a religion, that religion would cease to exist. Religion helps communities by teaching morality, nurturing its culture, and making people compassionate towards one another, as well as the environment around them. On the other hand faith begins with belief. When we start trusting someone or something faith begins. It helps us to hold on to something that we believe in, though it may be irrational to others. We should let our children learn about different faiths, let them notice their incompatibility, and let them draw their own conclution about the consequences of that incompatibility and finally let them make up their own minds when they are old enough to do so.

We should not indoctrinate our children. Let us teach them how to think for themselves, how to evaluate evidence, and how to disagree with us. We should know and understand that faith can be very very dangerous, and deliberately to implant it into the vulnerable mind of an innocent child was a grievous wrong. Religion and faith survives from generation to generation because something else is surviving. This something else appears to be the concept that children are taught to listen to and trust what their parents tell them. If parents say something is true, the children believe. The trust and obedience that children tend to naturally have is vital to their survival. A child is likely to believe what parents say, even if the child does not completely understand.

Certain children have been indoctrinated with the idea that silly myths are to be taken seriously. Batubatse children, like any other children, grew up, procreate, and, having learned from their own parents, continue similar ideas. Children have a right not to be forced to be fed bullshit by anyone, even parents who believe they have the right to teach them what they want. Because of the recent rights that Batubatse children had and the emergence of biblical and other religions, some have lost the idea that Nature, not god, is the father of everything. Christian and Muslim religions were gross religious errors to many African children when they grew up. If this means we are going to be called heathens, then so be it.

The creation of heavens and Earth and other planets through Nature was the establishment of the entire order of creation, the development of the Earth to prepare it for living creatures, and the forming of the living creatures which were to inhabit it. No one knows the beginning and the end of the creation. Of course anyone of us may come out with his or her own thinking, view or opinion about this and write down, just like those who wrote the Bible, Quran, Book of Mormon and other religious books. People will exercise their rights to agree or disagree with him or her. We don't desire to insult anyone, but we will be damned if we are going to stand by and do nothing while lame-brained clerics attempt to harm our children.

Many people will be deceived by religious innocent-looking-but-deadly enemies of righteousness and other religious institutions. Those who had elected the mythical Biblical God as the creator have made a disastrous election. Don't forget this remark and be on guard. It is matter of life and death as provided by Nature. Whether one follow a particular religion or faith many things, good or bad, will naturally continues to disappear, while at the same time new things, good or bad, will naturally continues to emerge as has happened in the past with no ending. Nature needs no prayers, pleas, begging or requests. Tshimangadzo Benedict Daswa was a Venda man of Mbahe village who, because of his Christian faith, feared and respected the Biblical God. He was regarded by members of the Catholic Church, of which he was also a member, as a man of God.

Today he is considered as a sort of their Ancestor- a Saint- a holy or officially recognized person by his church as having won by exceptional holiness a high place in heaven and veneration on Earth. He is still to be declared a saint if he qualifies. He refused to contribute five rand (R5.00) for a sangoma to identify the "dark forces" behind lightning strikes in his village that had caused several huts to burn down. On the 2nd of February 1990 he was caught at a roadblock residents had erected and fled as they stone him. He tried to hide in a hut, but was cornered. After begging his attackers to spare his life and not succeeding, he prayed before a steel knobkerrie landed on his head and killed him.

His attackers continued pouring boiling water through his nostrils and ears despite the wellknown belief that a powerful God is always there to protect his children, particularly those who believe in Him. Daswa's uncle Tshipenga Matshikiri was later accused of being behind the lightning stories. For this he was hacked with pangas and died in flames after his house was set alight with him inside. Why these gruesome and disgusting murders? It was the Unknown Creator God or Nature. Without Nature nothing was made that has been made. No prayer, wish or request can avoid what the Unknown Creator God or Nature provides.

There are many false prophets, priests, pastures, believers and teachers in our present day who will deceive many people about God, Ancestors, Devil and other deities. They will interpret their dreams wrongly in order to start new churches. Though these people might claim to know and communicate the truth, they will be spreading lies. They will inspire fear in our minds making us to succumb to their false wishes, hoping that we will be saved on the unknown and non-existance last day. They will do everything available to them to defend their lies and point of view. These people are really hungry, dangerous, selfish and ferocious wolves dressed in sheep's skins. Like any other person many of them want to become rich. Many are very popular, good speakers and friendly.

Some can even produce miraculous signs and accurately predict an event. False prophets, priests, pasters, believers and teachers of religions speak with conviction sweating, since they expect their lying words to be fulfilled. Stories have been reported in some parts of Africa, South Africa included, about how religious leaders with names like Bishop, General Overseer, Daddy, Papa, Mummy and many others train young ministers, pay them good salaries and send them to establish branches of their churches in a foreign countries, not necessarily to spread gospel, but to generate income. These ministers are then asked by their churches to collect offerings and tithes and send this money to church headquarters. In most instances, these ministers or priests are sent to countries with a booming economy so they can send good returns back home. The river water only rolls where the stones sleep, poor people.

This group of people has natural powers to predict success and victory in the name of Biblical God at the expense of our Ancestors. Of course, it is acknowledged, that certain religious practices can reduce stress or cure certain ailments. The world benefits much from all different religious beliefs. The personification and elevation of one aspect of the divine as the only God leads to the births of a multiplicity of conflicting spiritual traditions. Let us not upset the Ancestors. Belief in single Biblical God is a delusion- an aggressively-held belief that is evidently false. Single Biblical God and Devil or Satan never existed among the Batubatse people.

The people of Israel had no difficulty in acknowledging the ability and the willingness their Super Ancestor (Biblical God) to perform acts of power on their behalf and this is reflected throughout the Old Testament. These mighty acts of power were revealed in Christ (another Ancestor), who in his ministry, and later through that of his disciples in Palestine, not South Africa, and the apostles throughout showed his victory over the power of sin to distort and ruin. These mighty acts we find recorded throughout the New Testament. According to their culture, belief and religion, Christians believe that their God is the father of creation, while other people, according to their culture, belief and religion believe that the Unknown Creator God, Nature or Ptah, is the father of creation. Thomas Pain, one of the Founding Fathers of the American Revolution, wrote "All the tales of miracles, with which the Old and the New Testaments are filled, are fit only for imposters to preach and fools to believe". A number of Batubatse people subscribe to these remarks.

The existence of the Devil cannot be divorced from this discussion. The Devil is sometimes called Dragon, Serpent, Lucifer, Heathen God, Satan, clever or knavish person, luckless or wretched person, wicked person, and many other names by deferrent denominations. It is believed in many religions, myths and culture to be a supernatural entity that is the personification of evil and the archenemy of Biblical God and Mankind. This interpretation may be correct only if the Devil is not considered supernatural since, as indicated above, there is nothing beyond Nature. The Batubatse had no such a thing as the Devil. While the Batubatse mainstream contains no overt concept of a Devil, Christianity and other religions have variously regarded the Devil as a rebellious fallen angel or jinn that tempts humans to sin. As such, the Devil is seen as an allegory that represent a crisis of faith, individualism, freewill, wisdom and enlightment.

In mainstream Christianity and Islam, God and Devil are usually portrayed as fighting over the souls of humans. The Devil is believed to command a force of evil spirits, commonly known as demons. Whether these assertions are true or not, the Batubatse regard that as the work of Nature since both God and Devil are its products. In the Bible, the Devil is represented as the one who brought death into the world. There is no evidence to support that. No one can bring forth hard facts about this allegation and no one can describe the physic of the Devil. Death and many other bad things has been there before the orgin of Christianity and other religions and continues to visit us despite the allegation of the existance of the socalled Almight God. Therefore to say the Devil, if ever He exist, was defeated at the cross cannot hold water. Those who goes on to allege that the Devil was defeated are motivated by forces of darkness brought by nature and nothing more.

According to the Bible, Quran and other religious books, Biblical God or Quranic Allah created Heavens and Earth. One may ask as to who saw these happenings and who created God or Allah if all these did not naturally come to light. There is no evidence to answer this question. None of us can describe the structure or image of Nature; however, God could be something like an object. An object can be described and be given a name. An object can be associated and connected to a particular Ancestor, depending upon an ethnic group of a particular society on Earth. No one should elevate his/her own Ancestor, God, Allah, Camagu, Ganesha, Anu, Jah, Jahweh and all other deities that our people believe in into the position or status of Unknown God or Nature, above other people's ancestors.

But if one gives the nameless Nature a name such as God or Unknown God one may understand, only if that person does not refer to the Biblical God worshiped by the Jews, Israelis and Christians because the God referred to in the Bible is the Ancestor of certain Jewish and Israelis community. If someone undermines someone's understanding of his or her own God, Ancestor or any deity subject to the will of Nature one may not let that undermining go by without any challenge.

Sometimes it is loath to speak ill of other deities and the dead, even when it comes to telling hurtful truths. Suffice to say that many rich and poor people and anointed and not anointed priests had left the Earth to their resting place in disgrace, incidentally not before they fulfill their promises or achieve anything, while others did the opposite and succeeded. On Earth we are just like an elephant in the room in a prolonged gestation that has lasted more than thirty six (36) months. When its due date arrives, there are fears that the elephant might actually give birth to a mouse. Such thoughts are the outcome of the Unknown God, Nature or Ptah. The truth is always a stranger than fiction in action. Many people today are misled because they lack information about who wrote the Bible. Bible is a collection of books written by different authors based on their religion and faith. Some people don't know what information to accept because the Bible has been rewritten and reinterpreted many times.

The plain fact of the Bible narrative is that the Jews went to Babylon barbarians and came back more civilized after about two generations. This is born from the fact that when the Jews had returned to Jerusalem from the rule of King Nebuchadnezzar ll in Babylon, they re-wrote the first five Books of the Old Testament by depending on their memory and gradually added other writings over the years. The Books contained a certain amount of unreliability because they depended on human memory. For instance on the flood myth Genesis 6:20 and 7:14-15 states that there were two of each kind of fowl and clean beast, yet Genesis 7:2-3 states they came in seven. How could Noah have gathered male and female of each kind when some species are asexual, hermaphrodites (having both male and female sex organs) and parthenogenetic (only females)? How can a literal interpretation be appropriate if the text is self-contradictory?

The Bible as we know it today does not contain all the Books it contained at first, and some of the Books it once contained were thrown out by priests who decided what the Bible should contain. The genesis myths in the Bible proposing that the world was created in six days, the story of Adam and Eve, the flood story about Noah Ark, and many others have been plagiarized or borrowed from past Egyptian and Mesopotamian myths by changing almost nothing but the heroes. If the Bible (or the Quran, the Book of Mormon) is contradictory and mistaken about many things and where we came from, how can we trust it to tell us where we're going? It is time for Christians, Muslims and Mormons people to recognize that the defense of this modern earth, flood-geology creationism, based on the Noah myth and other myths is simply not truthful and must be abandoned before harm is done. The task of trying to identify sources of Biblical myths is like trying to uncover origins of some crazy TV cartoons. If the Biblical God is omnipotent, why not kill what he wanted killed directly, than resorting to a roundabout method that requires innumerable additional miracles?

The atmospheric conditions of the Earth have been significantly altered from the original conditions by the presence of life-forms as indicated by scientists who got their knowledge of this information from Nature or Unknown God, which the Batubatse believed. Despite the wide regional variations in climate by latitude and other geographical factors, the long-term average global climate is quite stable or sometime not. All these are due to the miracles of Nature, which Nature can be referred to by different persons in different names such as countryside, flora, fauna, landscape, environment, creation, creator, earth, view, cosmos, world, macrocosm, generation, scenery, spirit, humor, mood, universe, classical, and many others. These names do not make a difference because Unknown God or Nature will remain so by any other name. A rose is still a rose by any other name.

When one studies Genesis in the Bible, one will become convinced that the book is not about human origin. Humans were already in existence before the book was written. The book is about the origin of Messianic expectation by certain group of people. It is about their faith in the promise that their creator made to their ancestors in Eden. Long before the emergence of people called Israel, ruler-priests controlled vast areas of the ancient world. They built kingdoms and at the center of their kingdoms they built temples and shrines where they worshiped their Unknown God, Maker of all things in heaven and earth. They practiced animal sacrifice and offered prayers with incense. They regarded water as the element of purification. They observed sacred laws and spread all over across the earth. The biblical injunction to multiply and spread across the earth was apparently taken seriously by Abraham's ruler-priest ancestors.

James Keller asserts that "If God intervenes to save your life in a car crash, then what was he doing in Auschwitz concentration camp?" where at least 1.1 million innocent Jews prisoners died. Another six (6) million Jews, among them three (3) million Polish Christian Jews in Poland, were exterminated in the gas chambers in the extermination camps by Nazi Germany between 1933 and 1945 due to anti-Semitism (irrational hatred of Jews). During 2013 or 2014 about two hundred (200) innocent Nigerian girls and two famous respectable Nigerian Christian priests in August 2015 were kidnapped in Nigeria by the Nigerian militant rebel group. This was not a miracle, but an eye- catching event in the eyes of a so-called powerful God, who openly failed to save His lovely children and two faithful priests. These three examples above are not exhaustive.

According to Wikipedia Nature in the broadest sense, is the natural, physical, or material world or universe. It can refer to the phenomena of the physical world, and also to life in general. It can also refer to non-physical and non-material world or thing. The study of Nature is a large part of science. Although humans are part of Nature, human activity was and is still often understood as a separate category from other natural phenomena. Within the various uses of the word today Nature often refer to geological and wildlife. For this reason Nature can correctly refer to the general realm of living plants, animals, people according to their different races and ethnicity, and to the processes associated with inanimate and non-living objects -- the way that particular type of thing exist and change of their own accord, such as weather and geology on the Earth and other planets discovered by human beings through Nature or Ptah.

APPENDIX I

SERETO SA BATUBATSE (PRAISE POEM)

Agee Tlou Mohlakwana, Agee Tlou mokwa Bosega Agee Tlou Motubatse, Agee Tlou Motsubye Ke
batho ba Shai ya mabu Ba ba rego ge ba ba reta bare:

Ga Shai ga gone batho Batho ba gona ke mabyana Dihlogo ke maratetšwana.

Ke batho bao ba boyago Tsubye Sediba se Bore Tubatse
La bo Marakapula le bo Phetole Seleteng sa Mamokgadi bohlaba thaka Wa hlaba phodi e a
mela
Wa tsoga o e kga morogo ka motswana.

Ke batho ba Mmathelo Mmamokhala Benyi ba Mmammola molamodi wa ntwa Bare
molamodi ke motswara thoka
Wa se tsware thoka o a lohlanya.

Re boya Sediba se Bore Tubatse Se rego go tlala ka metsi sa phukhula
Ke batho ba go dula dithabeng Re boya Maakene matšhema Thaba mabye madula a tšhemile.

Gona kua gabo Shinamela oje moratha Dikgomo di ile o di bona
Re batho ba bo Mmakanaga Tubatse Ba bina tlou phookgo
Tlou tša go ja dihlare ka godimo.

Re batho ba bo Kgoshi Mashishimale a bo Khashane Kgoši se dula gare ga dithaba
Ke Kgoši se ja ka lekgwana
Ke bo Majatšebotse abo Tsemole.

Batho ba tshese ya Mpofuwa Maakene Ba Shai bare wa ja mpja o lle
O tšea mosela wa dira seala
Re batho ba taola ye ntso le ye khubedu
Ba re taola ye ntso ke thokola seretwa ke basadi.

Re Ba-Shai wa Motswi mokgabene Wa pitšana ya Mamoseki Seapeya mahabyahabya Makhura
a tšwa ka dibete
Nna re Matebele matsitswa mashweu Magana ke bohulwana, madumela boswana.
Ke batho ba go gana nnete ba e bona.

SERETO SA MMOLA (PRAISE POEM)

Agee Tlou, Agee Tubatse ya go boya Tsubye Tsubye la maraka pula
Yena monye molohlanyi, ga a lohlanye o lamola ntwa Agee Mamokgala, motho yo a boyago
Tubatse.

Tubatse Mohleng Mmola a mothei
Ke motho wa lehlako le legolo la Mmamoloro Wa go lora thotlwa e hwile
A tsoga a thopola nama.

Ke Mathelo ke Mamokgala, ke Mmammola molamodi wa ntwa Molamodi a tšie thoka a lamole
A se tšie thoka o a lohlanya, ke tlou ye e boyago Tsubye Tsubye la maraka pula le letšatši.

· · · · ·

SERETO SA MASEGARE SHAI (PERSONAL POEM)

Kgomo e a swa e gama ke mang?
E gama ke nna Tawaneng was masogana Kere ke gata kotse ka gata bogale
Sepimpi se a tuka, kare ke tima ka meetse sa gana Ka ba ka tima ka sebelebele sa mmele
Šewe pere e tshweu ya Masetshepi, e gata e gatoga
E lebile Ga-Mafeefee go ya go theetša taba tša maaka le tša nnete.

Lena maisimane le a loya, le roma tladi e phapha dikgong Mmutla wa tšwa ka kgorong
Banna ba šala ba swere ditedu Mma le tate le ntsware gabotse

Ke galase ke a thubega, ke tshaba moditi.

· · · · ·

"The great and glorious masterpiece of man is to know how to live to purpose."
– Michael Montaigne

APPENDIX 2

BATUBATSE NAMES

Based upon the culture and law the following are some of Batubatse common names to choose from and are recorded alphabetically for easy references:

1. Basentseng,
2. Boyi
3. Booyi
4. Butane,
5. Choma
6. Daola
7. Dintweng
8. Dipholo
9. Kabu
10. Kgabashayi
11. Kgabu
12. Kgariši
13. Kgashane
14. Kgokongtona
15. Kgopamoshodi
16. Khashane
17. Kokontona
18. Khahamedi
19. Kotipo
20. Kgopi
21. Khopi
22. Koloto
23. Kongkong
24. Kudumela
25. Lebeko
26. Lebobe
27. Leeto
28. Legaro
29. Legashe
30. Lekeke
31. Leshweni
32. Lethamaga
33. Letlaka
34. Letseke

M

35. Maabyale
36. Maalabi
37. Maalewe
38. Maatle
39. Maatloo
40. Maatsebe
41. Mabine
42. Mabja
43. Maboelele
44. Madingwane
45. Madume
46. Maebe
47. Mafedi
48. Magari
49. Magodiele
50. Magopalo
51. Mahlona
52. Mahlakwena
53. Maishago
54. Maitjeng
55. Majatšebotse
56. Makgatle
57. Makhoo
58. Makgwatleng
59. Makgwedi
60. Makutuma
61. Mamanyela
62. Mamohuma
63. Mamojele
64. Mamokgadi
65. Mamokhala
66. Mamoloro
67. Mamoseki
68. Mamothe
69. Mampai
70. Mampya
71. Manawa
72. Mangwedi
73. Mankete
74. Mankwana
75. Mantsana
76. Mapalakanye
77. Maphaba
78. Maphuthe
79. Mapiti
80. Marabe
81. Maphokwane
82. Mpofuwa
83. Mareane
84. Marebole
85. Mariti
86. Marotlo
87. Masegare
88. Masetle
89. Mashabake
90. Mashabane
91. Mashabakgole

92. Mashishimale
93. Masie
94. Masiye
95. Masoko
96. Mateane
97. Matela
98. Matheka
99. Mathepe
100. Matidimane
101. Mathoko
102. Mathukgwane
103. Matlabeya
104. Matladi
105. Matlakala
106. Matokolo
107. Matome
108. Matsakwe
109. Matshoshi
110. Matshubene
111. Matsolo
112. Mmakanaga
113. Mmamule
114. Mmanyaba
115. Mmerika
116. Modume
117. Moholoholo
118. Mohleng
119. Mohwalahwasa
120. Mokabatane
121. Mokantiana
122. Mokeketi
123. Mokgala
124. Mokgale
125. Mokgano
126. Mokgashane
127. Mokgona
128. Mokhokolo
129. Mokgwatjane
130. Mokibela
131. Molata
132. Moloto

133. Molotole
134. Monametji
135. Mongene
136. Montsane
137. Monyamane
138. Monyeleka
139. Morabudi
140 Morakane
141. Morake
142. Morakeng
143. Moriti
144. Moroubotji
145. Moshabela
146. Mosomedi
147. Motlatjo
148. Mothepe
149. Mpaseriti
150. Mphage
151. Mphaswa
152. Mphela
153. Mphera
154. Mpyanaiwa

N-Z

155. Nakampe
156. Ngako
157. Ngwako
158. Ngwanakgare
159. Nkabo
160. Nkale
161. Nkekolo
162. Nkgasetjeng
163. Nkurwane
164. Nnoi
165. Ntima
166. Ntimana
167. Ntsoane
168. Ntu
169. Pebane
170. Phaswane
171. Phetole

172. Podume
173. Polankete
174. Ponela
175. Ponele
176. Pududu
177. Pulankana
178. Ramatsi
179. Rabogale
180. Ramoshaba
181. Rathelo
182. Segopane
183. Segwate
184. Sekgasane
185. Sekwai
186. Sekwatapeng
187. Sekwekwene
188. Selota
189. Selote
190. Sereko
191. Serite
192. Setaki
193. Setlau
194. Setshube
195. Seyalenaga
196. Shema
197. Shinamela
198. Sodi
199. Thakadu
200. Taile
201. Thatale
202. Thelo
203. Tlowedi
204. Tobaka
205. Tsametse
206. Tshabakwane
207. Tsheetshee
208. Tshetludi
209. Tshobane
210. Tsemole
211. Tsetsetse

APPENDIX 3

BATUBATSE SURNAMES

The breaking into sections and the nicknaming of certain Batubatse members led them to assume new surnames. Some of those surnames, including SHAI, are the following:

1.	KGOAHLA	24.	MOGODI	47.	RAMAMPA
2.	MACHUBENE	25.	MOGONONI	48.	RAMONYATHI
3.	MADUME	26.	MOHALEAMALLA	49.	RAMOSHABA
4.	MAENETJA	27.	MOHLABE	50.	RASEKELE
5.	MAFOLOGELA	28.	MOHLOBUKA	51.	RATJATJI
6.	MAGODIELE	29.	MOKGOLOBOTO	52.	RATHETE
7.	MAHLAKWANA	30.	MOKGOMOLA	53.	RATLABALA
8.	MAHOLOBELA	31.	MOLEWA	54.	SEABELA
9.	MAKWALA	32.	MOLOISI	55.	SEANEGO
10.	MAMANYOHA	33.	MOSEAMEDI	56.	SEBASHE
11.	MAMPA.	34.	MOSHOLE	57.	SEKHULA
12.	MANASHANE	35.	MOTOLLA	58.	SELAELO
13.	MAPAILA	36.	MOTUBATSE	59.	SELOTA
14.	MAROBELA	37.	MPHAKANE	60.	SELOWA
15.	MARULE	38.	MOTSWI/MUTSWI	61.	SEOKOMA
16.	MASETE	39.	NAKAMPE	62.	SESHAI
17.	MASETLA	40.	NGOATJE	63.	SHAI
18.	MASHAI	41.	NGWAKO	64.	THEMA
19.	MASHAPU	42.	PHALADI		
20.	MASHUMU	43.	POPELA		
21.	MATLOU	44.	RAGOBOYA		
22.	MATOME	45.	RAKGOTSOKA		
23.	MMOLA	46.	RAMABOKA		

APPENDIX 4

BATUBATSE HOUSES/UNITS (DIKGORO)

These Units have been traced and are recorded hereunder in terms of their existence, but not according to their ranks.

SENIOR HOUSE/UNIT (KGOROKGOLO)-SHAYI/SHAI

7.3.1.   *KGORO YA MAMPA*

7.3.2.   *KGORO YA MAPITI/MOHLABE*

7.3.3.   *KGORO YA DIPHOLO/MMANYABA*

7.3.4.   *KGORO YA TEFO/MABINE*

7.3.5.   *KGORO YA TAOLA/MASHISHIMALE*

7.3.6.   *KGORO YA LETHAMAGA*

7.3.7.   *KGORO YA NKURWANE*

7.3.8.   *KGORO YA MASETLA/TLHOGOTLOU*

7.3.9.   *KGORO YA MATOME*

7.3.10.   *KGORO YA MMOLA*

7.3.11.   *KGORO YA MATLOU**

7.3.12.   *KGORO YA MPHAGE*

7.3.13.   *KGORO YA MUTSWI/MOTSWI**

7.3.14.   *KGORO YA SEANEGO*

7.3.15.   *KGORO YA MOHOLOHOLO*

BIBLIOGRAPHY / REFERENCES

Acocks J.P.H Veld Types of South Africa. Memoirs of the Botanical Survey of South Africa No 57 (Botanical Research Institute, Pretoria, 1988);

Aristotle Politics and The Athenian Constitution, John Warrington's translation, 1st Edition (London 1959);

Attenborough David, Collins Mark The Last Forests: A World Conservation Atlas;

Ayisi EO An Introduction to the study of African Culture, 2nd Edition, Nairobi: East African Education Publishers (1992);

Barclay Philip Zimbabwe-Years of Hope and Despair, (Bloomsbury Publishing Plc-London WID 3QY 2010);
Bennett TW Customary Law in South Africa, Juta and Company Ltd (2007)

Biesele Megan, Barclay Steve Ju'/Hoan Womrn's Tracking Knowledge and Its Contributions to Their Husbands' Hunting Success (March 2001);

Dahlberg Frances Woman the Gatherer (1975);

Dawkins Richard The God Delusion, Bantam Books, October 2006)

Dayhoff I Pioneering in Pediland, (Kansas City, Missouri: Nazarene Publishing House, 1964), 29ff;
De Traci Regular The Mysteries of Isis, (Minnesota 1995) 37, 90;

Edward Schure Die Grossen Eingeweihten, (Wien 1982) 39-40;
Esmo nd Wright The Ancient World, (New Jersey 1979) 255;

Freke Timothy and Gandy Peter The Hermetica- The Lost Wisdom of the Pharaohs (London 1997) 11-12, 45;

Freke and Gandy Peter A Complete Guide to World Mysticism (London) 72-73, 93,116;

Frits Jean et al The World in 1492, 94-95;

Gilbert Magi The Quest for a Secret Tradition, (1996) 115;
Herold Nelson Sudan- A Country Study, (March 1982) 2;

Hotema Hilton The Mystery Man of the Bible, (New York 1956) 40;
James The Stolen Legacy, (New York), 139;

Keller James A Moral Argument against Miracles, Faith and Philosophy vol. 12, no 1. Jan 1995- 54-78

Krige Jensen E African: Journal of the International African Institute (Cambridge University Press, Vol 11, No 3 July 1938)
Krige Jensen E and Krige JR The Realm of a Rain Queen, (Juta and Company Ltd Cope Town 1980);
Le Roux Magdel The Lemba-A lost Tribe of Israel in South Africa, (Unisa Press 1st Ed, 2005) Lindgren, Bjorm Academic Journal Article, (Africa, Vol. 74, No 2, Spring 2004)

Mandela Nelson The Struggle is My Life, (Idaf Publication Ltd, London-Revised April 1980);

Marlowe F.W Hunter-gatherers and human evolution- Evolutionary Anthropology: Issues, News and Reviews 14 (2) (2005);

Monnig H.O The Pedi, (1st Edition 1967);

Morton H.V A Traveller in Southern Italy, (Methuen & Co Ltd London 1969);
Motshekga Necherofho Dawn of the African Century, (Kara Publishers 1999); Motshekga Kherofo Mathole Mudjadji Dynasty, (Kara Books, Midrand 2010);
Mucina L and Rutherford M.C The vegetation of South Africa, Lesotho and Swaziland (Strelitzia 19, SANB I, Pretoria, (eds) 2006);

Pain Thomas The Writings of Thomas Pain, Volume 4, page 289, Putnam & Sons, 1896 OCLC 459072720;

Rev. Fritz Reuter, Berlin Mission, "Modjadji, a Native Queen in the Northern Transvaal", South African Journal of Science, (Marshalltown, South Africa: South African Association for the Advancement of Science, vol.3, 1906-07), 249;

Sharp Samuel The History of Egypt vol I, (London 1885 bb) 171-172;

Skinner J.D and Smithers R.H.N The Mammals of the Southern African Sub-region 3rd Ed (Cambridge University Press 1990);

Tompkins Peter Secrets of the Great Pyramid-5ff;

Van Warmelo NJ Union of South Africa, Department of Native Affairs-Ethnological Publication, (Pretoria 1944);
Wikipedia History of Ghana- The Free Encyclopaedia;

Windeband The History of Ancient Philosophy, 361-363.

www.ingramcontent.com/pod-product-compliance
Lightning Source LLC
Chambersburg PA
CBHW051818090426
42736CB00011B/1549